IMAGES
of America

VERONA

On the Cover: The Whaley Cheese Factory on the Erie Canal in Higginsville is pictured here. (Photograph courtesy of the Verona Historical Society.)

IMAGES
of America

VERONA

Dorothy M. Cmaylo, Thomas A. Beaver,
Kenneth A. Regner, and Sheila B. Hoffman
for the Town of Verona Historical Association

ARCADIA
PUBLISHING

ISBN 978-0-7385-7236-9

Published by Arcadia Publishing
Charleston, South Carolina

Printed in the United States of America

Library of Congress Control Number: 2009933573

For all general information contact Arcadia Publishing at:
Telephone 843-853-2070
Fax 843-853-0044
E-mail sales@arcadiapublishing.com
For customer service and orders:
Toll-Free 1-888-313-2665

Visit us on the Internet at www.arcadiapublishing.com

To our forefathers whose unselfish sacrifices, hard labor, and faith built this community.

Contents

ACKNOWLEDGMENTS

Many people gave generously of their time and talent for the publication of this book, including those who shared their pictures and stories of the town's history. Special recognition must be given to the members of the Verona Historical Association for their support and encouragement. All profits from the sales of this book will benefit the Verona Historical Association.

INTRODUCTION

In the years following the Revolutionary War, people from the New England states started to migrate west. Many came to settle the area now known as the town of Verona. In the early 1800s, many small hamlets were established, including Verona, Higginsville, New London, Churchville, Durhamville, Verona Mills, Verona Springs, Dunbarton, Scononda, State Bridge, Stacy Basin, and Verona Beach.

The first settler to the town was George A. Smith, as he made his way from the town of Westmoreland on Christmas Eve 1791. He and his family settled at the mouth of Oneida Lake near the abandoned Royal Block House, a fortification used by British troops.

Population within the township began to grow with improvements to the waterways. The Western Inland Lock Navigation Canal Company was established in 1792 and was the state's first canal company for the purpose of providing easier access to New York's rivers for eastern merchants and western settlers. The improvements it made connected the Hudson and Mohawk Rivers with Wood Creek, allowing travel and commerce to Lake Ontario through Oneida Lake. Wood Creek in particular had to be widened to allow passage of the bateaux and Durham boats.

On February 17, 1802, the township was established from the neighboring town of Westmoreland as more settlers arrived. The first town meeting was held at the home of Martin Langdon near Verona Village on March 2, 1802.

The opening of the Erie Canal in 1825 and later the railroads spurred economic development in the town throughout the 19th century. Canal-related careers were created and skilled craftsmen, merchants, and professionals were attracted to the area. New factories like the Durhamville Glass Factory and Dunbarton Glass Works also became a source of employment. The already established agricultural industry prospered with many small family dairy farms and small, independent cheese factories.

Efficient travel by rail also helped make Verona a vacation destination into the 1900s. Verona Beach, located on the shore of Oneida Lake, and the Verona Springs Hotel, with its healing mineral waters, were attractive locations.

Following World War II, the construction of four state highways, including an exit on the New York State Thruway, replaced the dependence on the canal and the railroads. It was convenient for residents of Verona to drive to their jobs at factories in neighboring cities, replacing the family farm as the main source of income. A migration of people to the town also made the hamlets more suburban.

With the closing of Griffiss Air Force Base in 1995, combined with the loss of manufacturing jobs, Verona began to develop the characteristics of a bedroom community.

In 1995, the Oneida Indian Nation established the Turning Stone Casino, the largest employer in Oneida County. With gambling, golf courses, professional sports events, and entertainers, Verona is once again becoming a tourist destination.

One

DURHAMVILLE

In 1811, Eliphalet Frazee of Manlius, New York, settled along Oneida Creek, becoming Durhamville's first inhabitant.

When Eber Durham, the hamlet's namesake, settled here in 1826, only four log cabins existed. But with the arrival of the Erie Canal, Durhamville prospered.

Many canal-related businesses were established, including dry goods and provision stores, warehouses, taverns, grist and feed mills, foundries, and tanneries. Some of the more notable businesses included the Kelsey clay pipe factory, Seibel's Store, Doran's Dry Dock, the Keller Feed Mill, and the Felt's Hotel. Several churches and missions were also founded to meet the spiritual needs of a growing population.

The largest enterprises in the area were two glass factories. In 1845, DeWitt Clinton Stephens established a glass factory in Durhamville before selling it to Fox, Gregory, and Son. It became the largest in the state. A second factory was located in nearby Dunbarton.

The construction of the canal and resulting economic prosperity was an invitation to Europeans to settle in the town. Irishmen helped construct and operate the canal, the Germans used their glassblowing skills at the glass factories, and the Welsh were skilled stonemasons for canal, bridge, and building foundations.

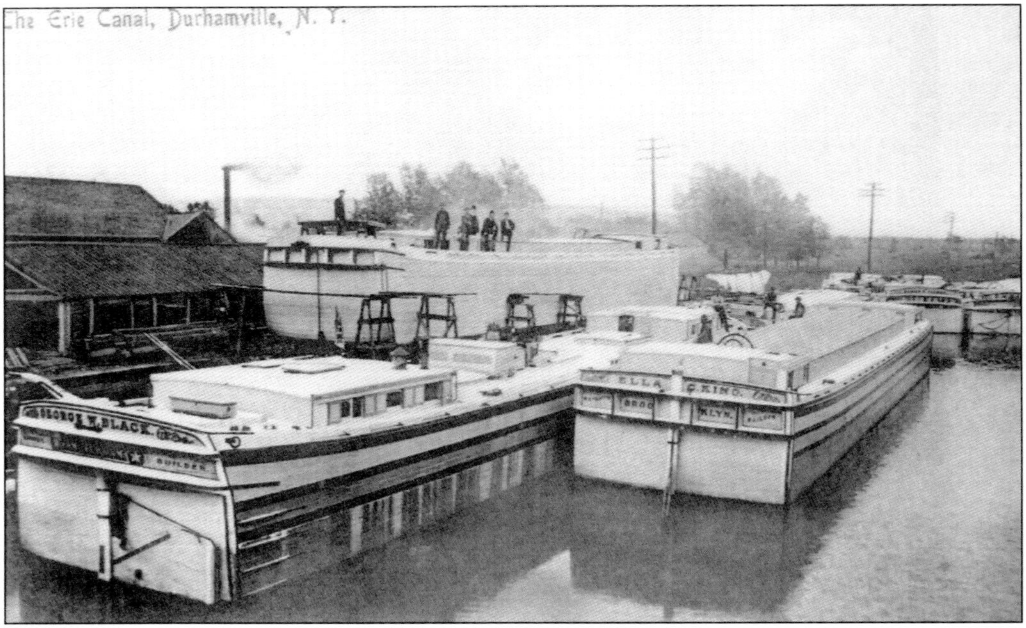

The Doran Dry Dock in Durhamville provided an essential service as it built and repaired canal boats that ran from New York City to the Great Lakes. The dry dock was comprised of 22 acres containing a blacksmith shop, pitch house, icehouse, and foreman's office. The business operated from 1863 until 1924, when the bridge over New York State Route 316 was lowered.

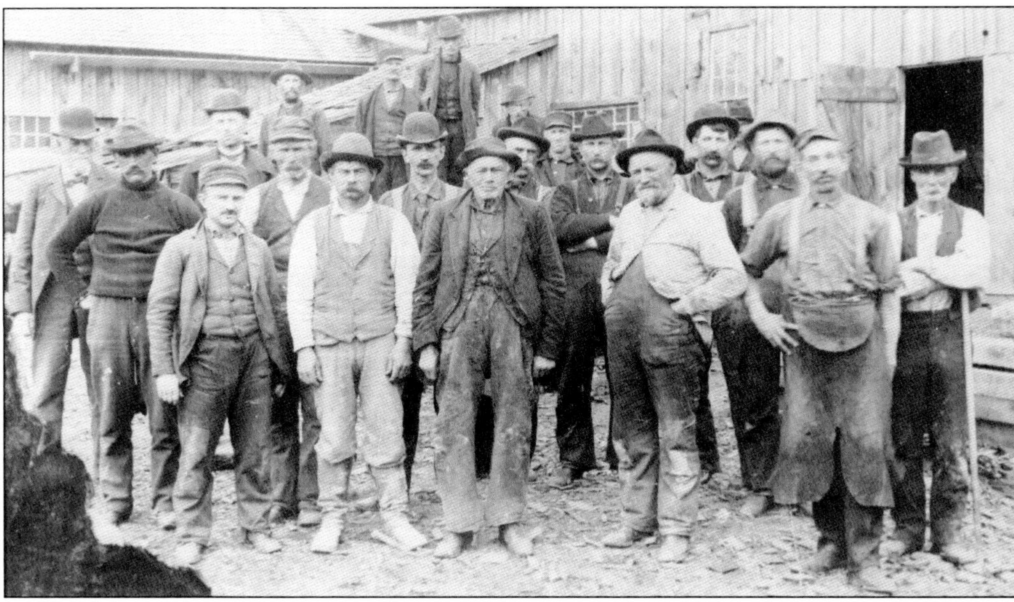

Pictured here are employees of the Doran Dry Dock. These men were local, skilled craftsmen that included carpenters and caulkers. Businesses like the dry dock were not only a source of employment for immigrants but also a reason to settle in the town. Pictured here are, from left to right, (first row) Walter Rice, Frank Ballard, Martin Fuller, John Doran, John Smith, and unidentified; (second row) Michael Doran (proprietor), Jesse Stedman (foreman), Orin Poppleton, Henry George, Dallas Jones, Charles Adams, Martin Cassidy, and Carl Merrell; (third row) Hiram Adams, Walter Eggleston, Alonzo King, Charles McCuen, and John Hook.

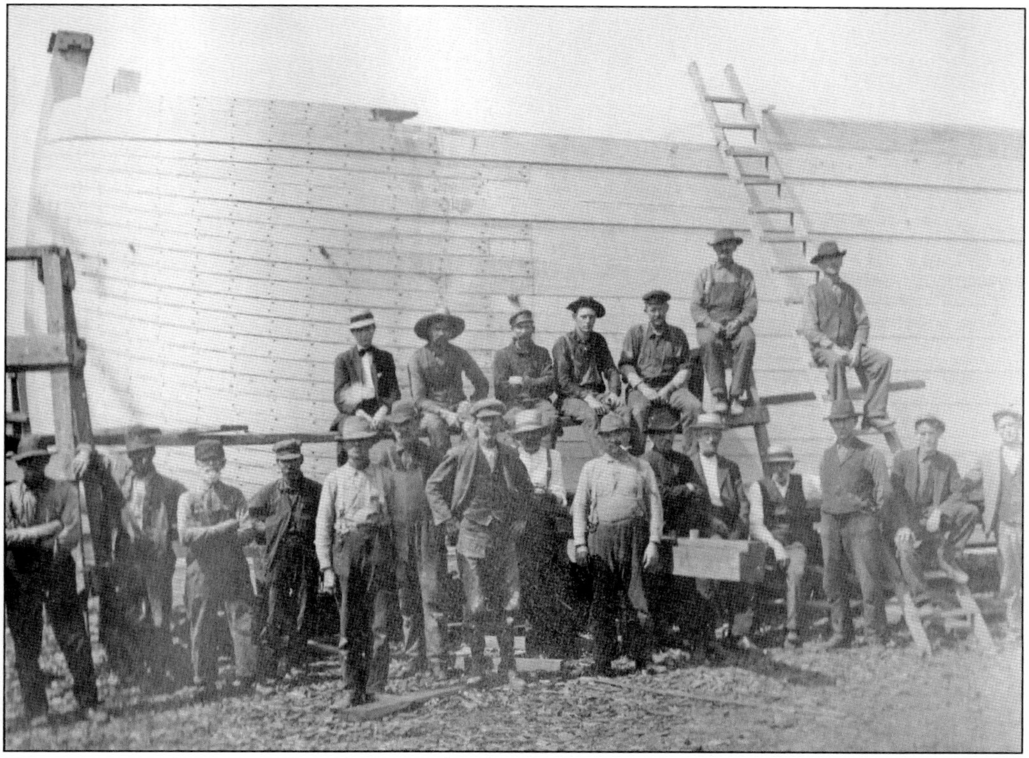

This is a second picture of workmen at the dry dock posing beside a boat under construction. Notice the size of the boat for the purpose of transporting tons of goods for trade on the canal, yet its flat bottom allowed travel in shallow water.

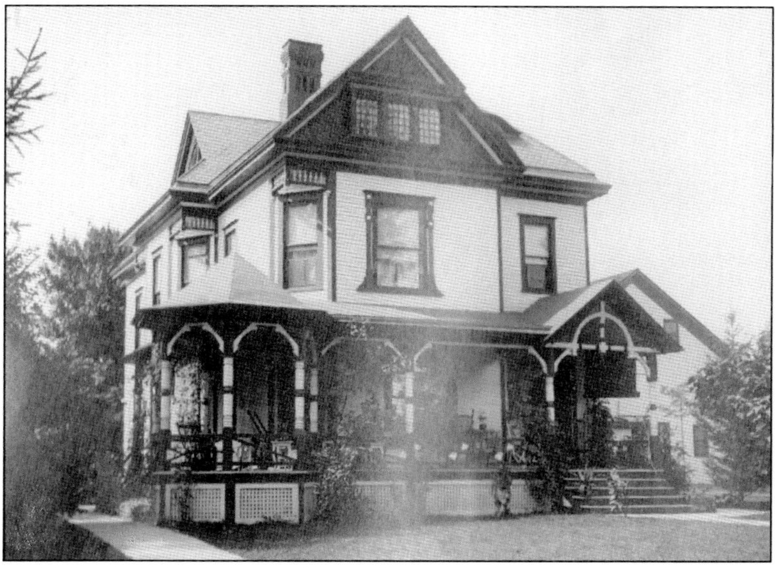

The residence of Michael Doran, proprietor of Doran's Dry Dock, is located on the present New York State Route 316 in Oneida. The home was originally considered to be in Durhamville until Oneida Creek became the new line separating Oneida and Madison Counties. The house is still a private residence.

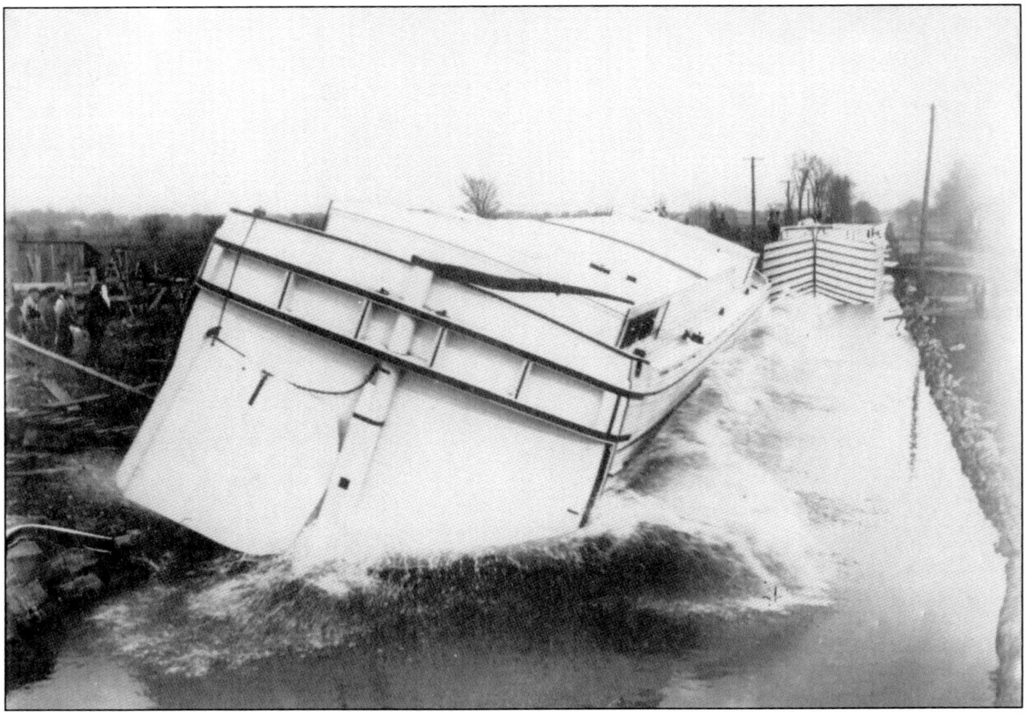

The arrival of the railroads was the death knell for the canal and its workers as the trains provided a faster and more efficient mode of travel. Doran's Dry Dock closed in 1924.

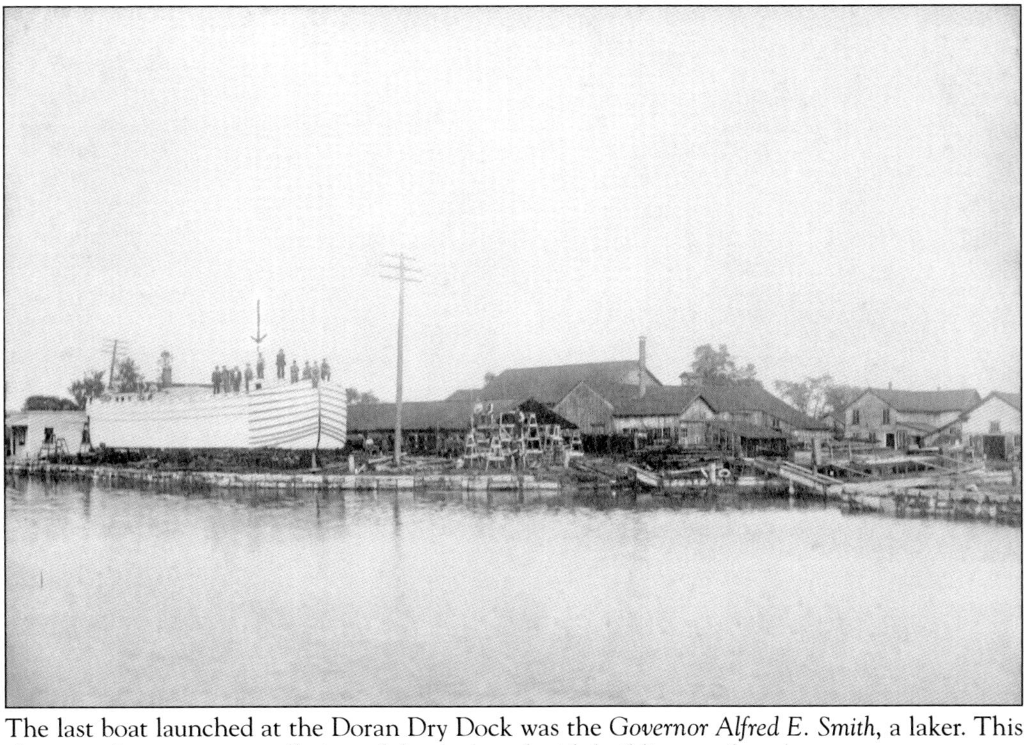

The last boat launched at the Doran Dry Dock was the *Governor Alfred E. Smith*, a laker. This photograph gives an overall view of the dockyard with buildings and workers.

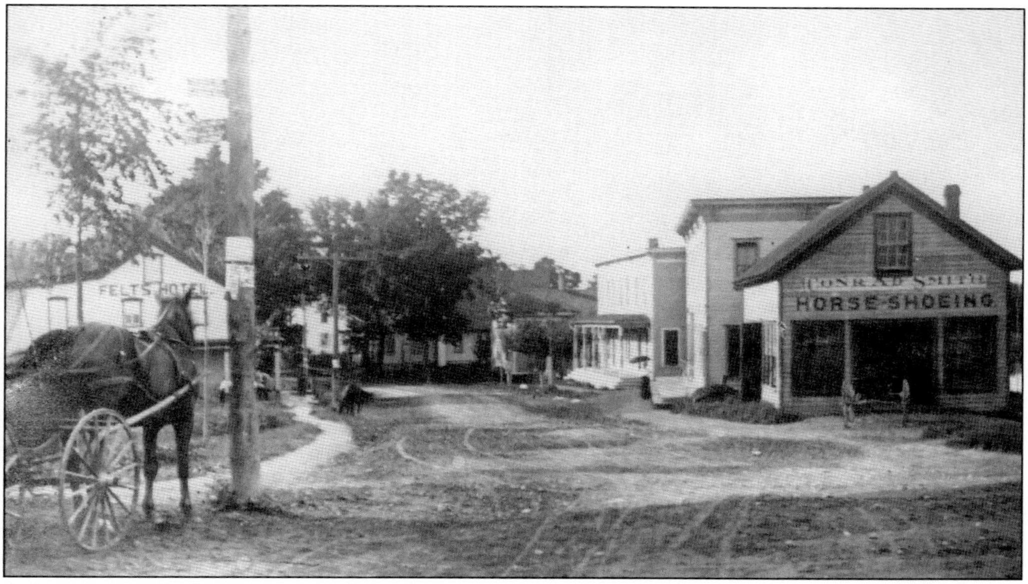

A horse waits before going northward on Main Street in Durhamville, 1902. The Felts Hotel can be seen on the left and Conrad Smith's Blacksmith Shop in the right foreground. Behind it are Order of the Odd Fellows Hall, a fraternal organization, and the Schaub Hotel, all near the towpath.

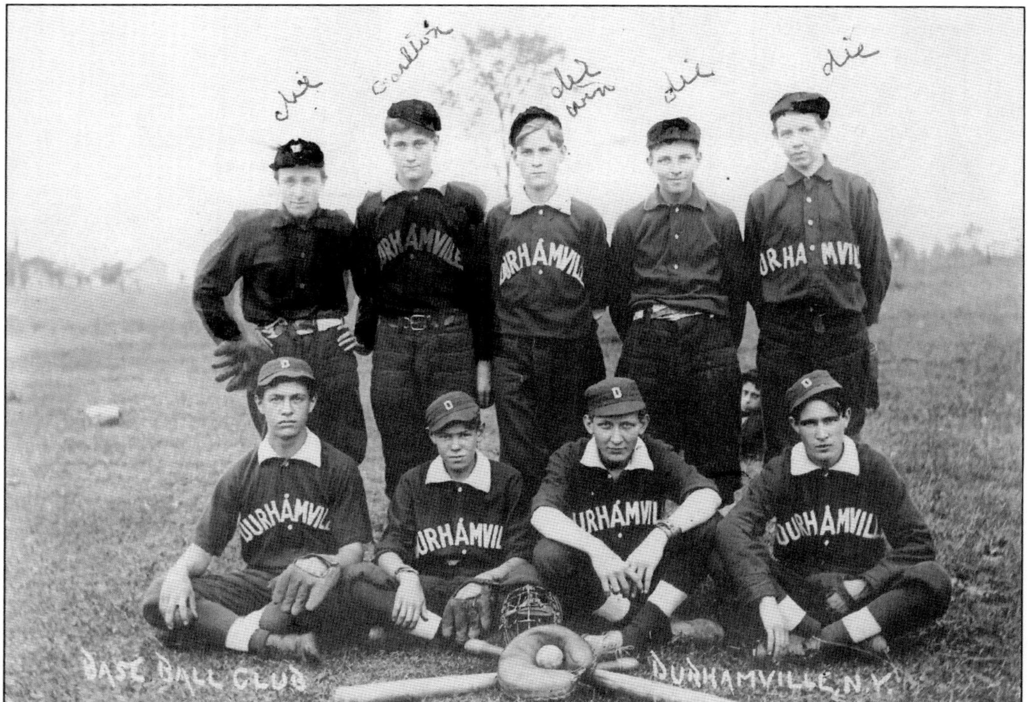

America's pastime was a common form of recreation, as shown in this picture of the Durhamville Baseball Club in the year 1907. From left to right are (seated) Will Gregory, Irving Smith, Stewart Schlernitzaurer, and Tom Tierney; (standing) Herold Mayer, Carl Merrill, Win Merrill, Carl Seibel, and John State.

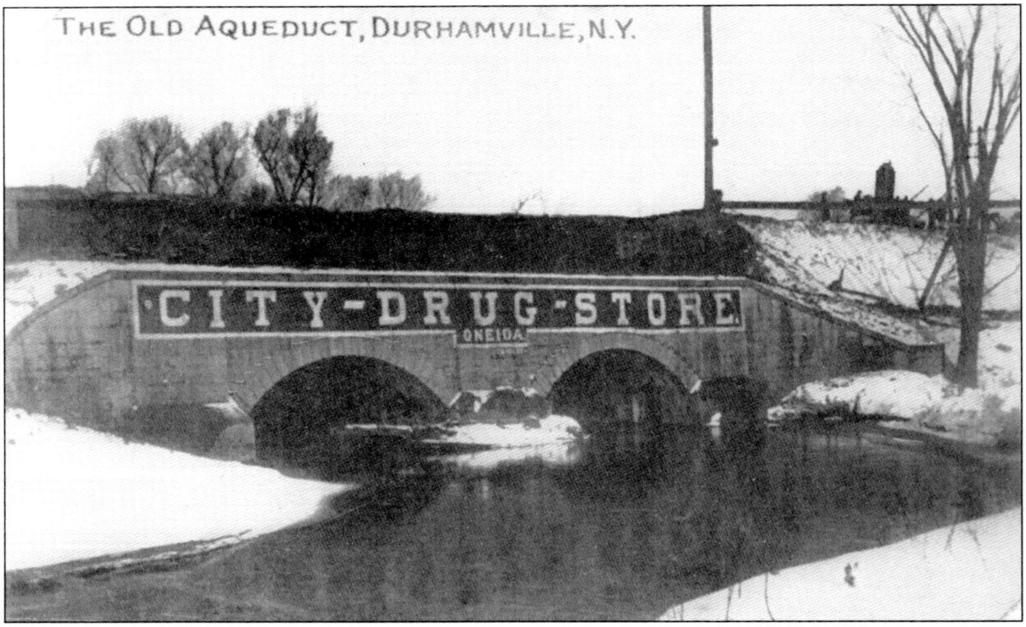

The above photograph shows the 60-foot-long aqueduct in Durhamville that carried the Erie Canal over Oneida Creek. Constructed between 1845 and 1855, it was a double-arch stone structure. The design proved inadequate for large water volume and was prone to frequent repairs. Pictured below is the new steel aqueduct that was authorized by the state legislature in 1907 and built at a construction cost of $76,600.

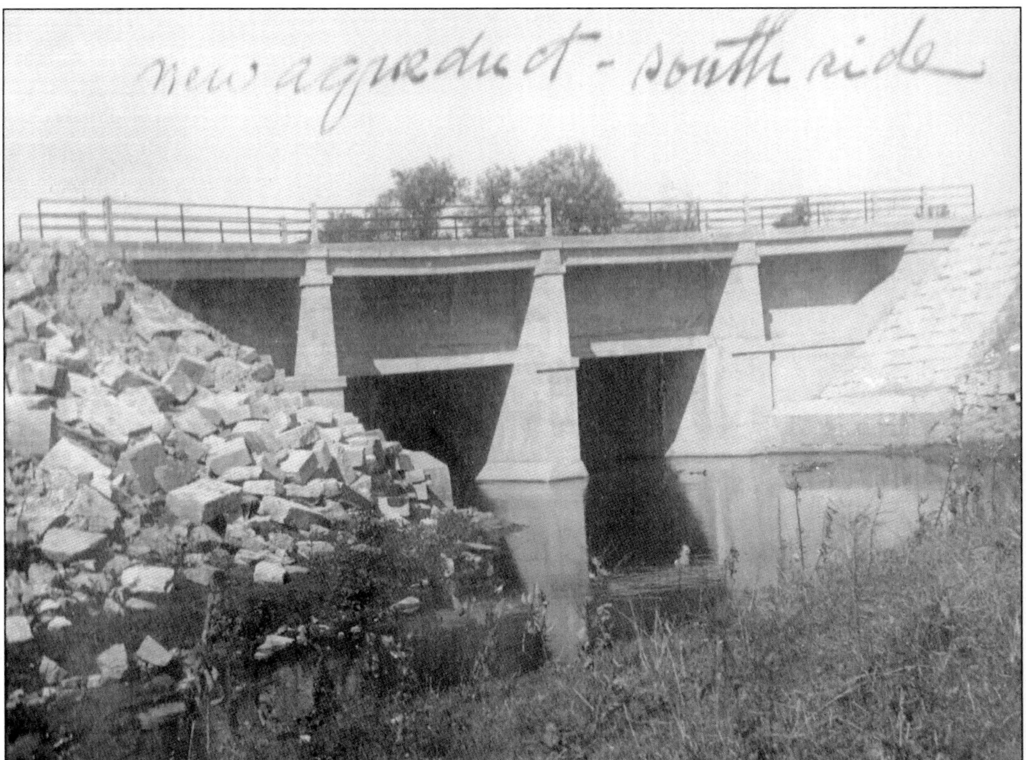

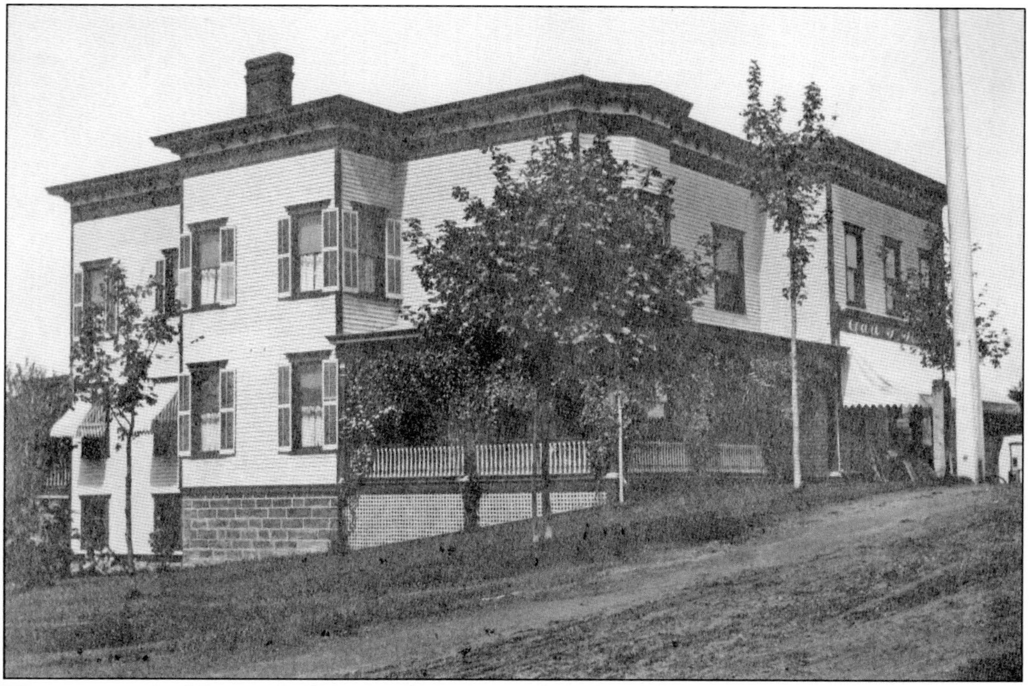

This spacious building is the home and store owned and built by Carl T. Seibel in the early 1900s and later enlarged. The store was a source of provisions for residents, boatmen, and canal travelers. The post office was also located here. Below is a photograph of Seibel's Store at election time in 1908. Note the huge flag and campaign flyers in the windows of the upstairs apartment. In the foreground is the end of the bridge over the Erie Canal and the base of a liberty pole.

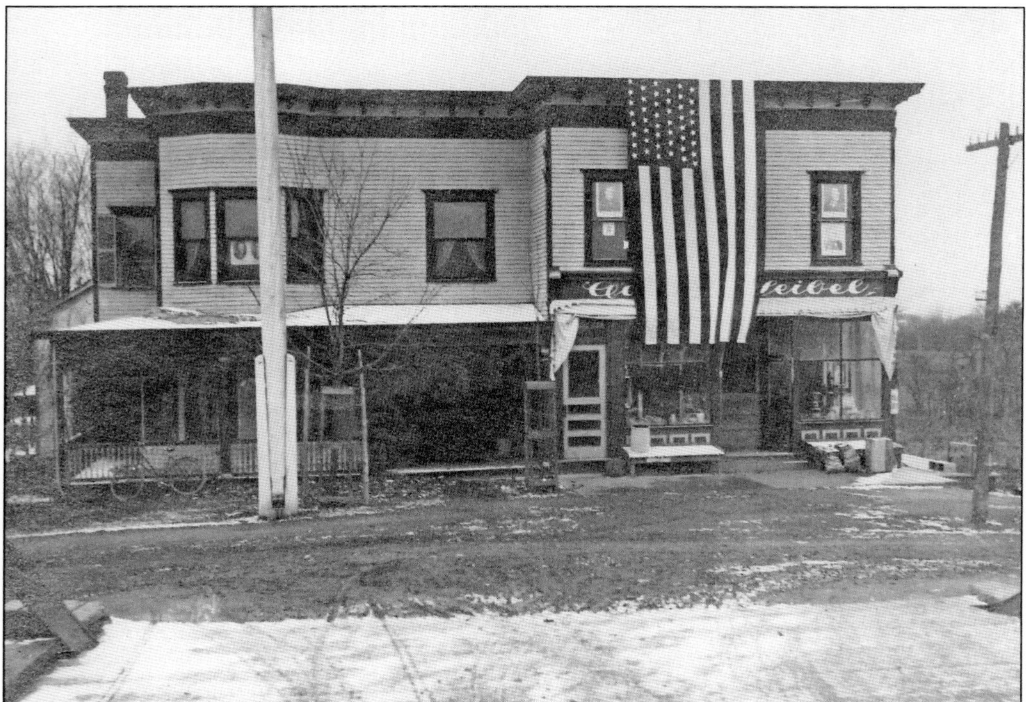

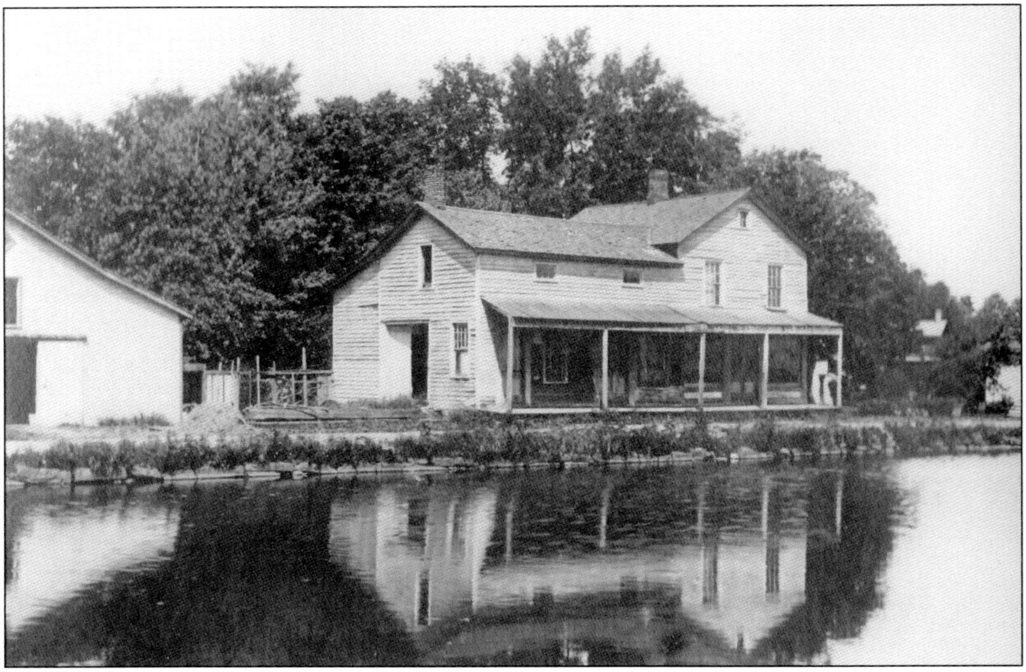

Known as Schaub's Shanty, this small house along the canal was near the home of George and Adelia Schaub. On January 5, 1929, the home was destroyed by a fire that also took the Order of the Odd Fellows Hall. The Schaubs moved what furniture was saved from their home to their hotel across the street. Schaub's Hotel was frequented by German migrants traveling northward by canal and was also important as a hospitality house during the height of the local glassmaking industry.

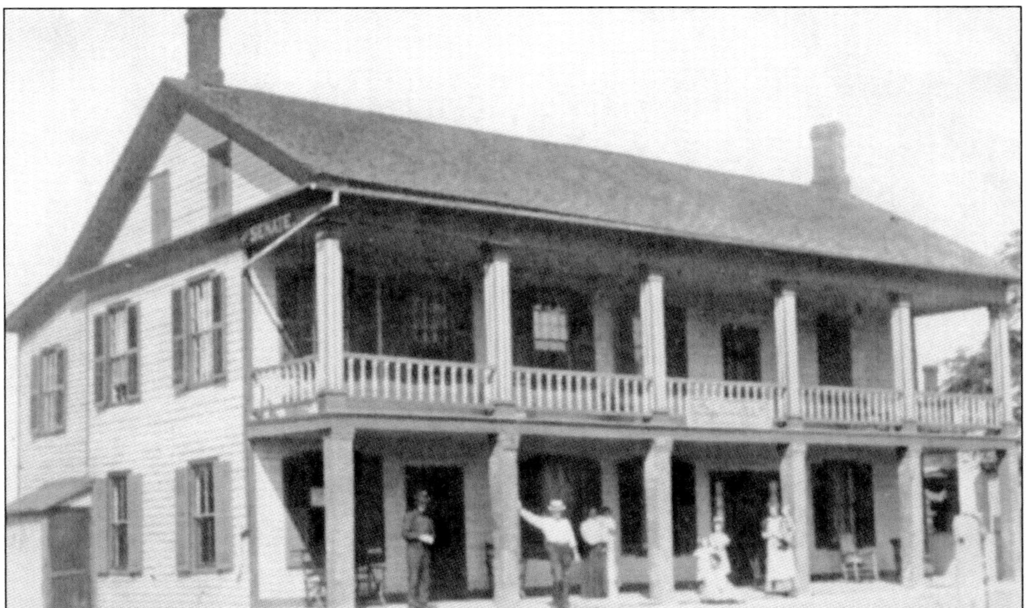

This lovely building was the Senate Hotel, owned by Thomas Shortell. It stood for many years and was owned by several different people. It was finally demolished for the construction of a convenience store on New York State Route 46.

St. Francis Catholic Church in Durhamville was erected by the Franciscan Fathers of Syracuse around 1858. These men were of the Order of St. Francis of Assissi, who supplied the pastors. The present-day rectory was first a school operated by the church, where lessons were taught in German, possibly due to the large number of German glassblowers in the area. Eventually the church came under the jurisdiction of the Roman Catholic Diocese of Syracuse.

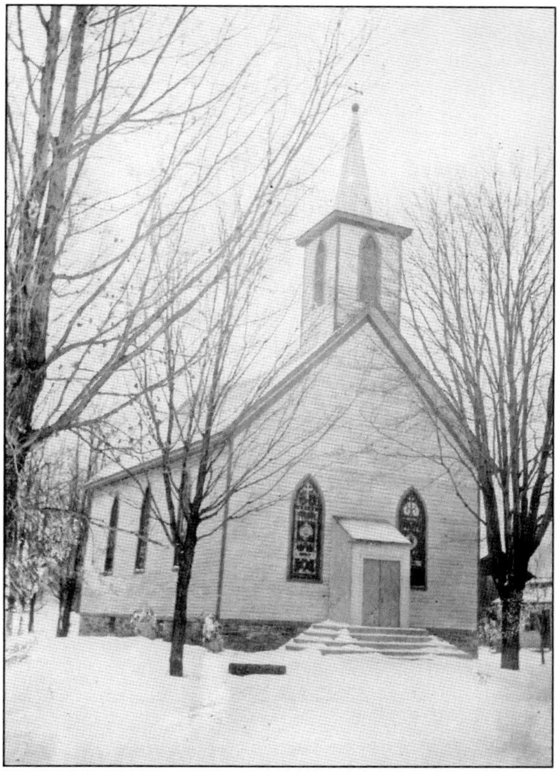

St. Andrew's Episcopal Church was located on Main Street. Built in 1886, it was later closed with its members joining the Episcopal parish in Oneida. With the reconstruction of New York State Route 46 in the 1950s, the building was moved to the northern end of Main Street and is now a private home.

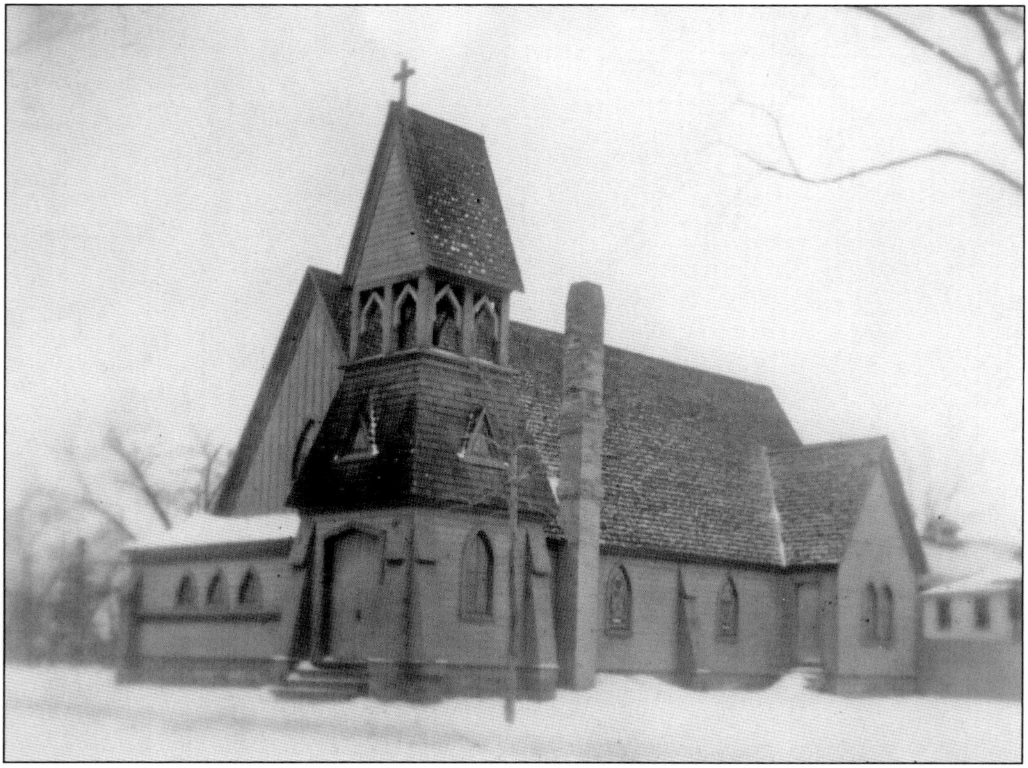

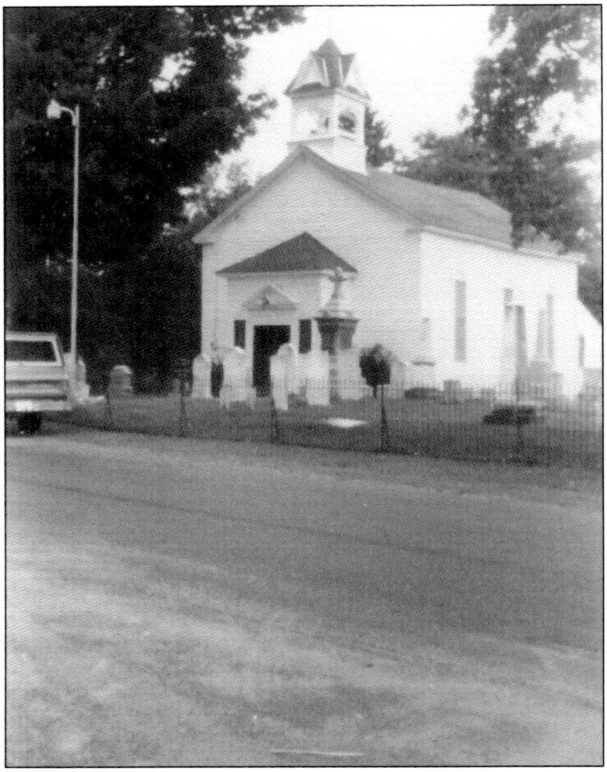

Built in 1831, St. Mary's Church at Irish Ridge was established by the Irish immigrants who came here when the Erie Canal was being built. Visiting priests from other churches came to lead the services. Eventually St. Mary's became a mission of St. Francis Church in Durhamville. Currently it is closed, but interested local people recently did major work to preserve this icon of the Irish Catholic community. Services are still offered on special occasions.

The Durhamville Baptist Church was built in 1815 and burned on November 8, 1824. It was replaced by the current building and parsonage.

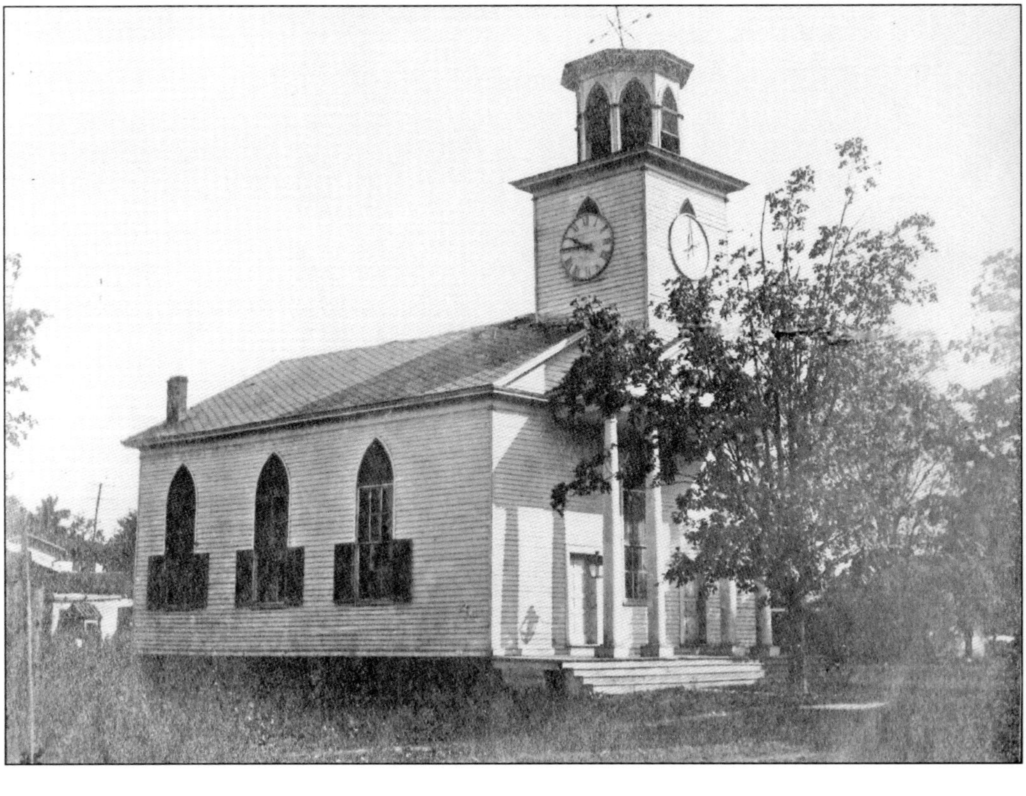

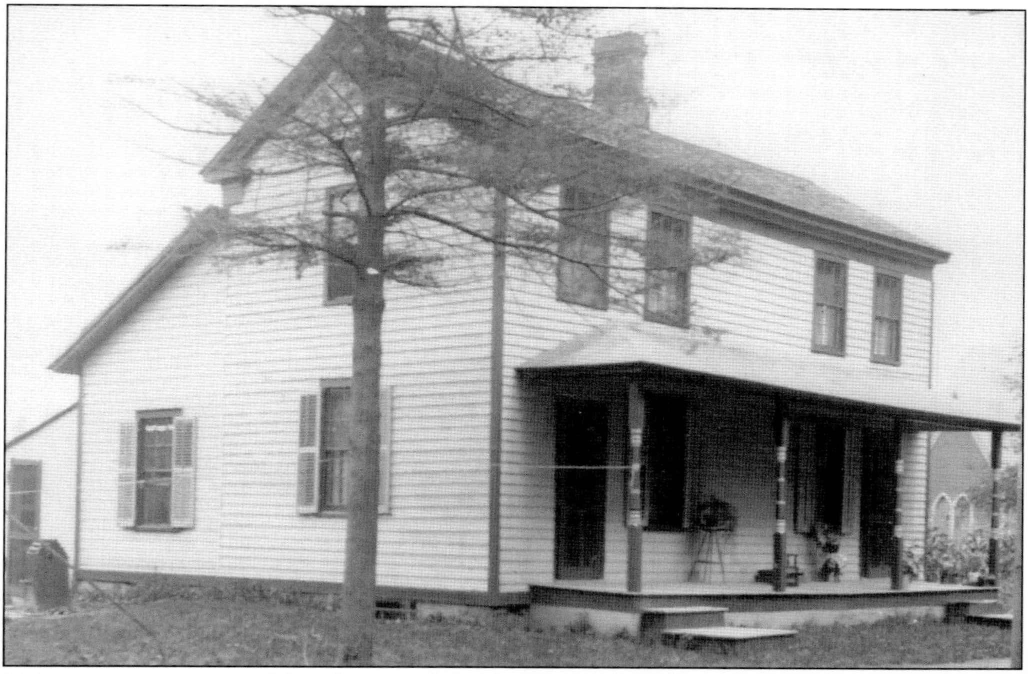

This private residence on Main Street still stands today and is still a private residence. The wooden pump in the left foreground was manufactured by the Nunn Pump Company. The Episcopal church can be seen in the background.

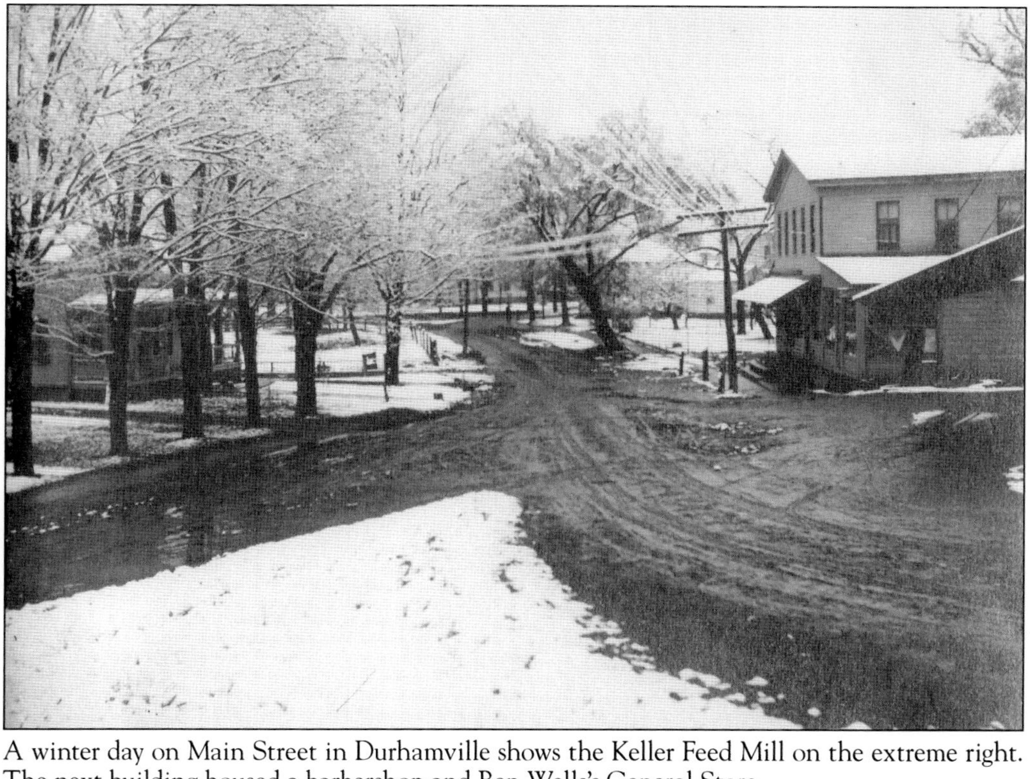

A winter day on Main Street in Durhamville shows the Keller Feed Mill on the extreme right. The next building housed a barbershop and Ben Wells's General Store.

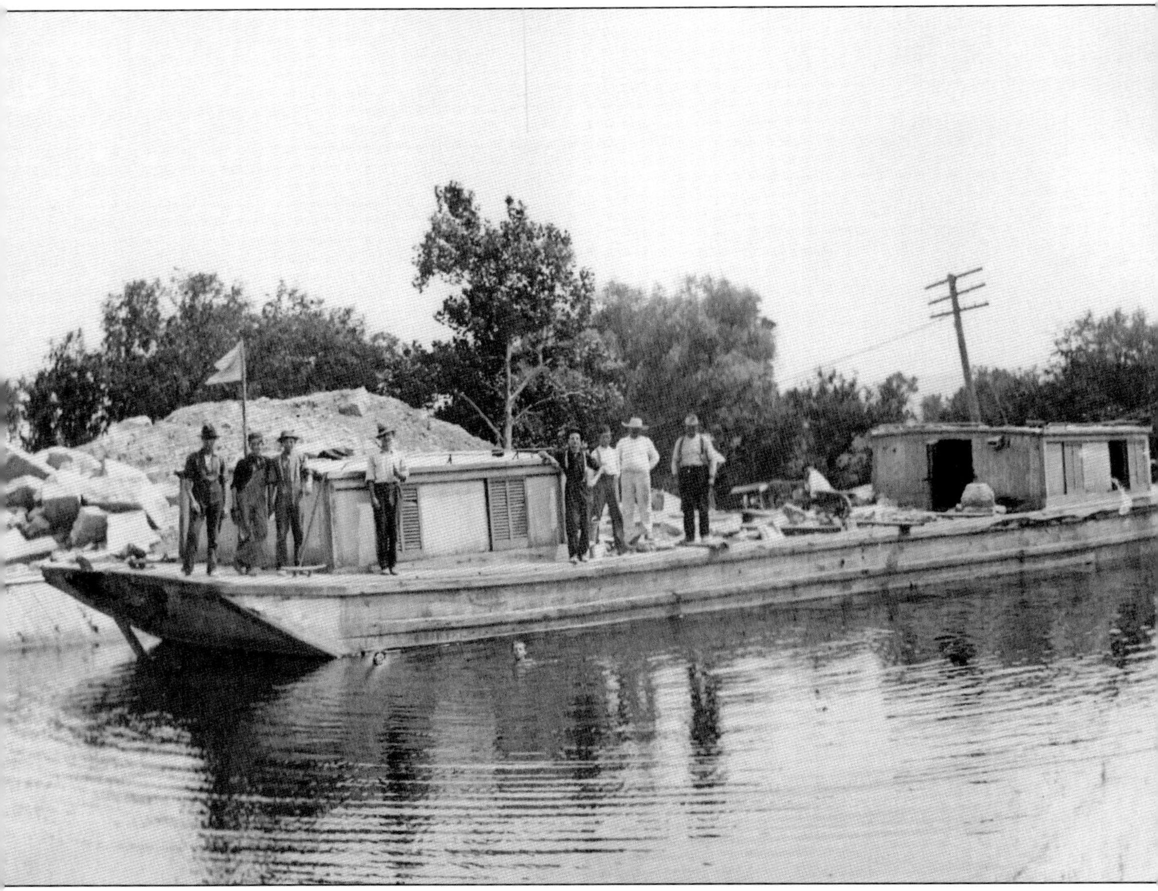

The *Dirty Ann* was a small boat used by workmen for making repairs on the Erie Canal. Note the load of stone to be used in reconstructing the canal banks.

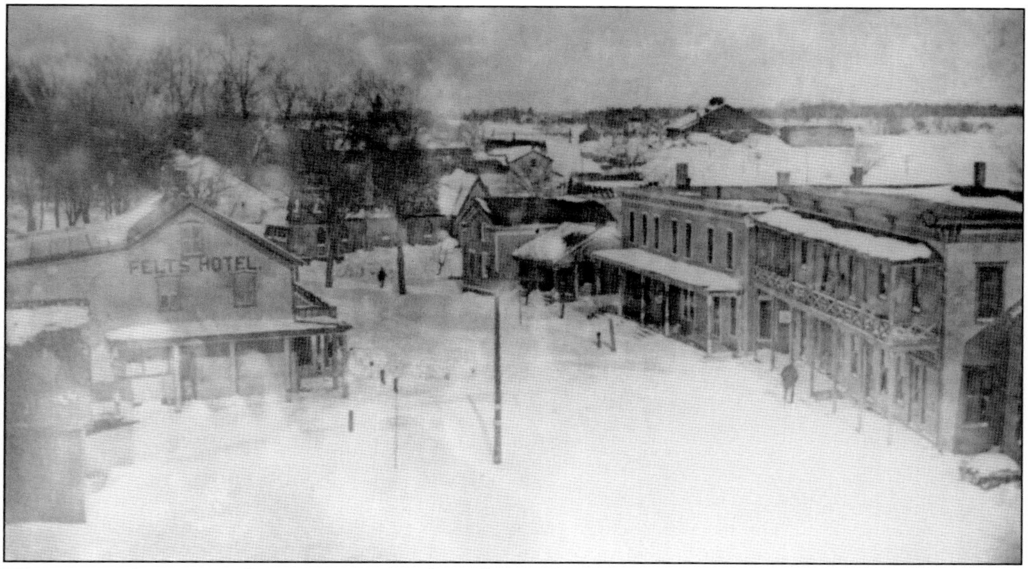

This is another view of Main Street and Durhamville on a winter day in 1902. The Felts Hotel, which is still standing today, is in the left foreground. On the right is the Odd Fellows hall with Schaub's Hotel next to it. Note the roofline of the Durhamville Glass Factory owned by the Fox family in the right background.

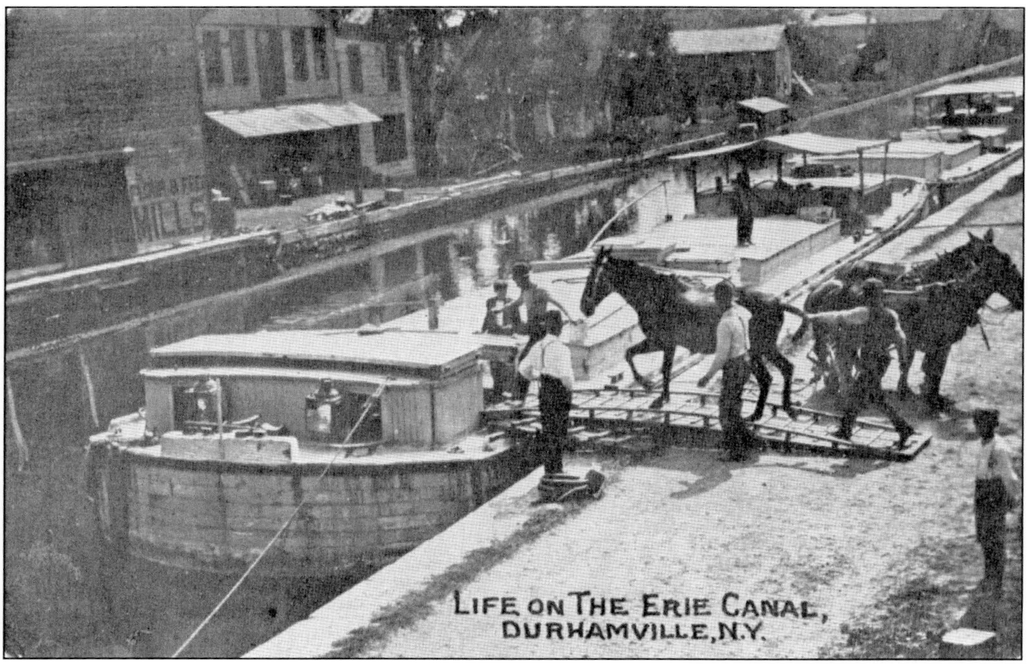

Drivers exchanging mules at the end of their six-hour shift was a familiar scene along the Erie Canal.

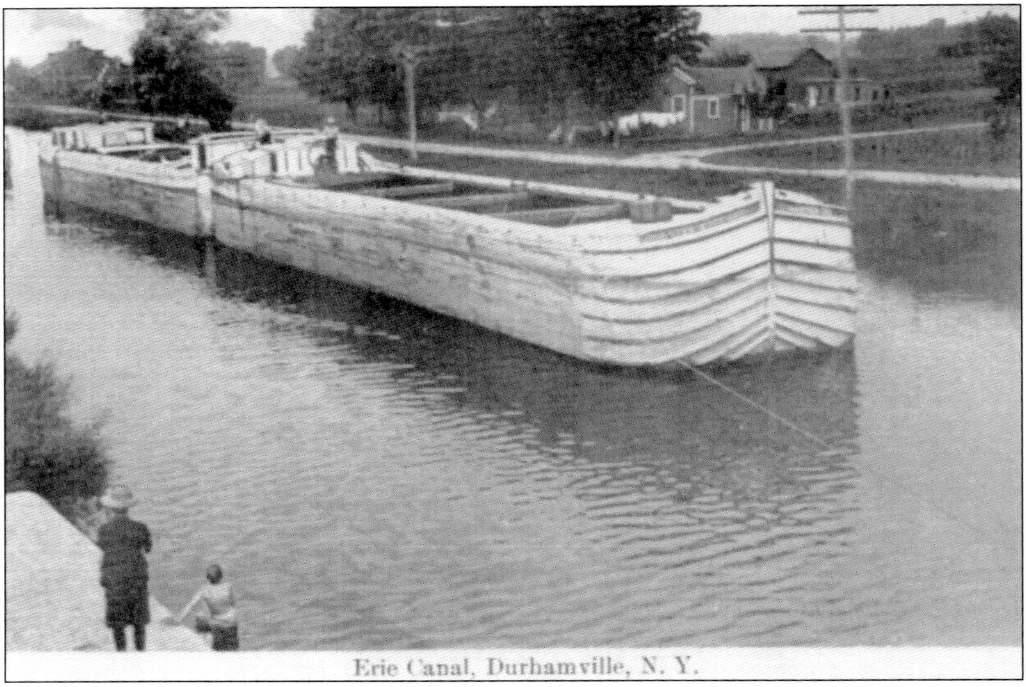

Pictured here are canal boats under tow passing through Durhamville. Two young boys are enjoying the sight. In the background is the Durhamville Glass Factory. In the near background is a home that still stands today.

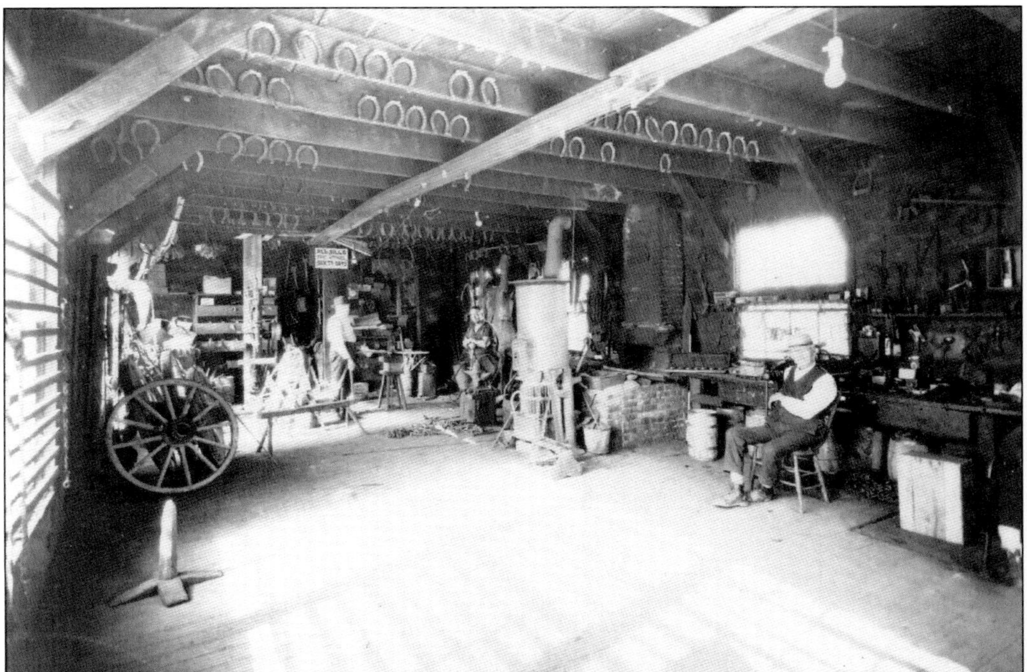

This is a picture of the interior of Ben Vaughn's Blacksmith Shop, once owned by Conrad Smith. It was located directly on the towpath in Durhamville, adjacent to the canal. Note the horseshoes hung on the beams.

These rare tickets were used on the New York State Electric Railway and the Ontario and Western Railway. The "Old and Weary" ended operations in 1957. The top ticket was issued for travel on the Ontario and Western Railway from Oneida to State Bridge. The bottom was for travel from Sherrill to Oneida.

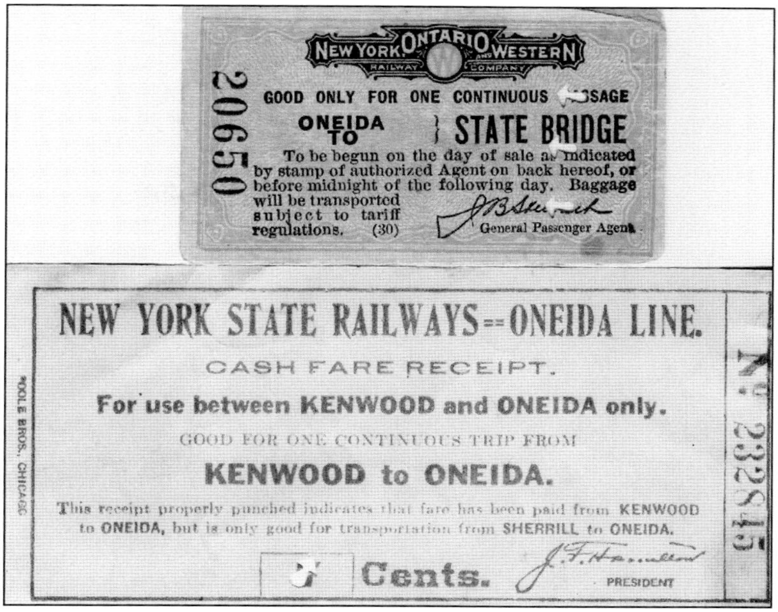

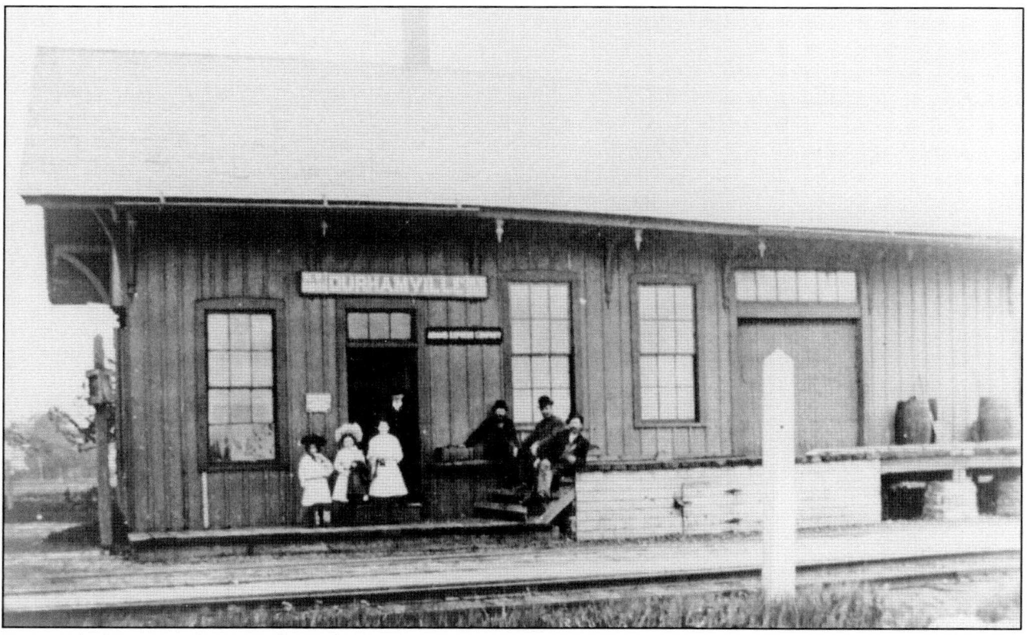

Young ladies are about to board the Ontario and Western Railway in Durhamville. The station was completed in September 1869 and was in use until September 1, 1931. In 1944, it was sold to Moses Brothers Feed Company. The building was later demolished.

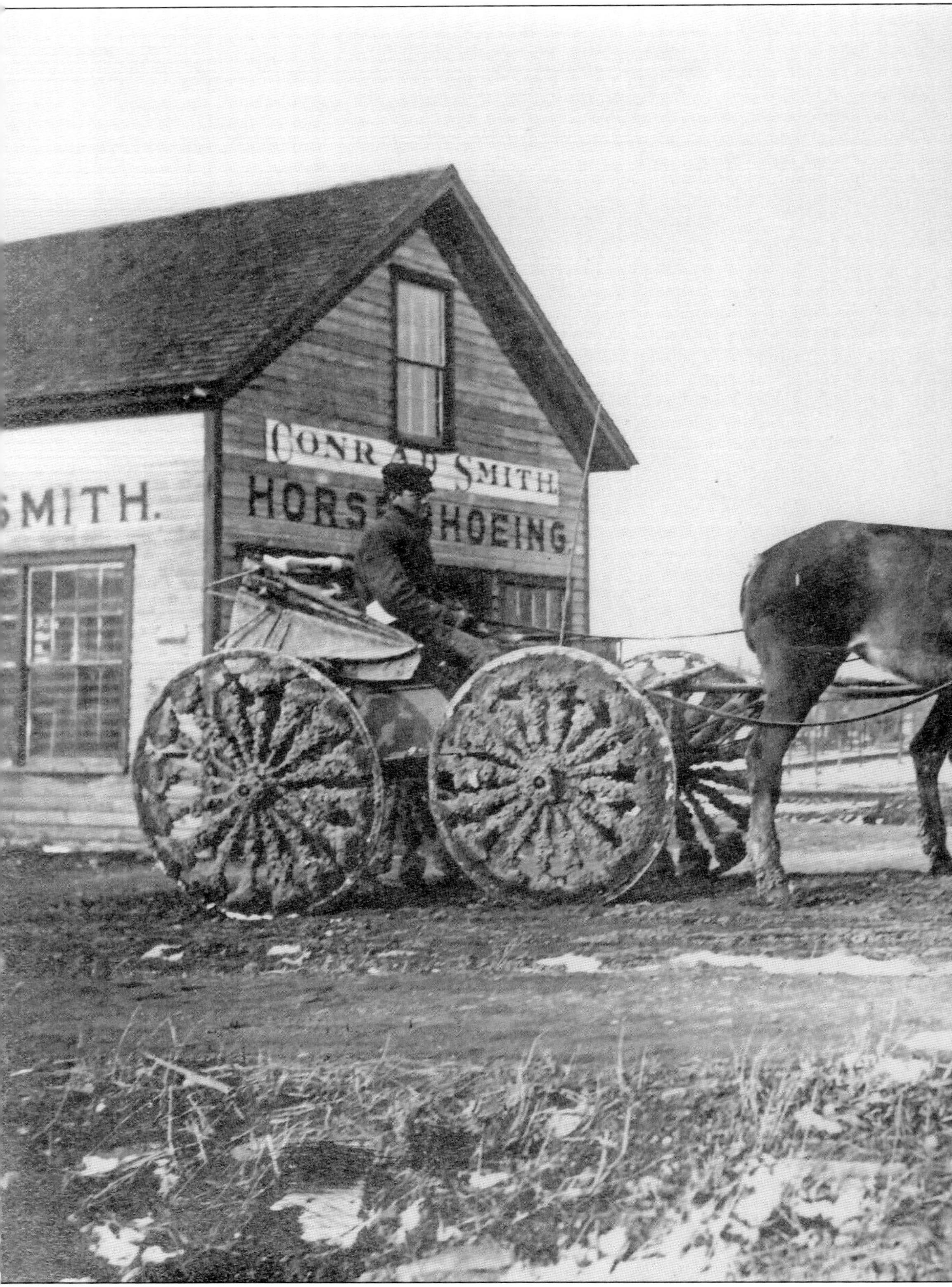
SMITH.
CONRAD SMITH
HORSESHOEING

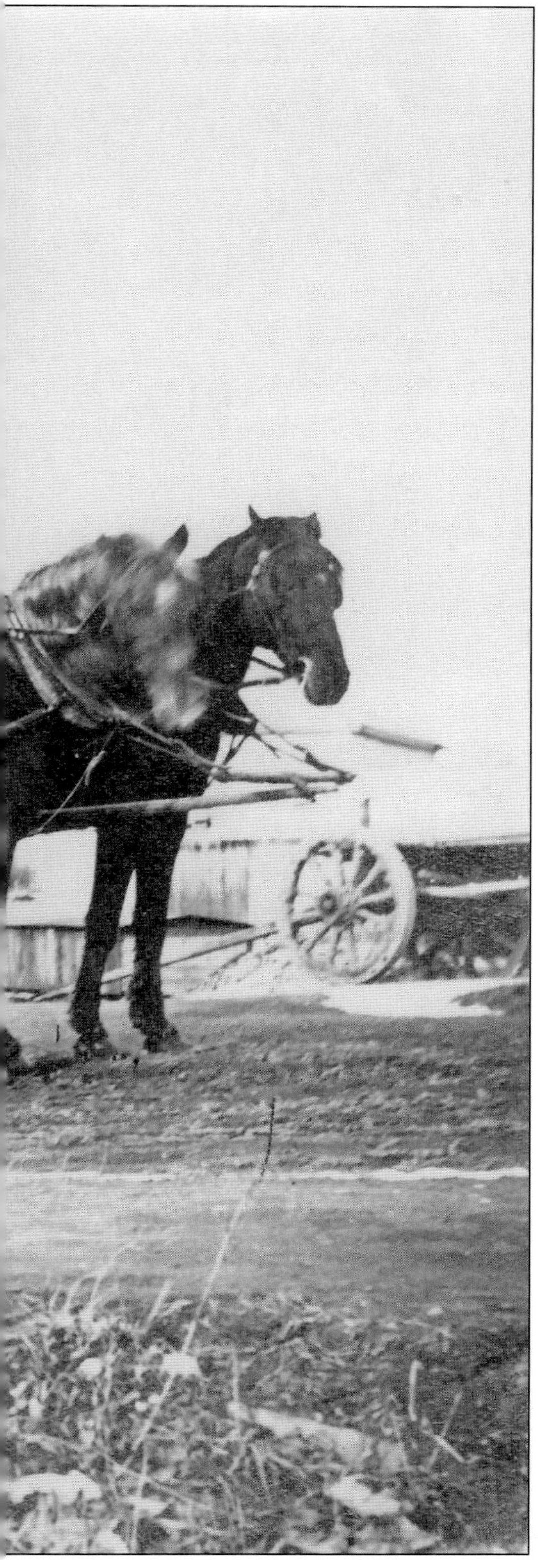

"Ernie" Lawrence was the Durhamville rural mail carrier. On this cold spring day, he found the country roads very muddy. Note the frozen mud on the wheels.

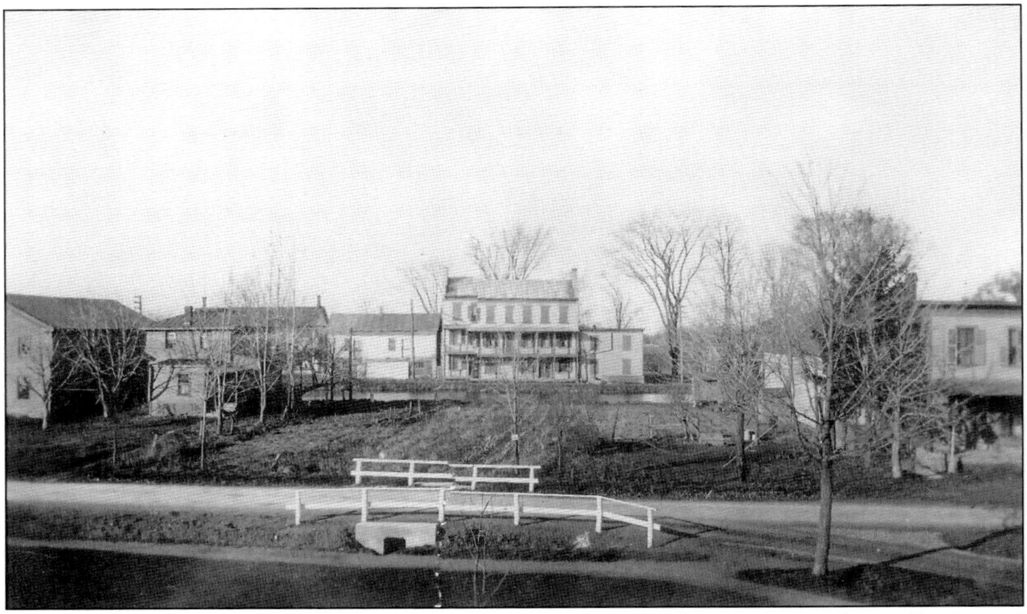

This is a unique view of the Pfeiffer Block from present-day Oneida Street in Durhamville. Owned by the Pfeiffer family, this building at one time housed the office for the justice of the peace, Teddy Briggs. Other rooms were used for rent and office space. This building was razed when the new New York State Route 46 was constructed.

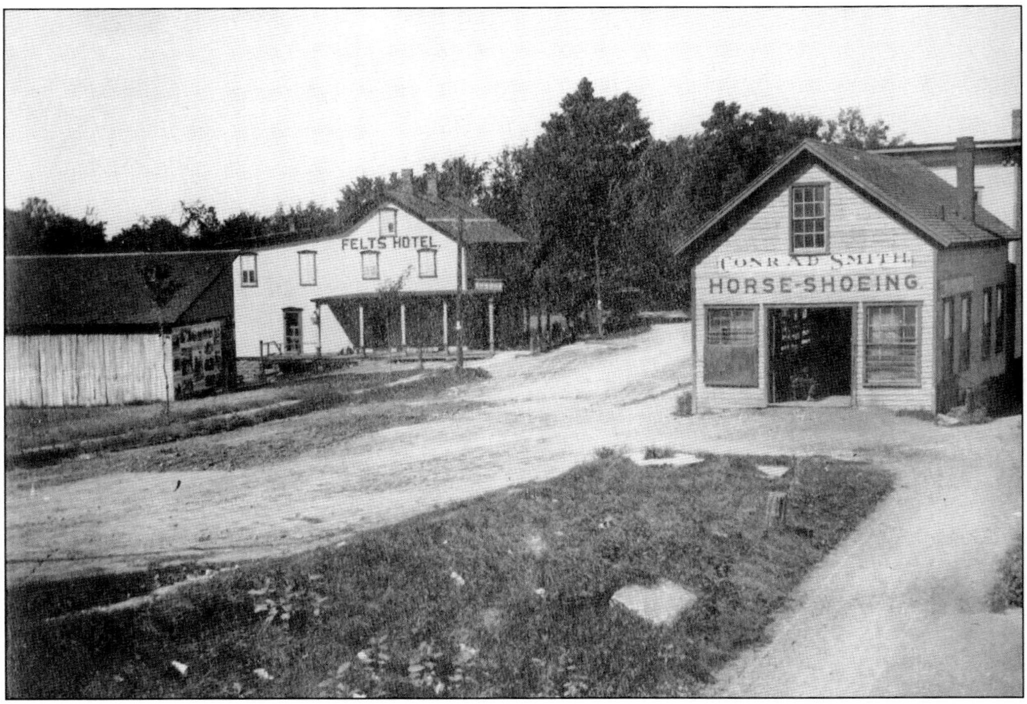

Pictured here are the Felts Hotel on Main Street and Conrad Smith's Blacksmith Shop. This photograph was taken from the bridge over the canal directly in front of Seibel's Store. The Felts building is still standing and in use. The blacksmith shop later became a gas station until it was demolished for construction of Route 46.

The residence of Elisha Norris Kelsey was located on Main Street in Durhamville. Kelsey established a clay pipe factory in 1877. While employing about 20 people, the factory produced 18,000 smoking pipes per day that were sold to all parts of the country. Durhamville suffered a severe fire in 1888 that included the destruction of the pipe factory.

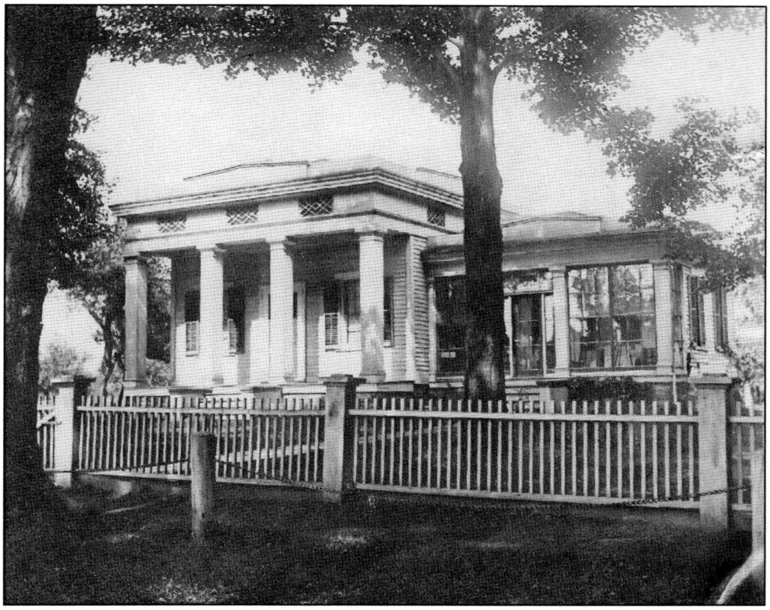

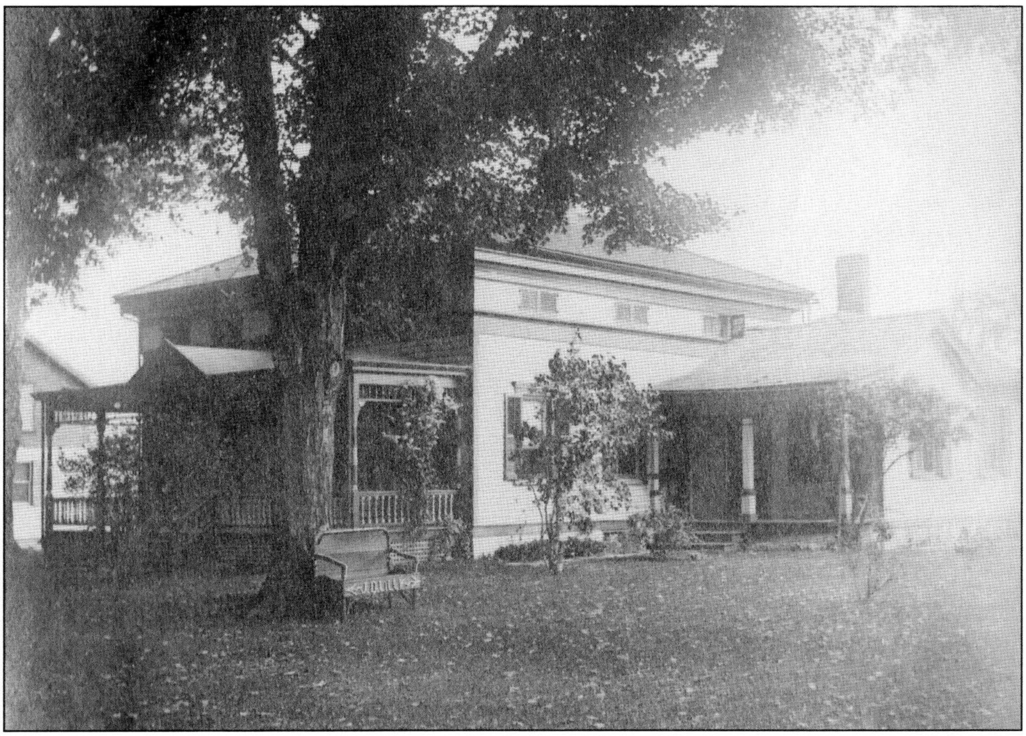

This home on Main Street in Durhamville was the residence of James D. Lilly. He served in the Civil War, and in 1876, was blinded in one eye when the Durhamville cannon fired prematurely during a Fourth of July celebration. Lilly was a glass cutter in the nearby Fox Glass Factory and lived to vote in 20 presidential elections.

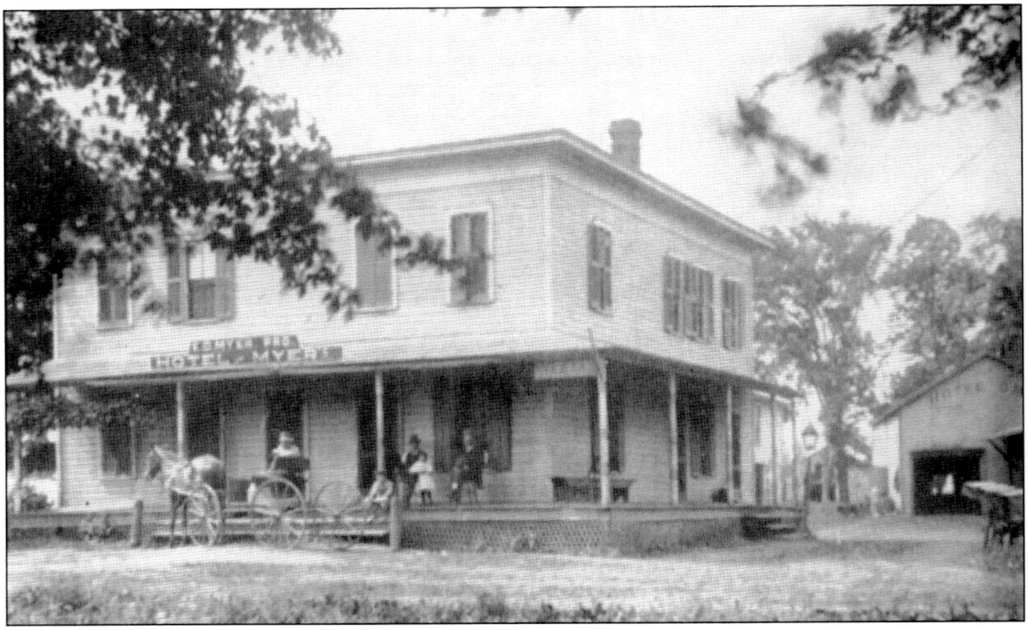

The Oriental Hotel, operated by Dennis Megan, was located on Church Street. It was later renamed Hotel Myer when it was sold to Enos D. Myer.

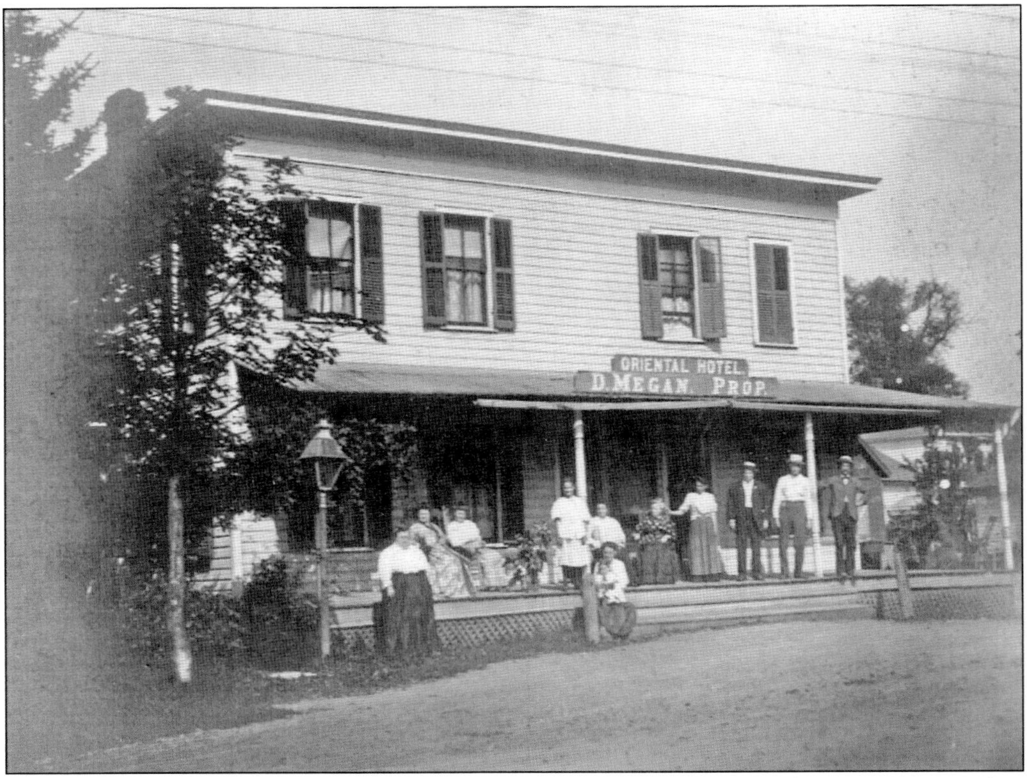

This is the same building as Hotel Myer. The Oriental Hotel was passed to Myer's son-in-law George Sixbury after Myer's death in 1917. After changing hands several more times, the building was razed to create a parking lot for the present location of the Durhamville Fire Department.

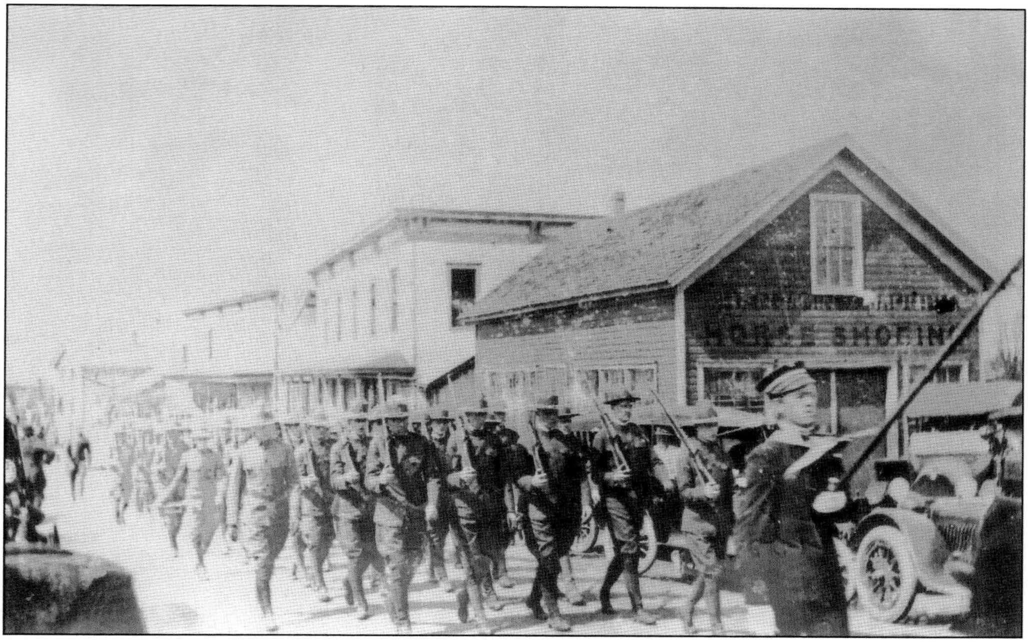

U.S. National Guard troops are shown marching in Durhamville on April 15, 1918. In the background can be seen the Odd Fellows hall and the blacksmith shop.

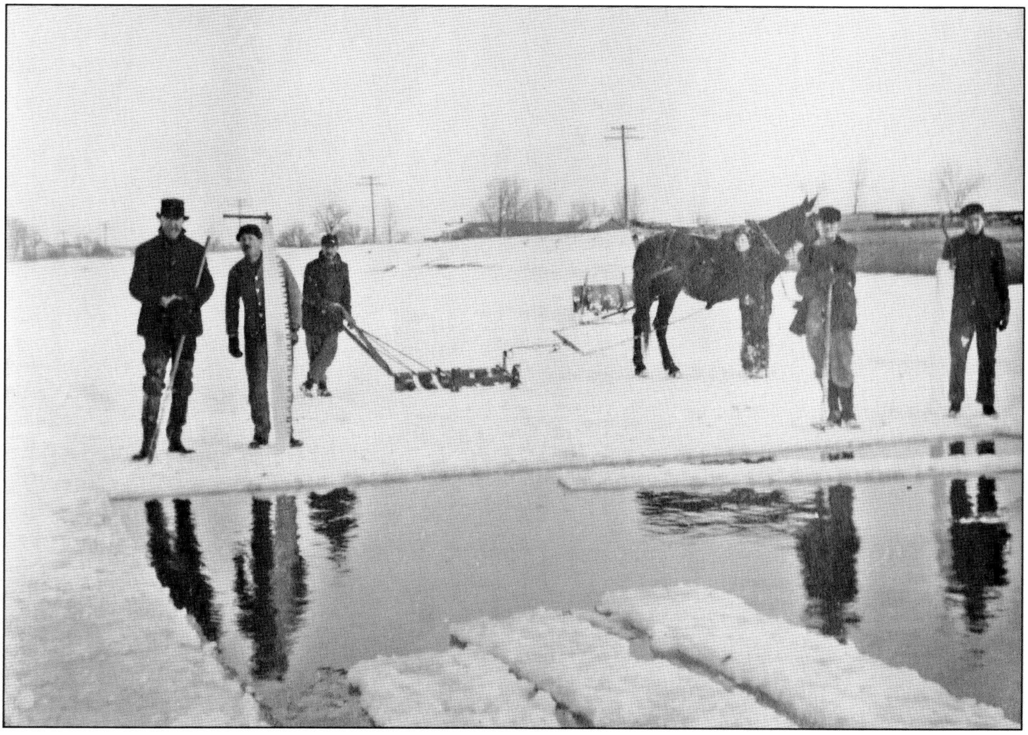

Ice harvesting took place on the Erie Canal as well as several ponds in the Verona area. The ice was cut into blocks of varying sizes and then stored in icehouses using sawdust as an insulator. The ice was delivered in the summer months for farm and household use. It was used on farms to refrigerate the cans of milk in the milk houses and in the iceboxes of homes.

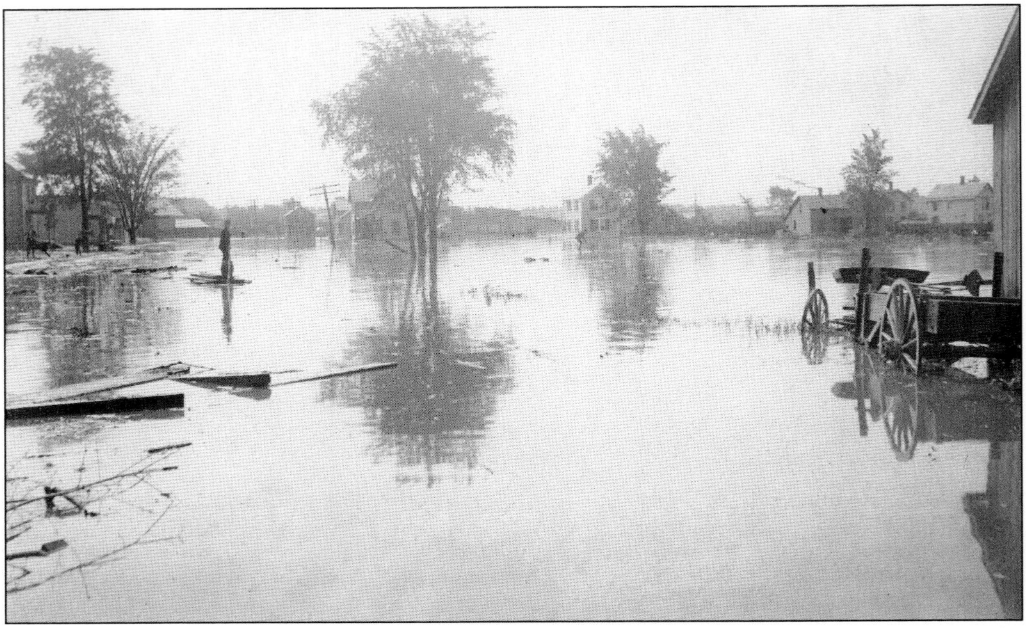

This was the scene of the big flood of 1922 in Durhamville. Although no lives were lost, the extent of property damage was incalculable. These conditions were largely alleviated by the straightening and deepening of Oneida Creek.

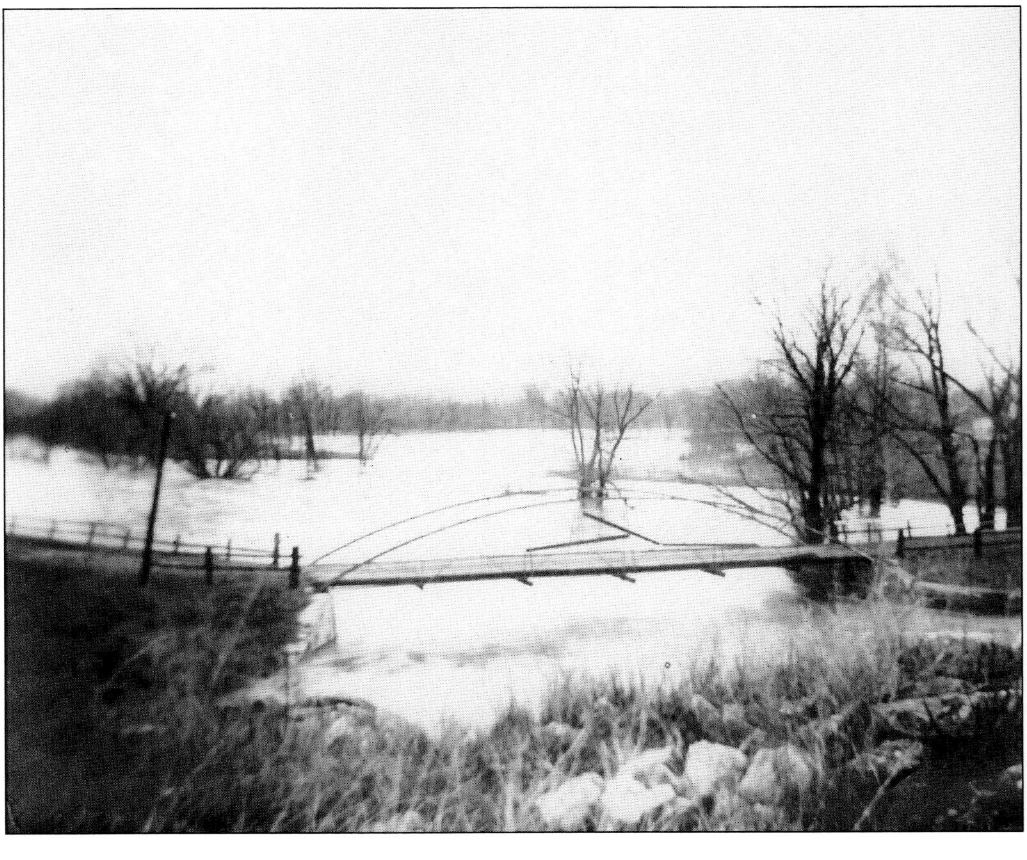

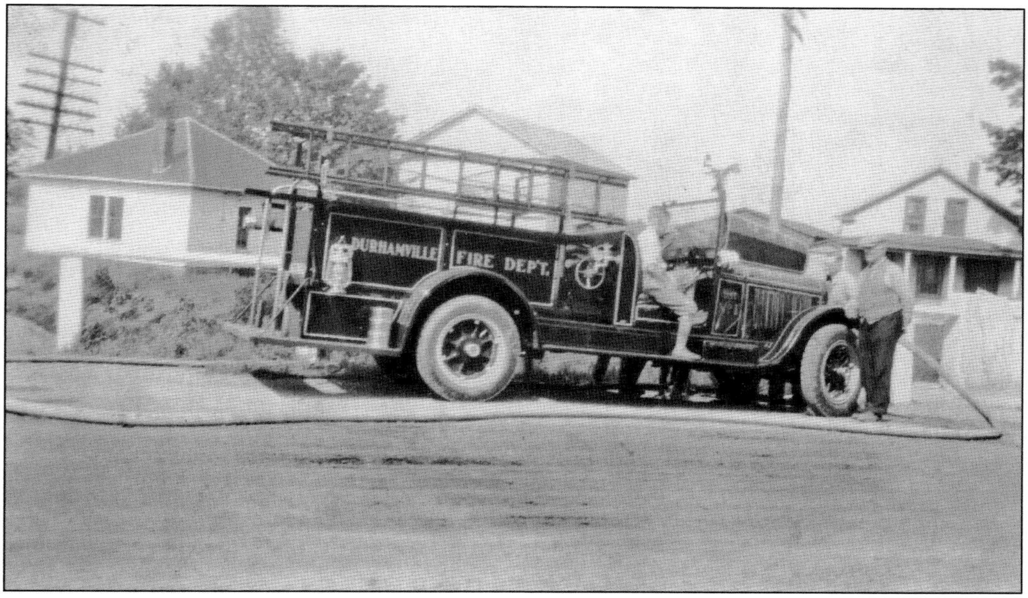

Using the latest in fire protection, volunteers from the Durhamville Fire Department are pumping water from the Erie Canal in the 1930s. In the background on the left is the old firehouse. The taller building in the middle is the former Methodist church, which is now the Durhamville Post Office.

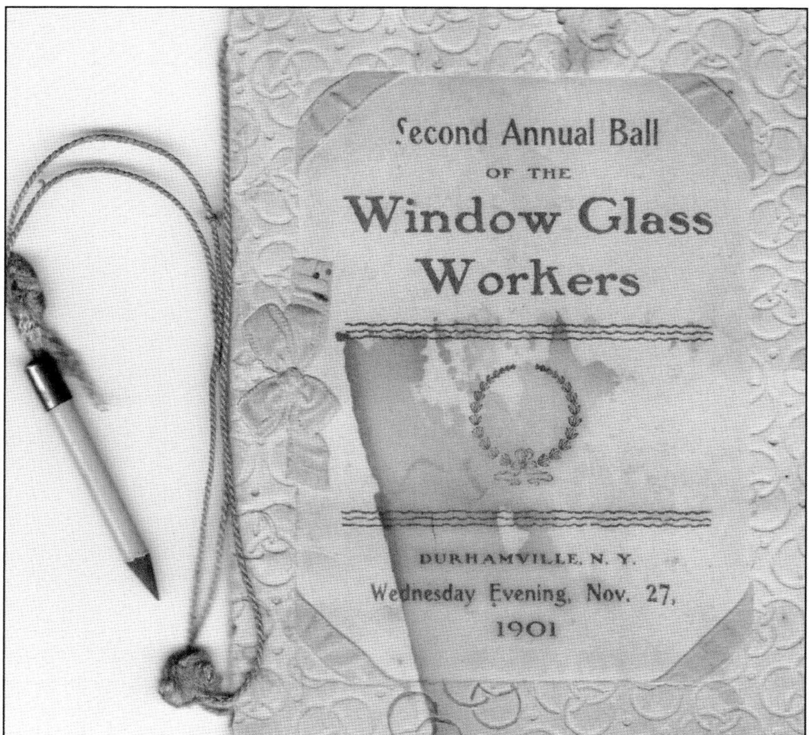

The Durhamville Glass Factory sponsored a yearly gala. This is a picture of a dance card from the Second Annual Ball in 1901.

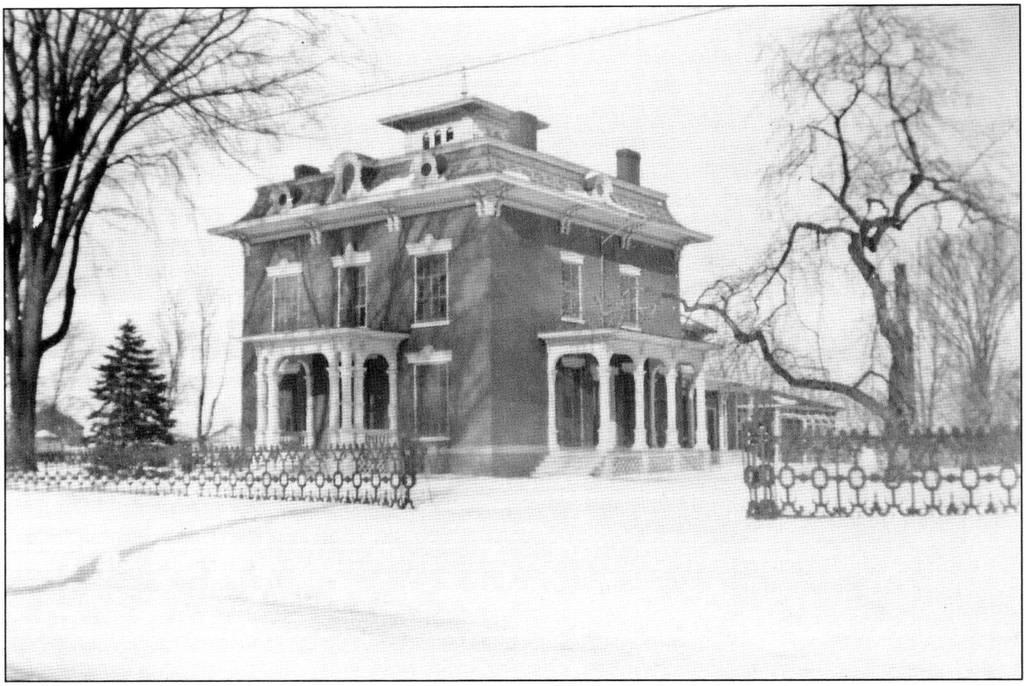

Pictured here is the Fox mansion located on Main Street in Durhamville. It was surrounded by beautiful grounds and bounded by a wrought iron fence. Sadly the upper floor burned and the Mansard roof had to be replaced.

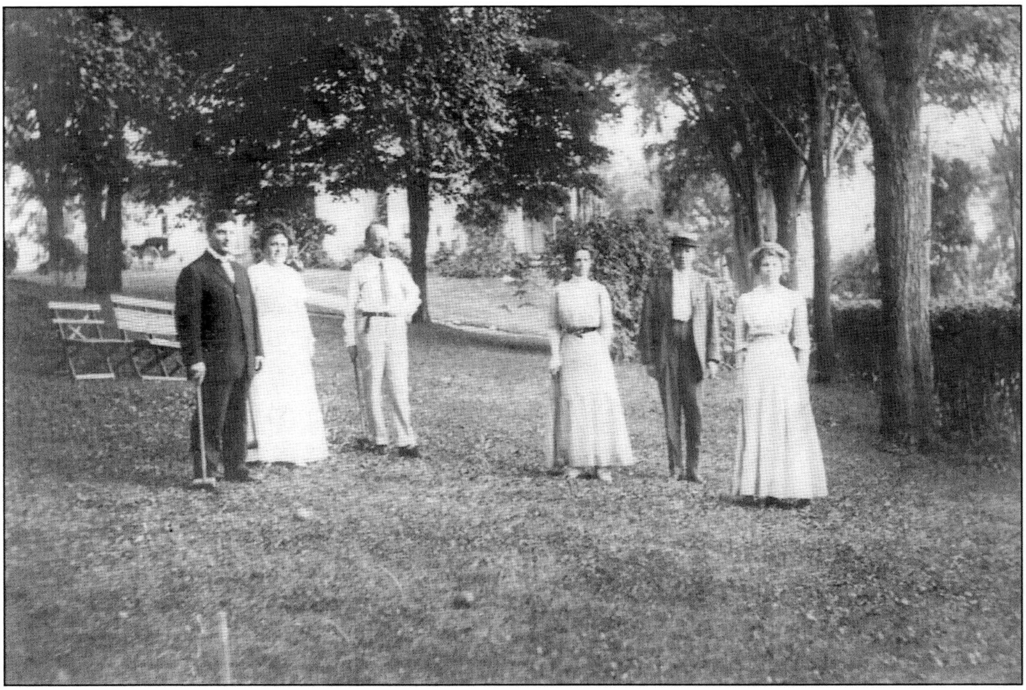

This picture shows members of the Fox family and guests playing croquet on the lush lawns of their mansion on Main Street in Durhamville. Croquet became a popular game to play in the late 19th century.

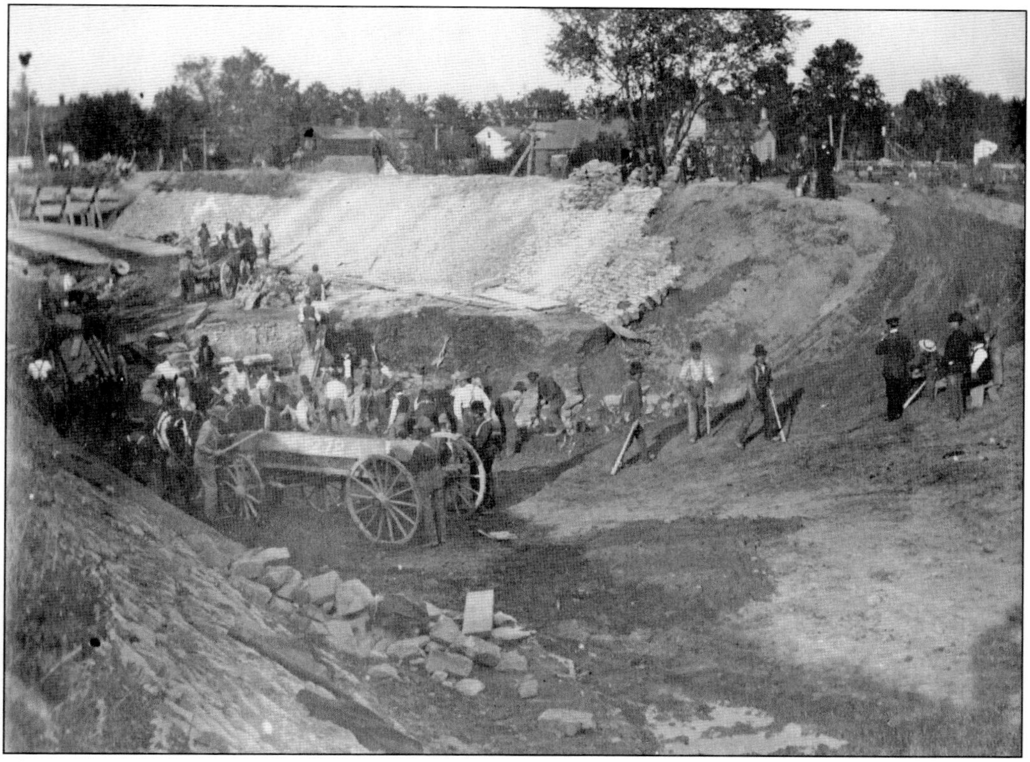

Shown here is a major break in the Erie Canal. The banks were reinforced with stone to prevent erosion. This provided employment for masons, many of whom emigrated from Wales.

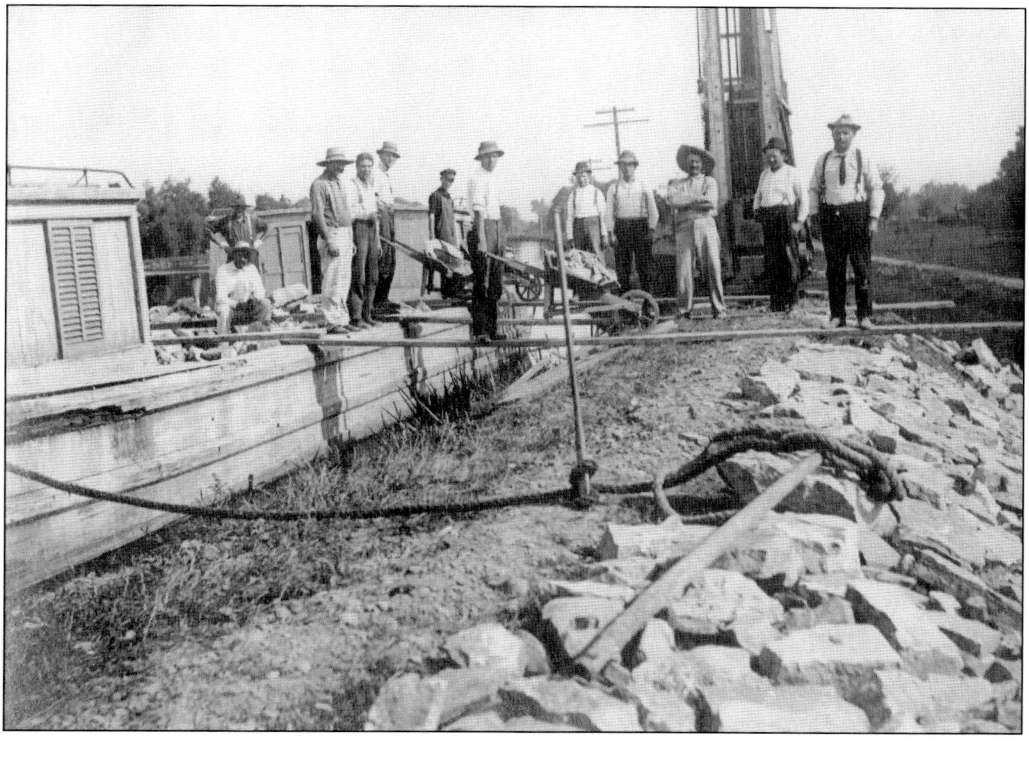

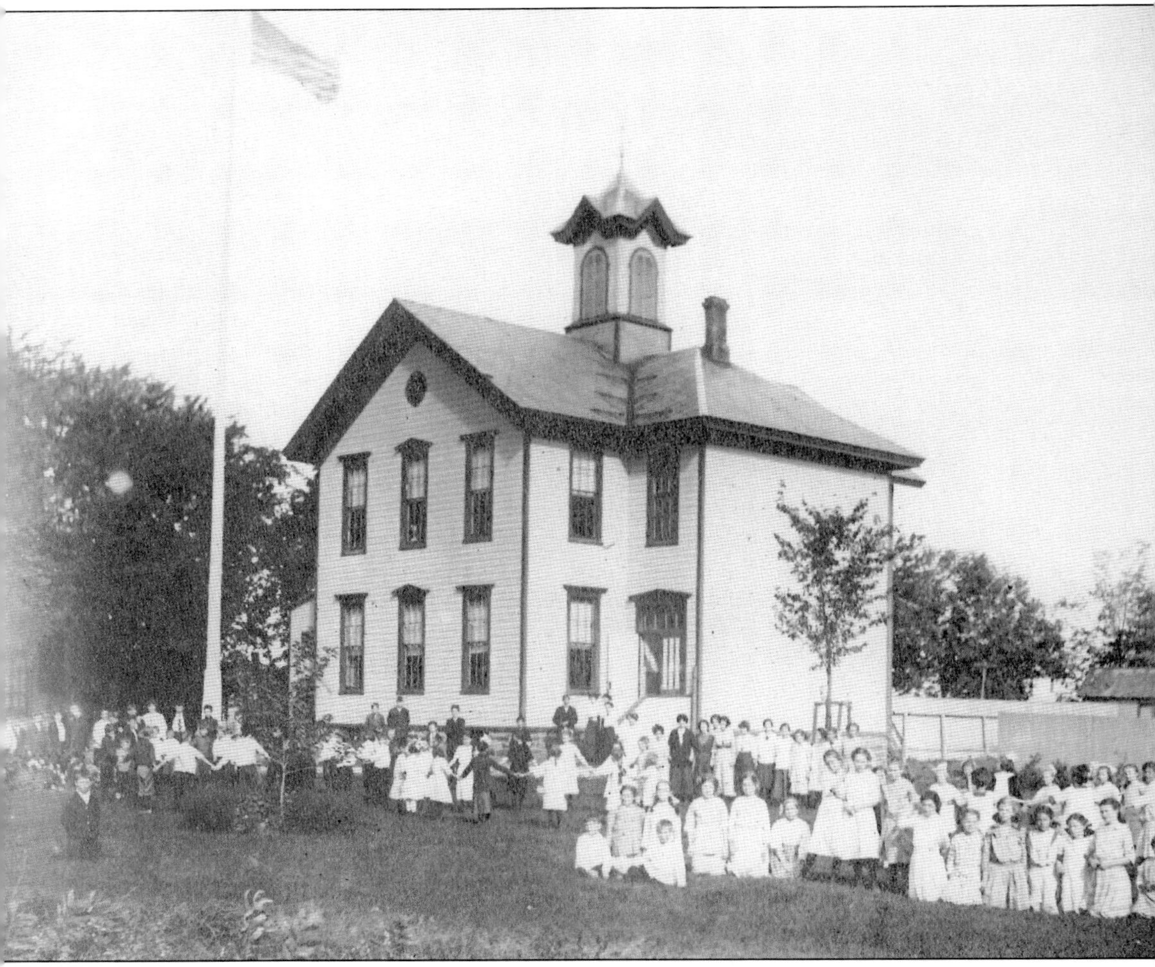

The old Durhamville school building looks much as it did when children were taught here through the eighth grade. The building consisted of four classrooms, with two grades to a room. It was closed when Durhamville consolidated with the Oneida City School District in the 1950s.

Two

Higginsville, State Bridge, and Dunbarton

The Higginsville Hamlet and its vicinity cover a large area of the central portion of the town and, at the canal's peak, also consisted of the nearby busy hamlets of State Bridge and Dunbarton.

Higginsville was basically a farming community until the Erie Canal helped introduce the typical canal-related commercial ventures of stores, hotels, boatyards, dry docks, and a post office. The state also located here a canal collector's office to calculate the amount of tax each boat owed based on the weight of its cargo.

Christopher Higgins, a native of Connecticut, gave this hamlet its name. He owned and operated the Higginsville Hotel before he died in a train accident in 1865.

One point of particular interest in Higginsville is Stark's Landing. Jabez Stark moved to Higginsville from Seneca Falls around 1820. He owned and operated many canal-related businesses, including a hotel, store, and blacksmith shop. The family homestead and hotel were common sites for social gatherings and dances. A state historical sign at the corner of Germany Road and New York State Route 46 marks the site of the buildings.

The Oneida Lake Canal, better known as the "Side Cut," was constructed to provide a shortened route for westbound travelers to reach the lake. Along it was a quarry from which the stone was used to build the support structures for canal bridges and walls. St. Patrick's Church in Oneida was also built using the same stone as it was taken and transported by canal boats to the construction site.

A state-maintained highway and canal bridge identified the nearby hamlet of State Bridge. Businesses included a hotel, provision stores, blacksmith shop, and post office. An original section of "Clinton's Ditch" is still visible near the intersection of New York State Routes 46 and 31.

A second glass factory was established in the town of Verona in the nearby settlement of Dunbarton, located just a mile north of State Bridge. This factory was owned by Loring Munroe and George Cowarden and employed 50 master glassblowers who produced a large amount of superior glass. Little evidence remains of its existence except for small shards of glass which glisten in the sun when the adjacent fields are being fitted for planting by local farmers.

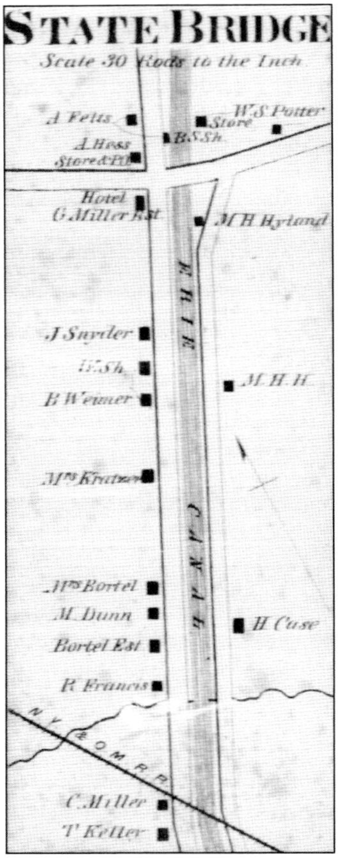

This 1874 map of State Bridge shows in detail the homes, stores, and shops where the residents lived and conducted their lives. Small hamlets like this in the town were dependent on the traffic created by the canal.

State Bridge was a bustling community. "Rollie" Potter's General Store, Feed Mill, and Post Office were located on the "heelpath" side of the canal.

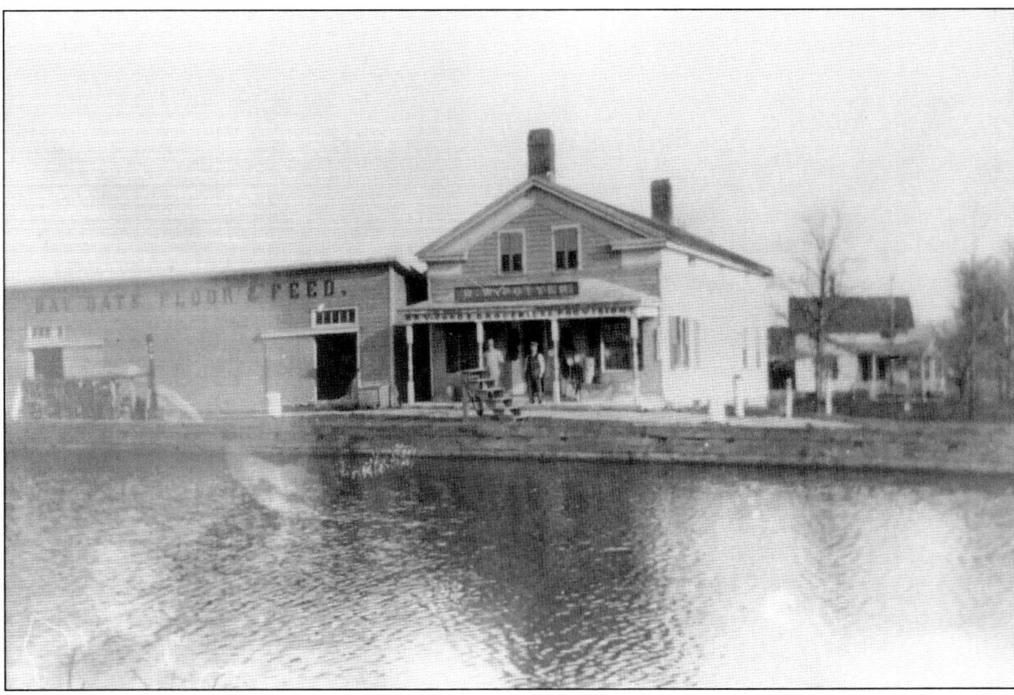

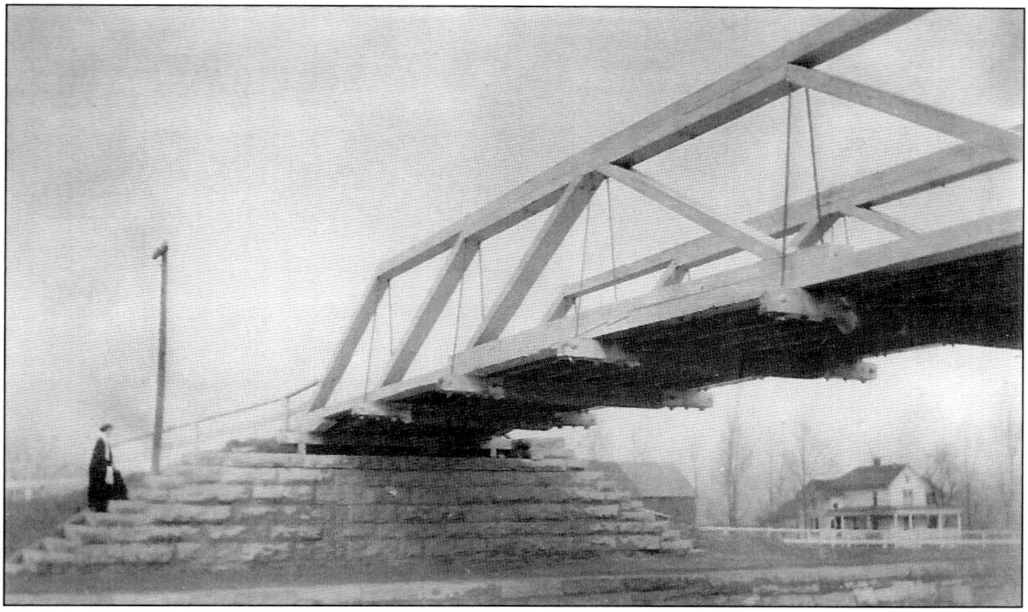

A woman climbs the masonry steps of the State Bridge hamlet's namesake to reach the other side of the Erie Canal. This picture is an excellent example of the skilled labor provided by the master masons to build the bridge stone-support structures and to secure the banks of the canal. Much of the stone came from nearby quarries in Higginsville.

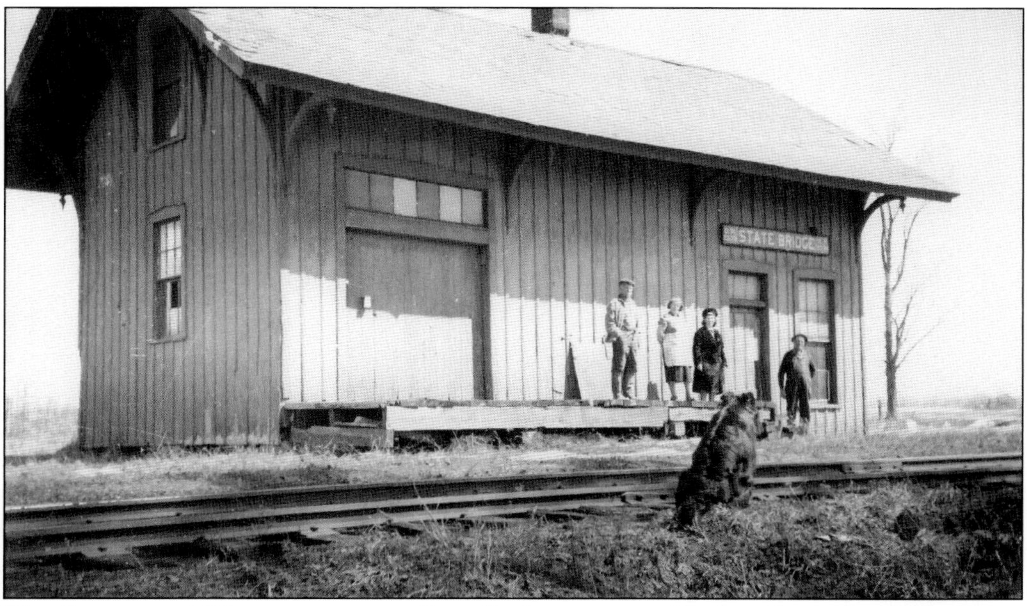

The Ontario and Western station at State Bridge was completed in September 1869. There was also a milk station and creamery across the road. This station was noteworthy because the stationmaster was a woman. Theresa Dunn held this position for over 50 years.

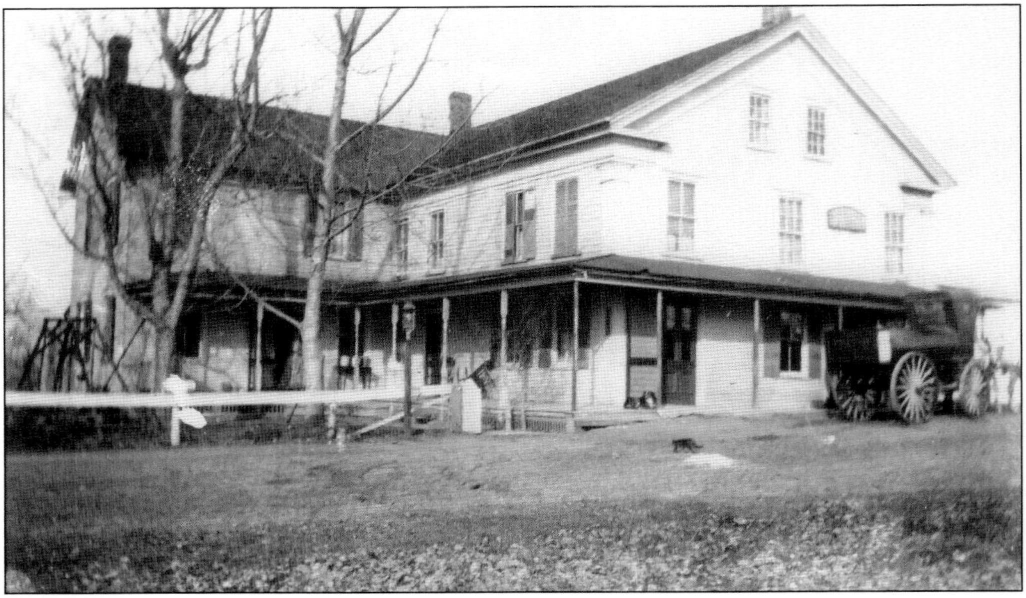

The State Bridge, or Collins Hotel, was operated by Sylvester and Althea Collins. Its location along the towpath and beside the State Road drew patrons from all walks of life. The three-story frame structure was destroyed by fire on October 13, 1917, due to a defective chimney. The loss was valued at $8,000.

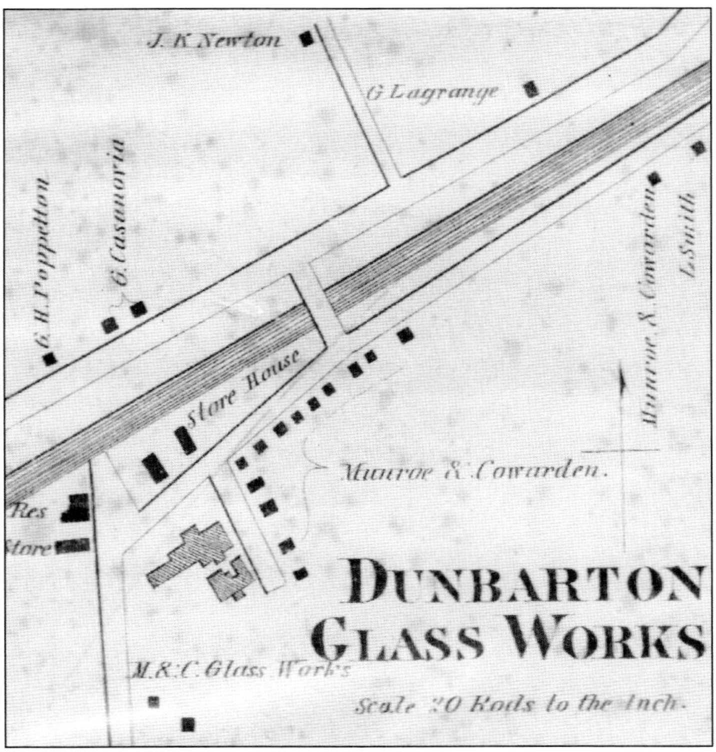

This map, taken from an 1874 atlas, shows the size and extent of the Dunbarton Glass Factory and the factory homes of some of the workers. It was common during the 19th century for entrepreneurs to establish factory communities within towns. Employee housing and company stores were typically built by factory owners to meet the needs of their workers and maximize company profits. Shin plasters, a form of money, were earned by the Dunbarton Glass Factory employees to spend within the factory store. The factory was owned by Loring Munroe and Anthony Cowarden and later by John Cooper.

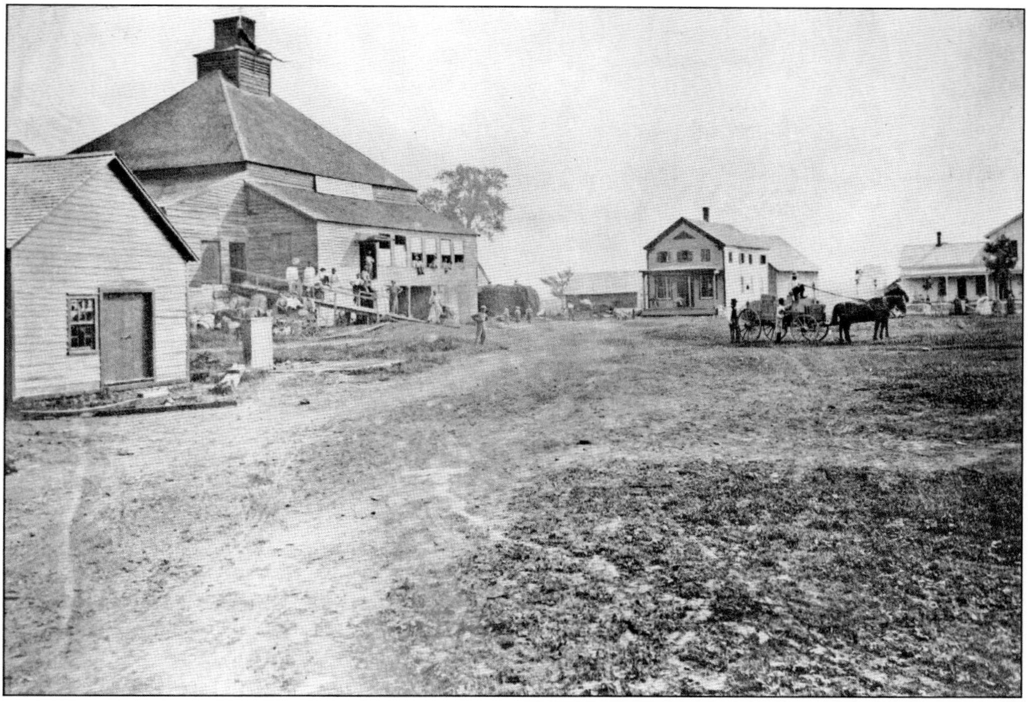

The Dunbarton Glass Factory was located north of the State Bridge on the Erie Canal. It produced superior glass items, including window glass. The business was purchased by the United Glass Company, one of the largest glass manufacturers in the country, and was closed in 1890.

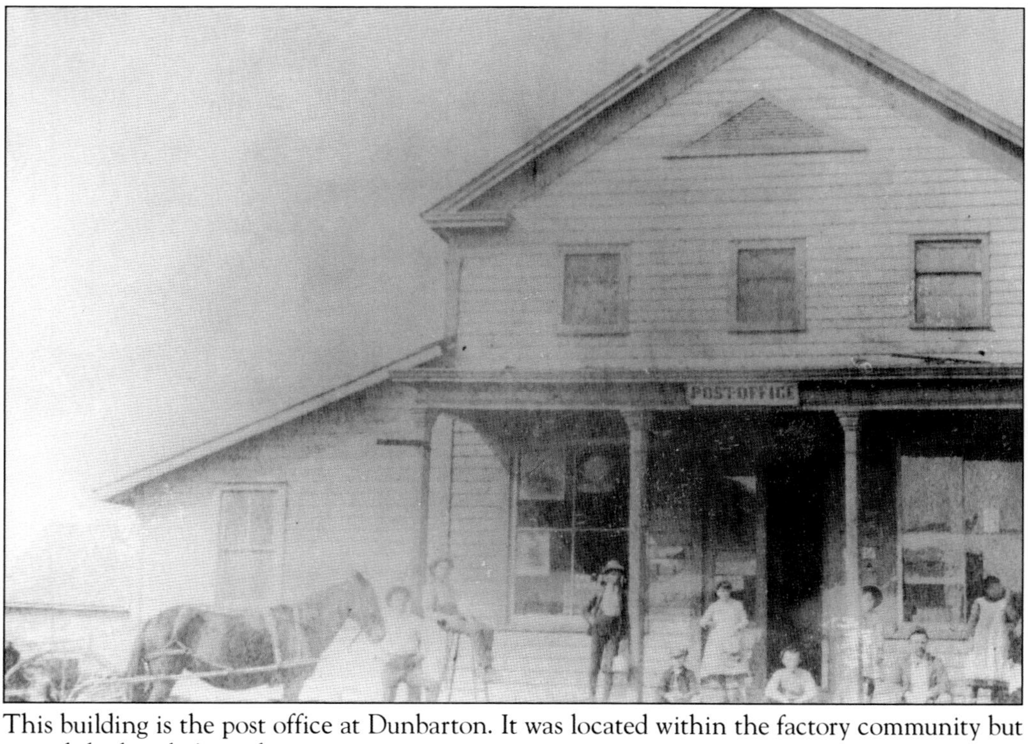

This building is the post office at Dunbarton. It was located within the factory community but served the hamlet's residents, too.

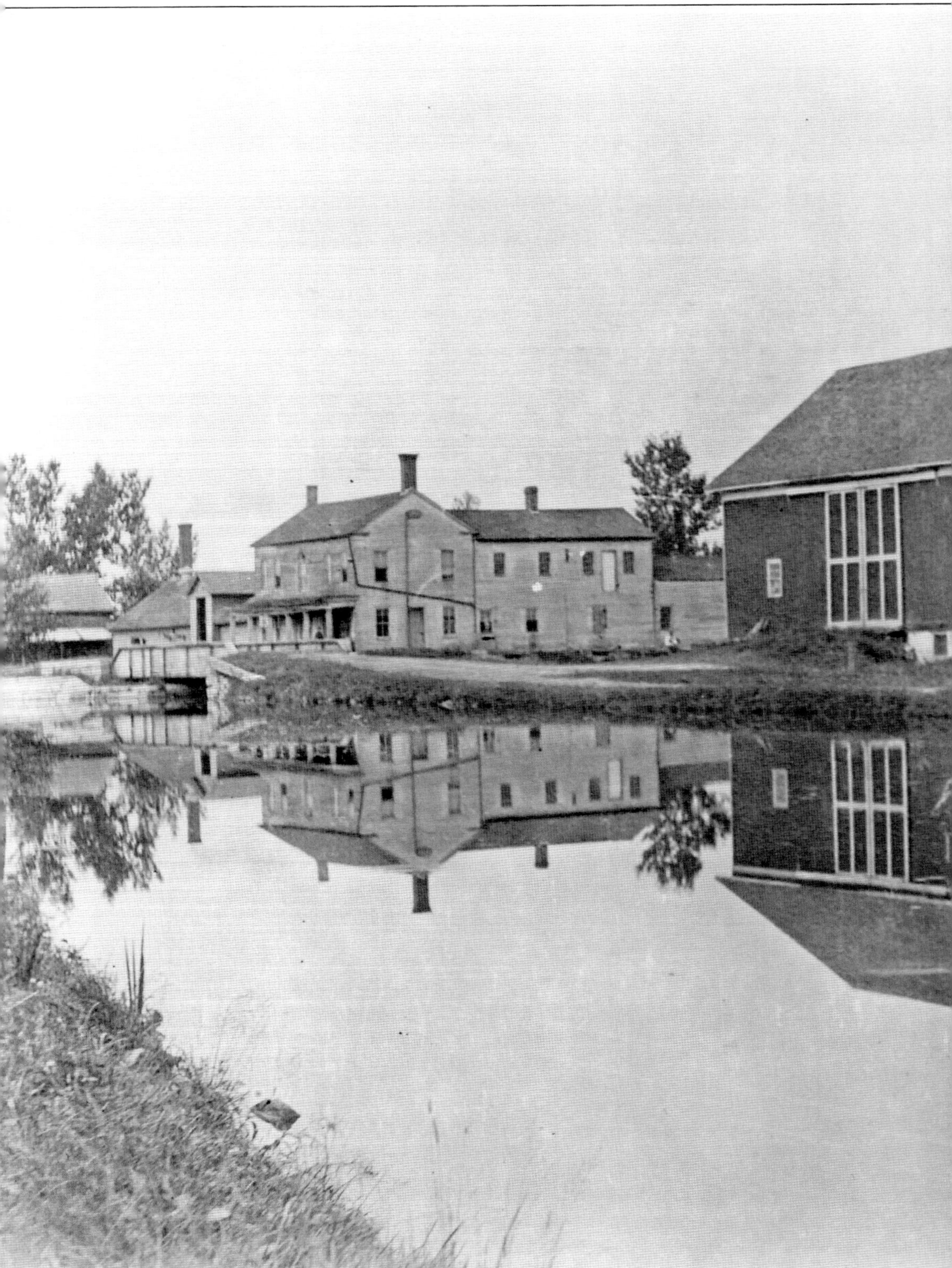

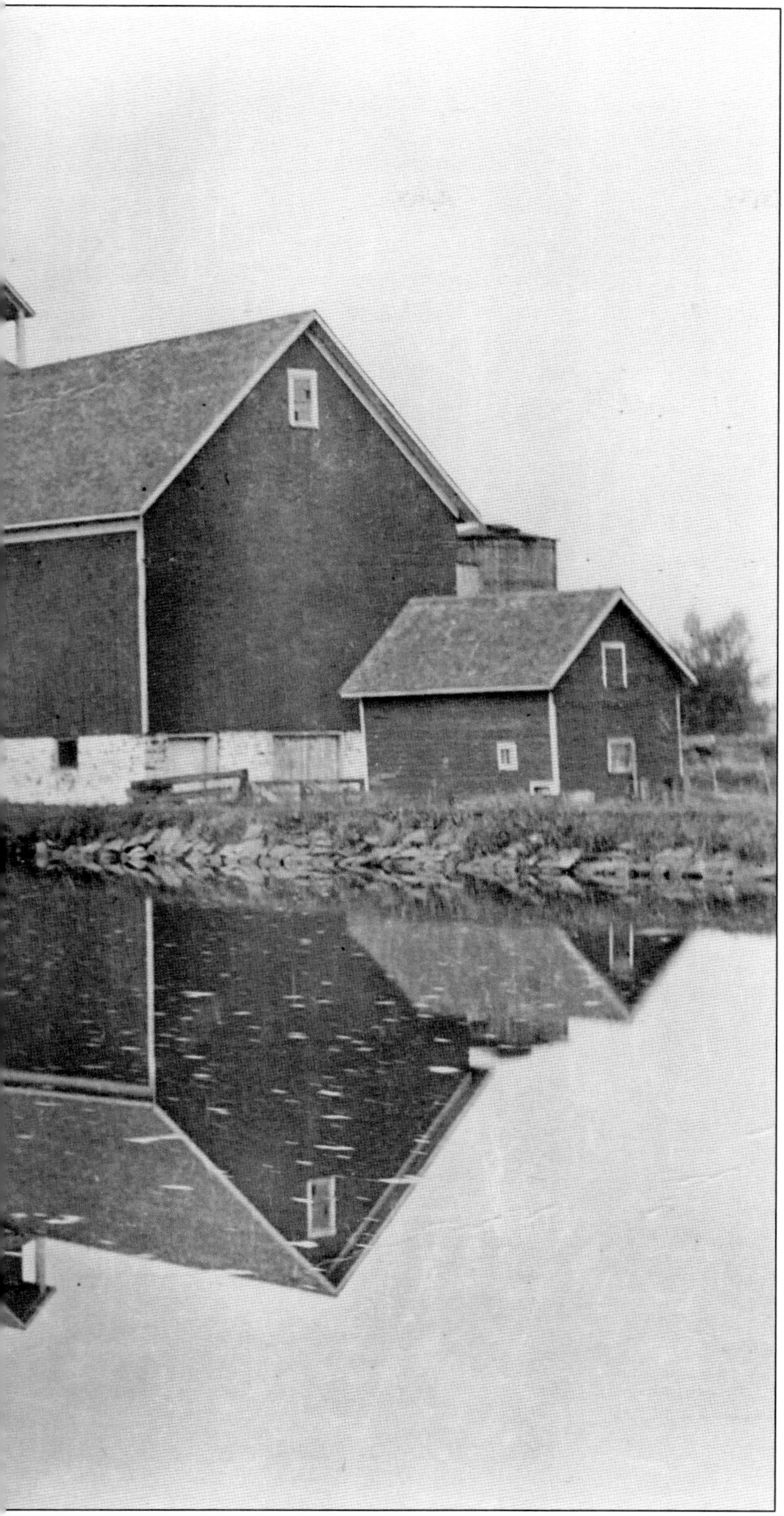

The Whaley Cheese Factory was owned by Dr. James Whaley, whose wife was the daughter of Christopher Higgins, the founder of Higginsville. The Higgins homestead, hotel, and cheese factory were located at the intersection of the Erie and Side Cut Canals. The factory operated until 1927. It was later torn down with the widening of New York State Route 46.

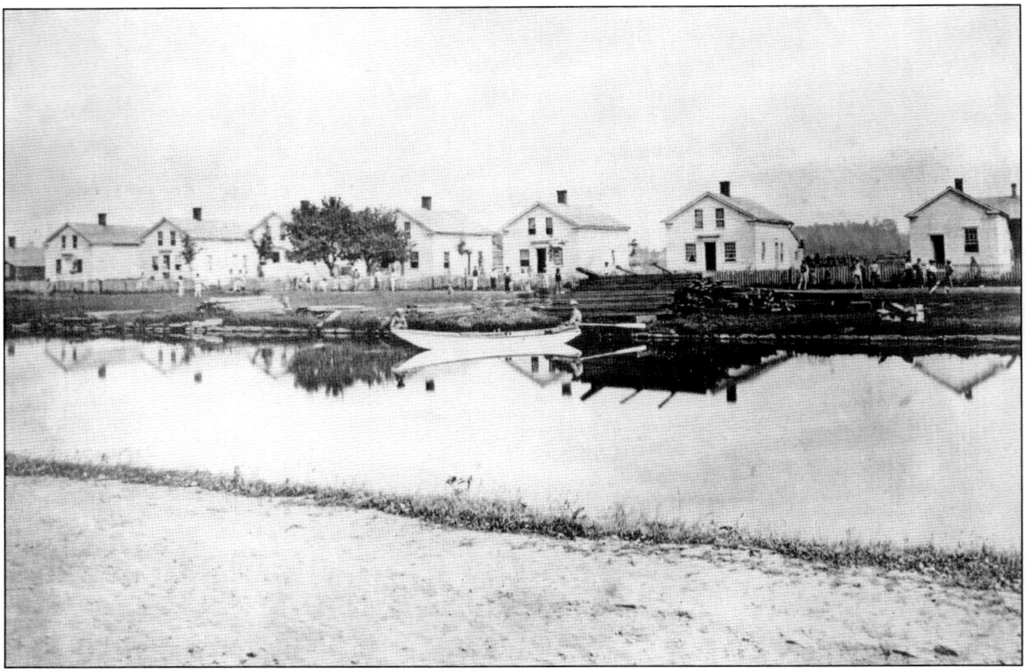

Pictured are the homes of Dunbarton Glass Factory workers. The Erie Canal is pictured in the foreground, and the photograph suggests that the canal may have been a source of amusement, too.

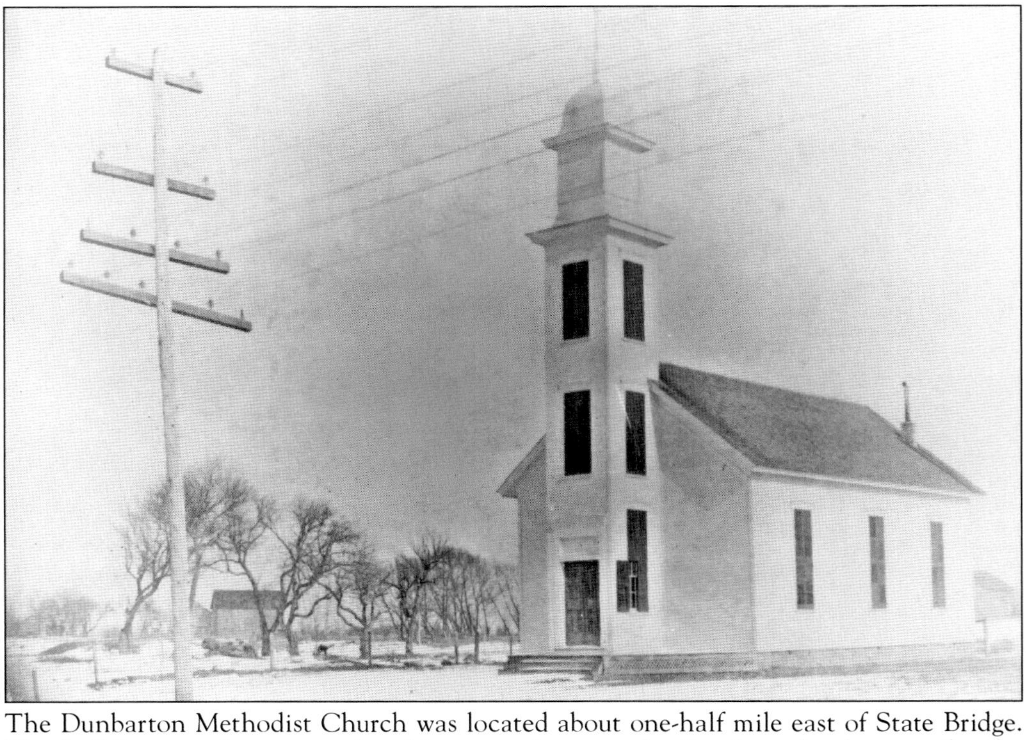

The Dunbarton Methodist Church was located about one-half mile east of State Bridge. The building was later moved to Verona to become the Sunday school rooms for the Verona Methodist Church.

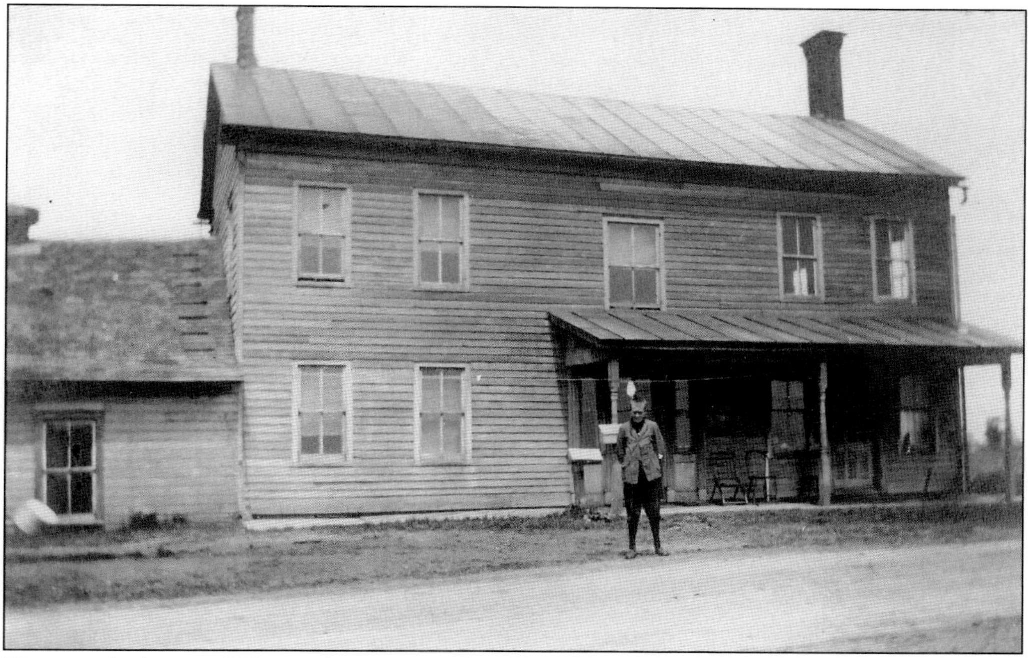

This was the home of Christopher Higgins, for whom Higginsville was named. Higgins, a member of the Whig party, served as town clerk in 1854 and actively represented the hamlet in all matters. In later years, a cheese factory was added to which local farmers brought their milk to be processed. This factory was then called the Whaley Cheese Factory.

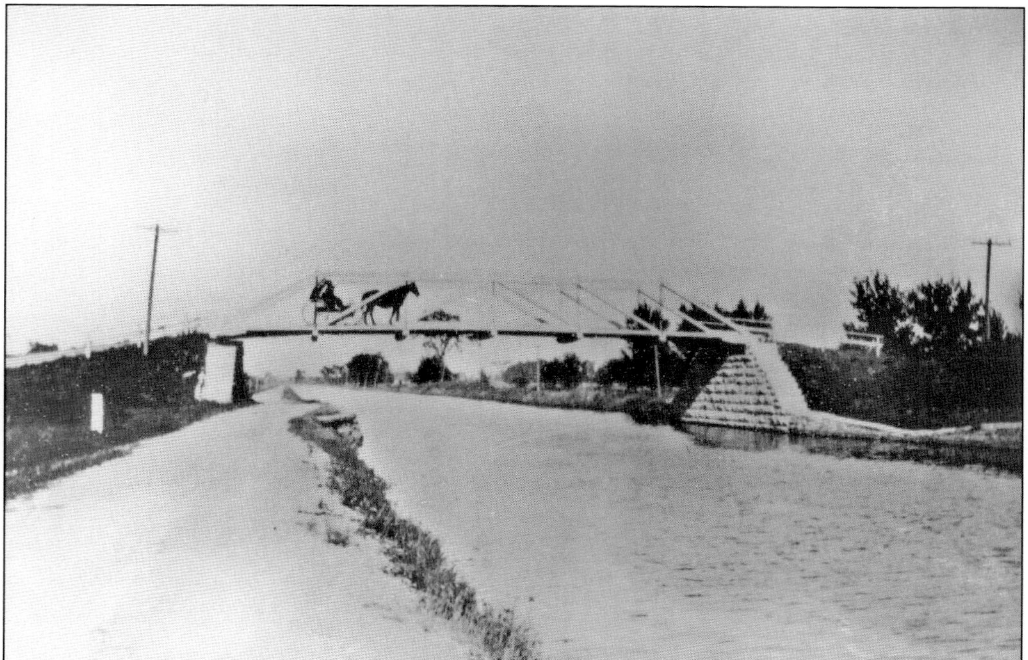

This view of the bridge at Dunbarton shows a horse and carriage crossing the Erie Canal. Note the width of the towpath in the left foreground and the height of the bridge. These were designed to accommodate teams and drivers.

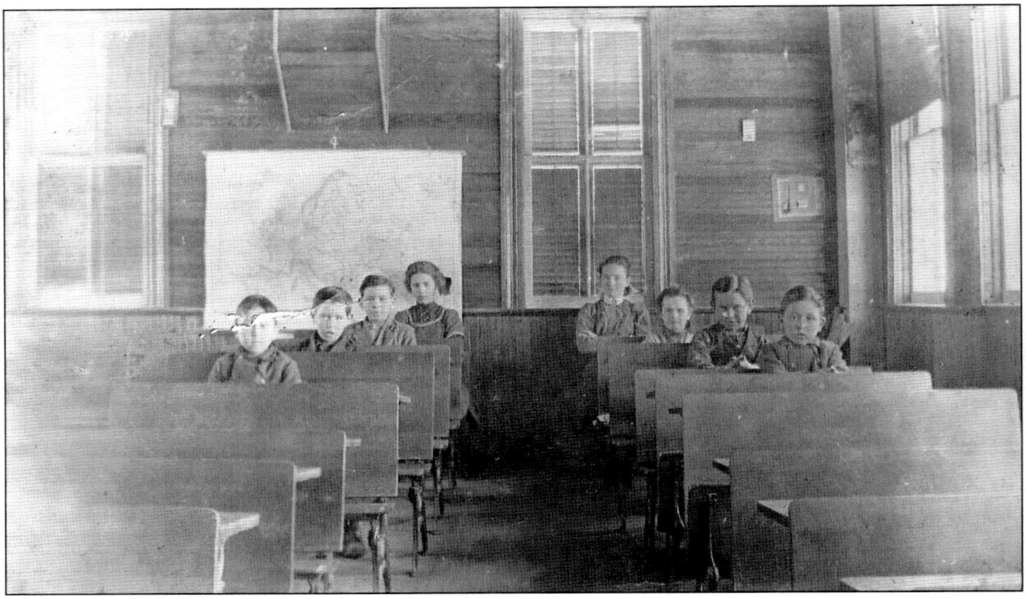

This is a rare glimpse inside the one-room schoolhouse on Jug Point Road in the early 1900s. Note the wooden desks and map on the back wall. One of the students pictured is Celia Brown. (Photograph courtesy of Sandra G. Fleming.)

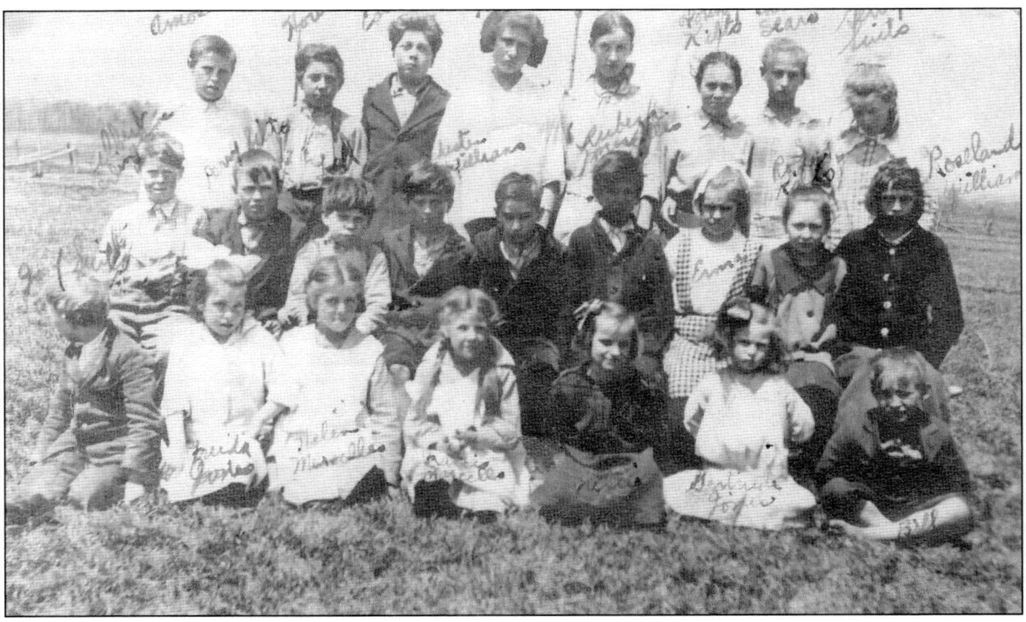

This photograph was taken in 1915 showing the students at the Jug Point Road School. Among the pupils are several children of the Brown, Jones, Marcellus, Sears, Suits, and Williams families. The school still stands as a private family residence. (Photograph courtesy of Sandra G. Fleming.)

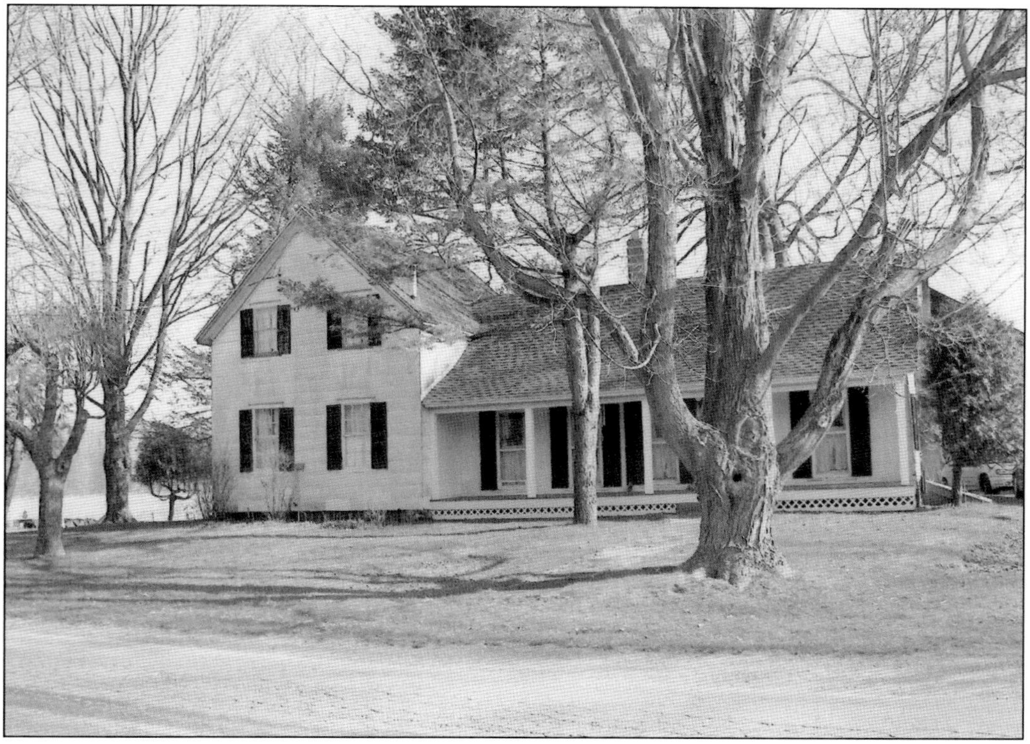

This quaint farmhouse (above) located on Mills Road was owned by Charles Felter in the early 1900s. He was a butcher who raised cattle and poultry for sale to customers in the Oneida area. The stone smokehouse and barn were essential to the butchering business. The farm was purchased in 1918 by Jacob and Alexandra Cmaylo who operated a dairy farm (below). The Cmaylos also raised geese and turkeys for sale during the holidays.

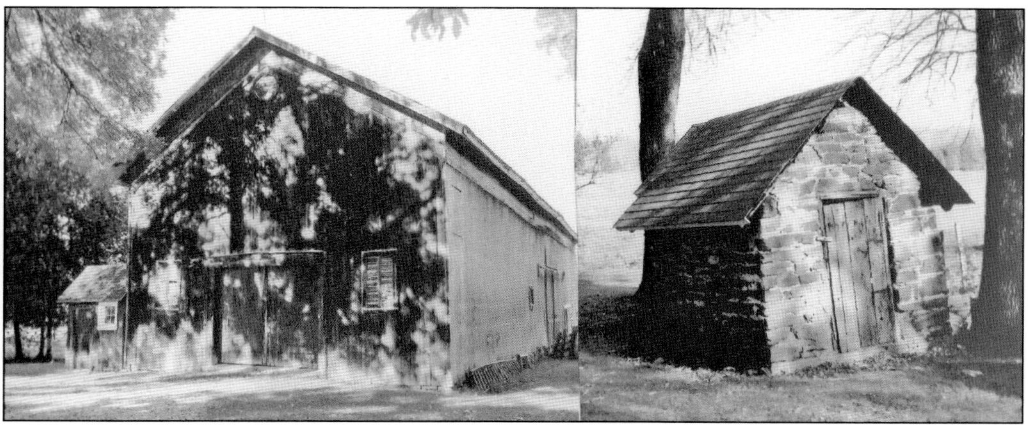

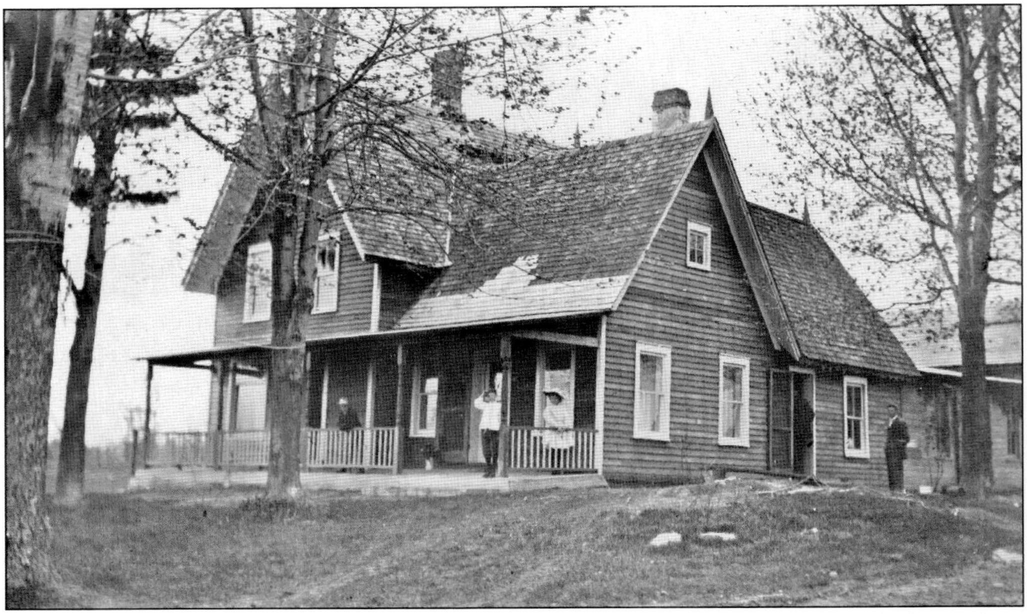

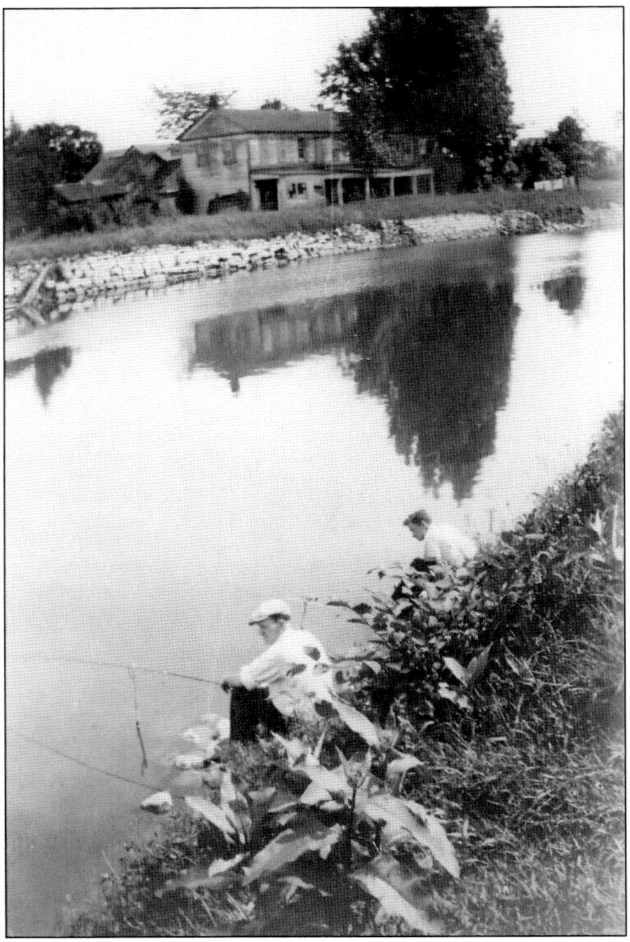

This 1912 photograph shows the Newey House on Higginsville Road. It was built in the 1800s by Arthur Newey, a farmer and a furniture maker. He came to America from Birmingham, England, where he was a church bell ringer. He also served as a private in Company C, 50th Regiment of the New York Engineers during the American Civil War.

In this photograph, two gentlemen fish in the Erie Canal. Pictured across the canal in Higginsville is a hotel owned by Tony Berical, which operated from the 1890s to 1910. Note the stonework, which helped to stabilize the canal banks.

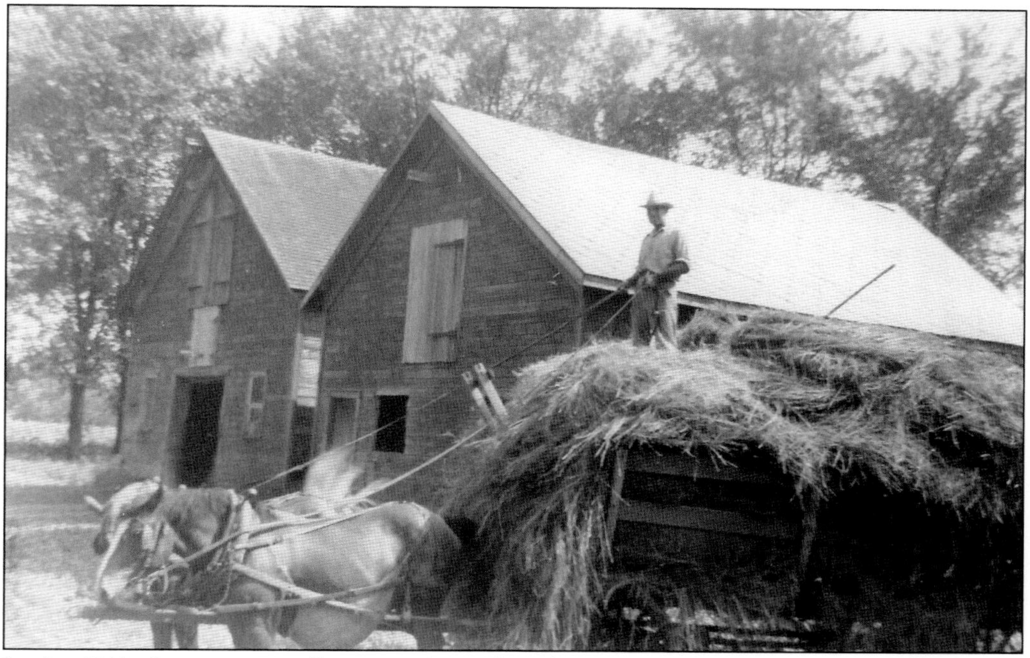

In the 1940s, horses were still commonly used on farms, as gasoline was being rationed during World War II. Pictured here, Henry Peploski with his team of Mustangs, Slug and Daisy, are bringing in the day's final load of hay. (Photograph courtesy of the Peploski family.)

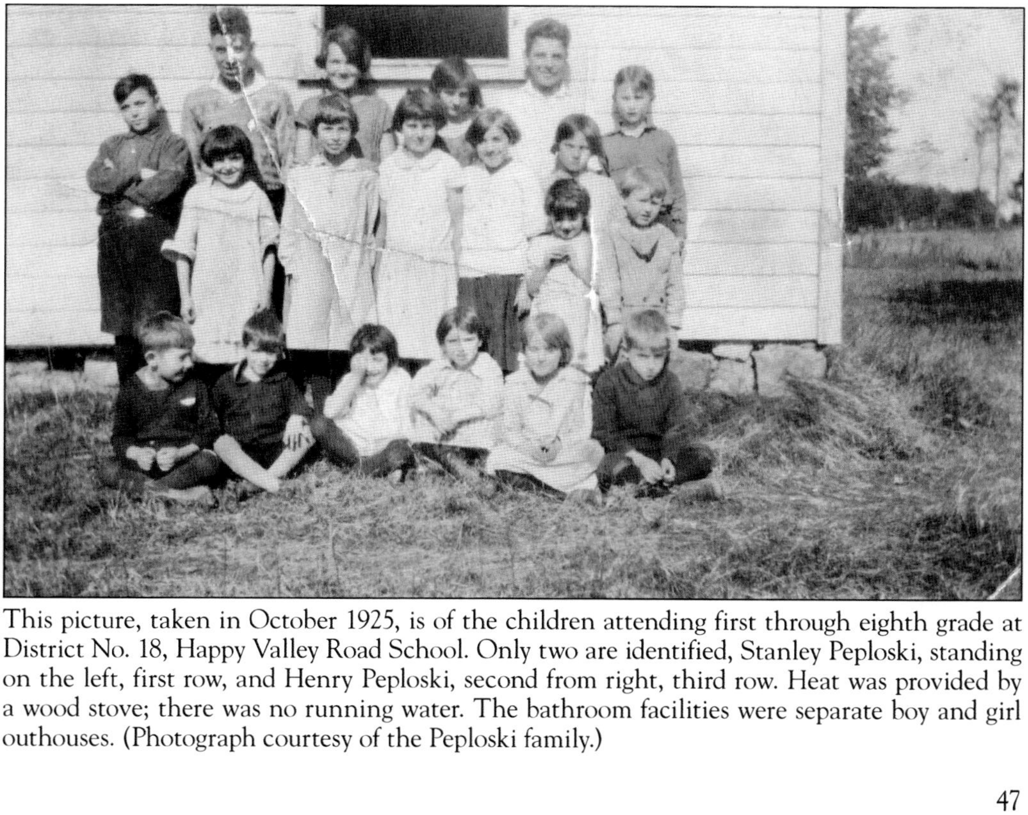

This picture, taken in October 1925, is of the children attending first through eighth grade at District No. 18, Happy Valley Road School. Only two are identified, Stanley Peploski, standing on the left, first row, and Henry Peploski, second from right, third row. Heat was provided by a wood stove; there was no running water. The bathroom facilities were separate boy and girl outhouses. (Photograph courtesy of the Peploski family.)

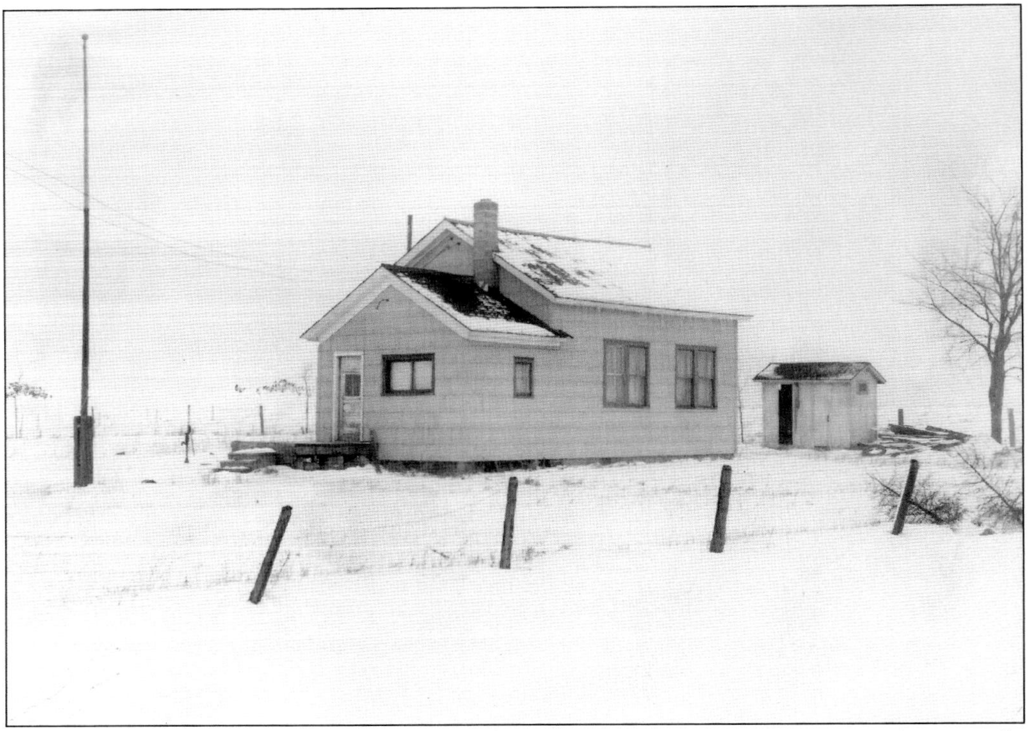

The White School was built in 1868 on White Road, now known as Poppleton Road. Originally known as District No. 29, it was changed to District No. 21 in 1881. Classes were previously held at a house owned by Henry White. The new schoolhouse measured 20 feet by 26 feet with a 6-foot square entryway. In 1925, children from the Seybold and Hyland families transferred from the Jug Point Road school in District No. 24, later the Wilcox home. In 1938, the school was wired for a power line. The school closed in 1943.

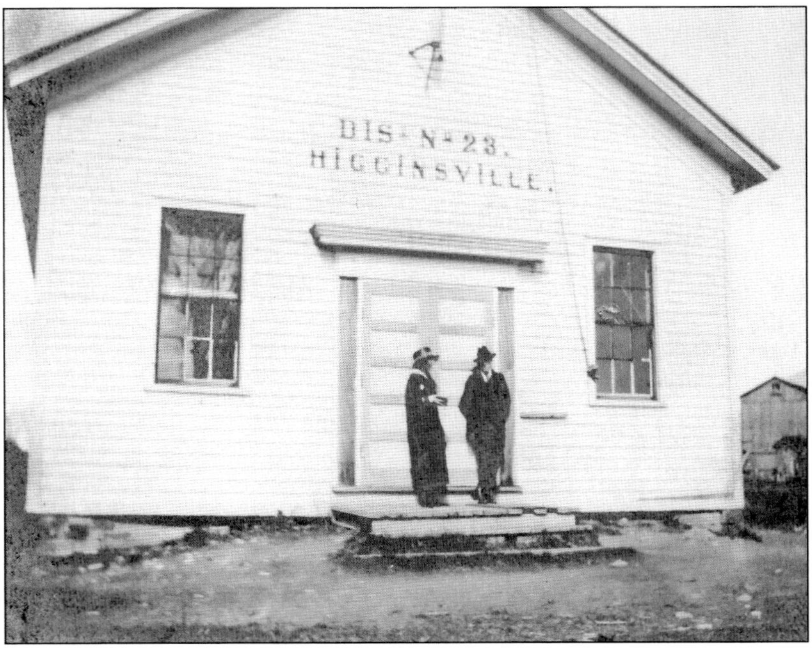

The Higginsville Schoolhouse was located on the banks of the Side Cut Canal. The students found great pleasure in riding on the swing bridge across the canal during their lunch break.

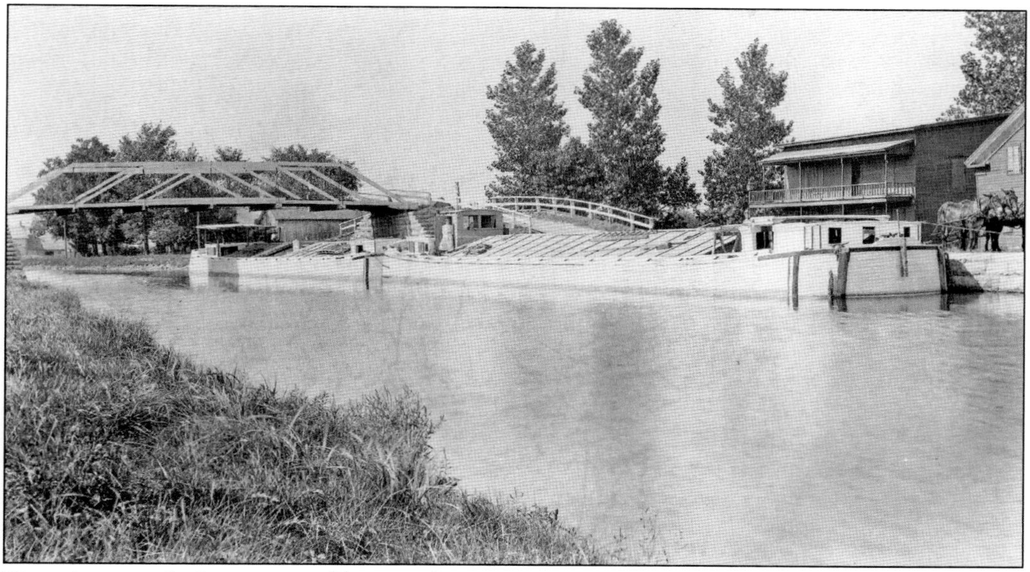

This photograph shows a canal boat tied up in front of the Higginsville Hotel along the Eric Canal. A young lady stands in front of the toll collector's office.

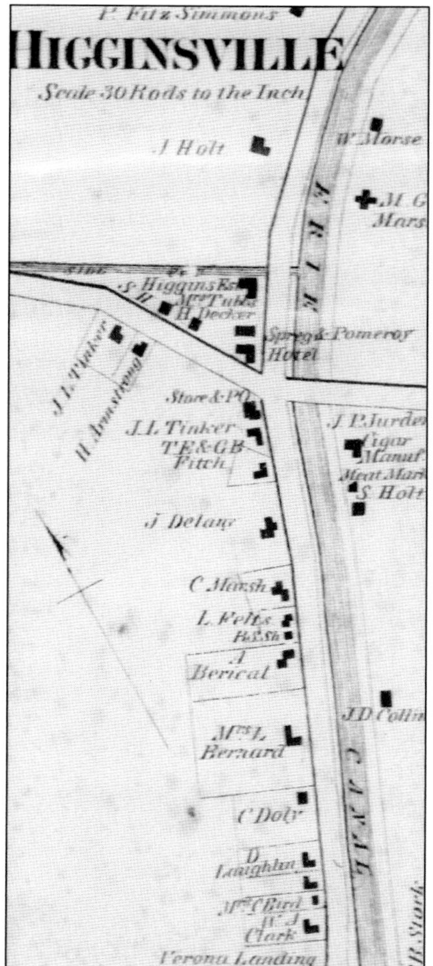

This is a map of the Higginsville area in 1874. Note the various businesses that included a hotel, meat market, cigar manufacturer, post office, and cheese factory.

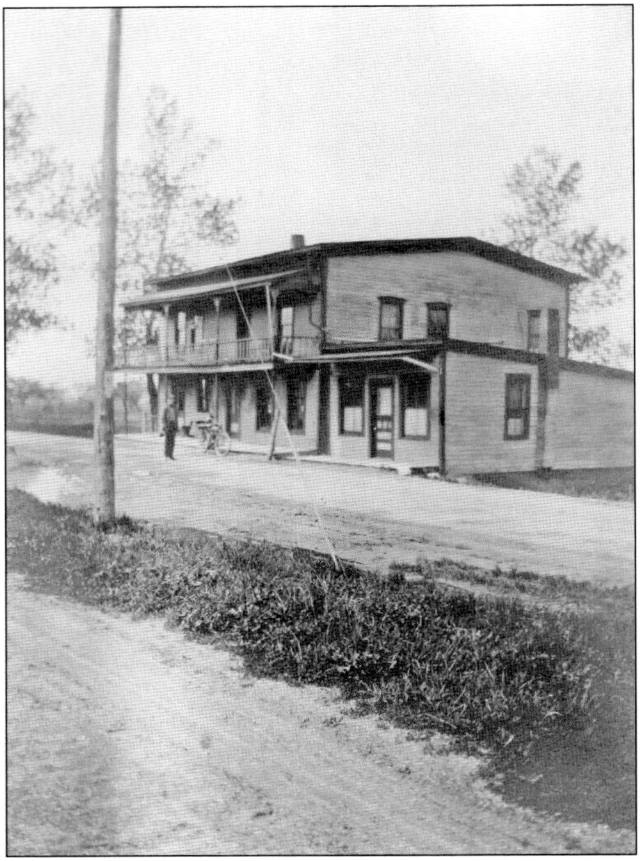

In 1850, Christopher Higgins was the proprietor of the Higginsville Hotel. In the mid-1900s, Charlie Daedlow operated the hotel for many years, followed by his son-in-law, Anthony Maiura. The building has since been demolished.

This small home on the Higginsville Road was occupied by Minerva Suits. She was a maiden lady, a member of the large Suits family in the area.

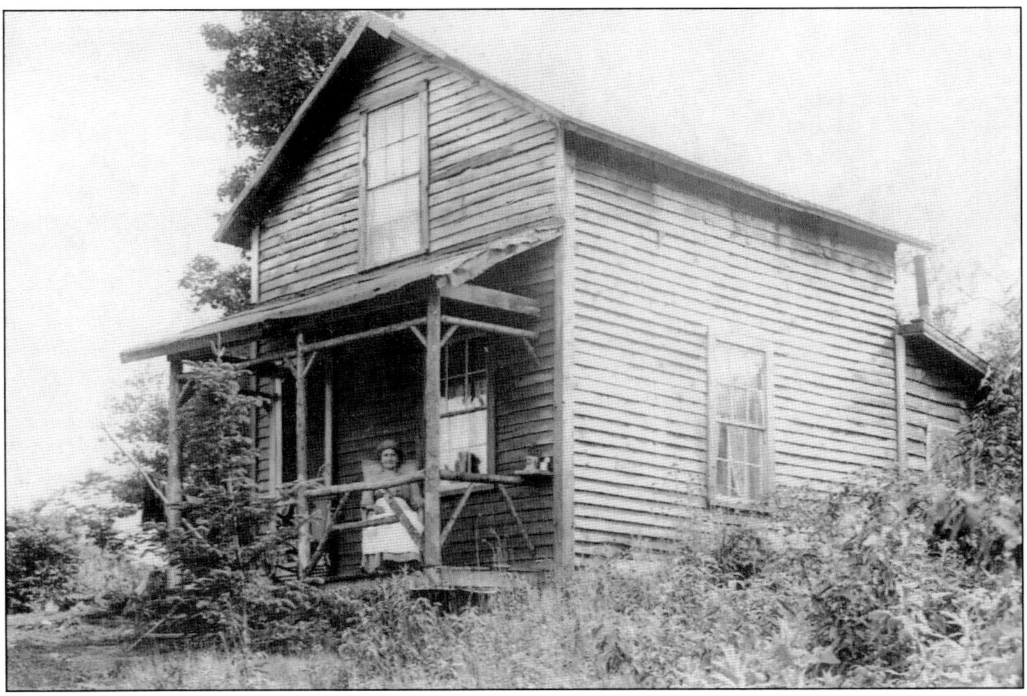

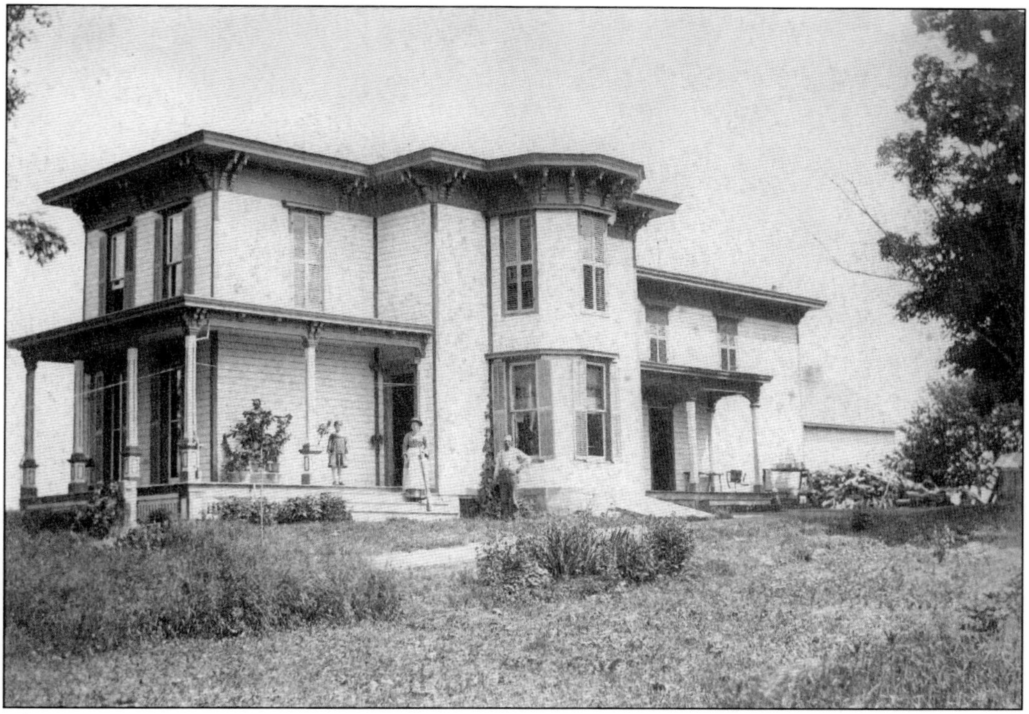

The Neverl Farm one Higginsville Road is a landmark in the town. Today it is operated by Kevin Angell, the fifth generation descended from the Christopher Suits family. (Photograph courtesy of the Angell family.)

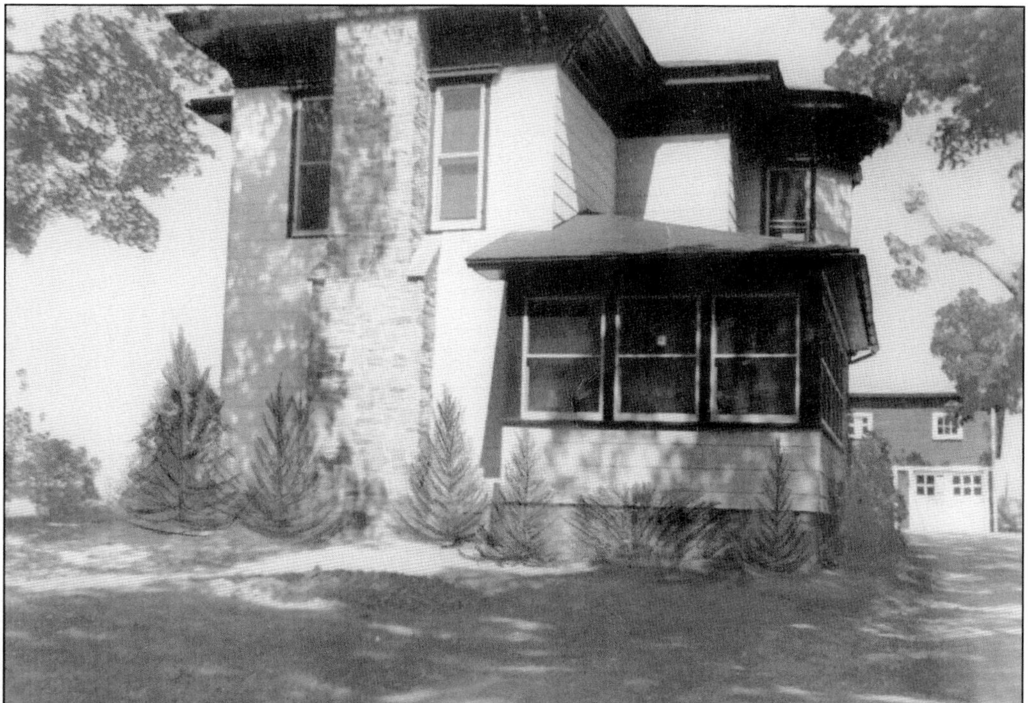

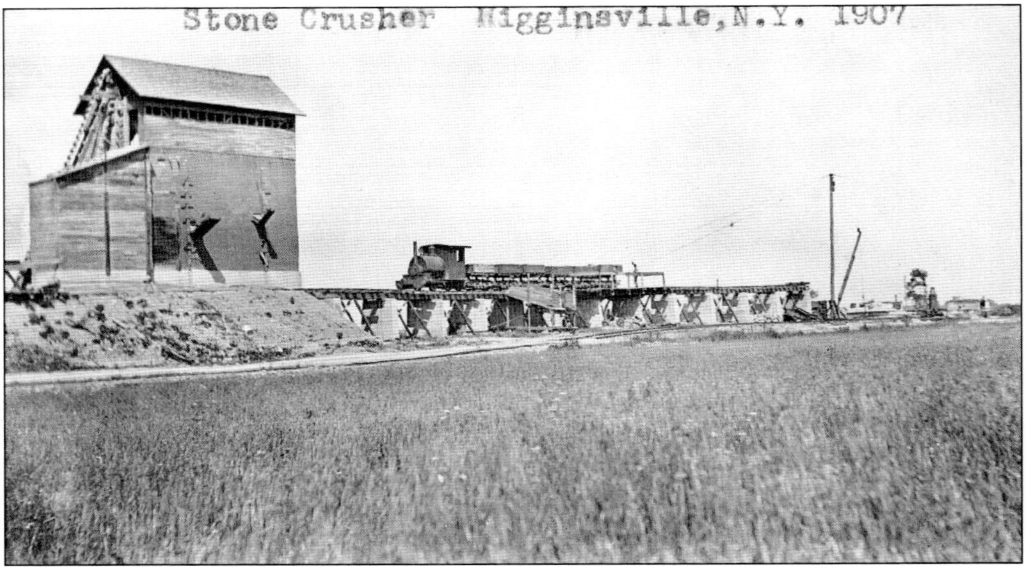

This is the stone crusher in operation at the Conley Quarry in the mid- to late 1890s. Stone was crushed and loaded on boats on the Side Cut and transported to market on the Erie Canal. The quarry was previously owned by Fidelis Hauck.

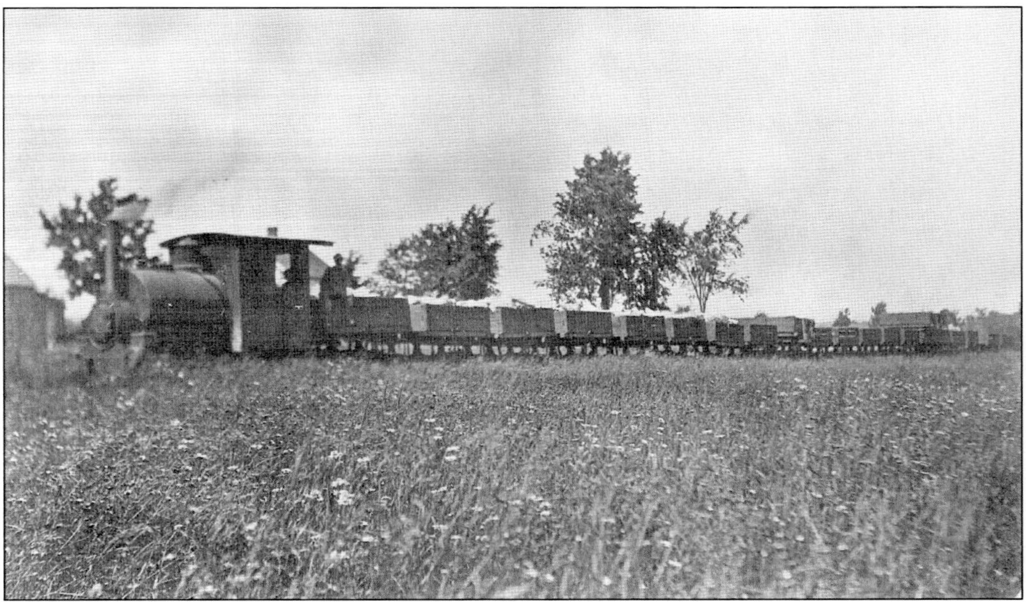

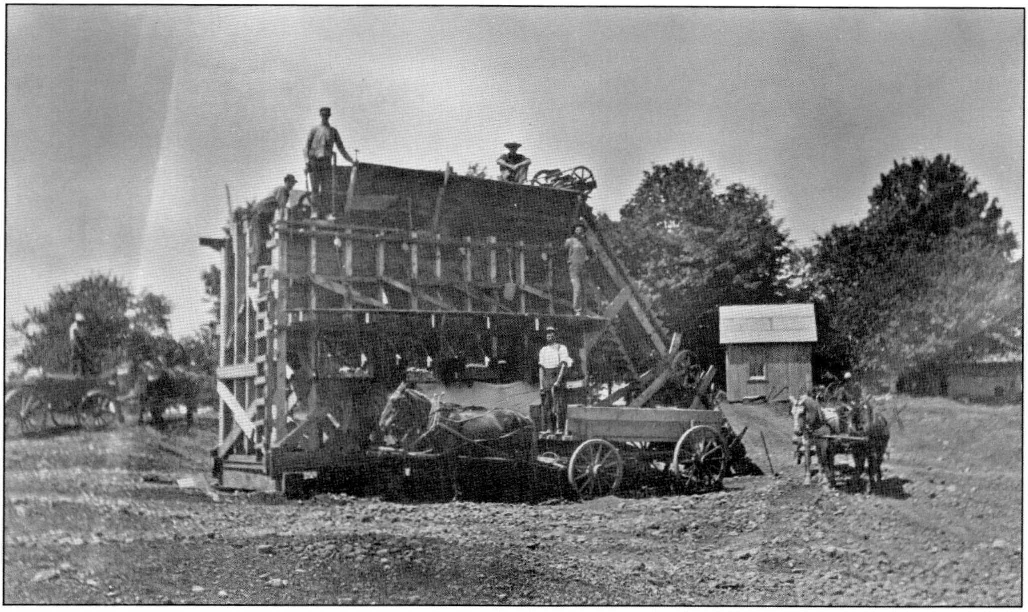

The Jackson Gravel Bed was located on the Jackson Farm on Germany Road near Irish Ridge Road. In this 1911 picture, horse-drawn wagons wait in line to be loaded.

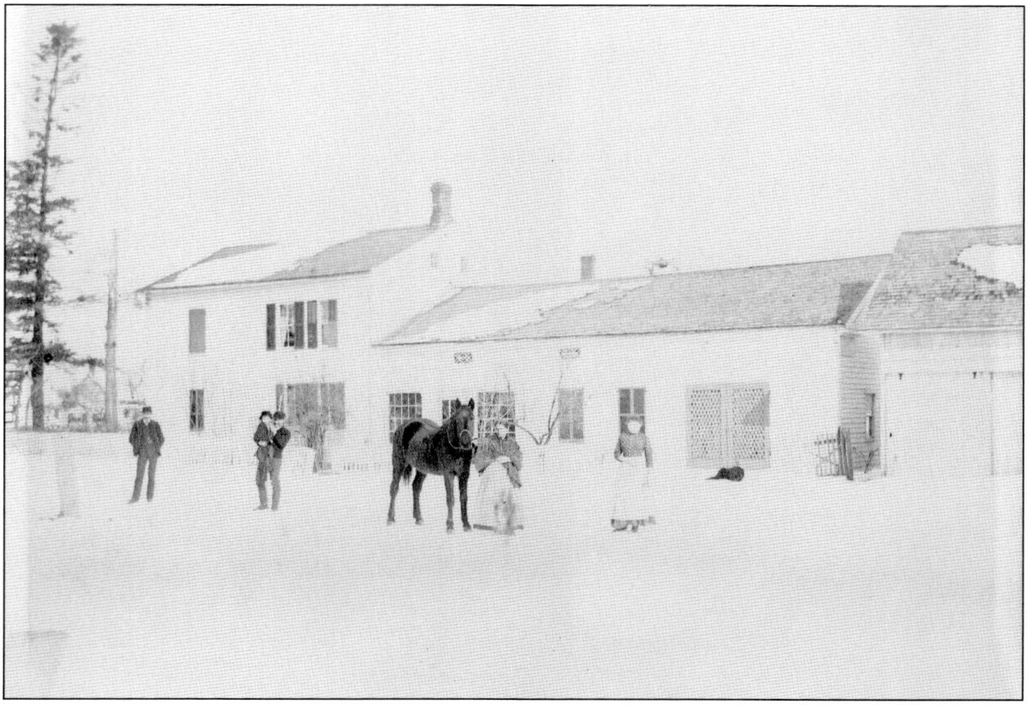

The corner of Germany Road and Route 46 is the location of the Stark family businesses, which included the Stark's Landing Hotel and store. Other endeavors of patriarch Jabez Stark were banking, a blacksmith shop, and a sleigh shop. The homestead was a common location in Higginsville for social gatherings and dances. Alcohol and card playing were not permitted by Stark.

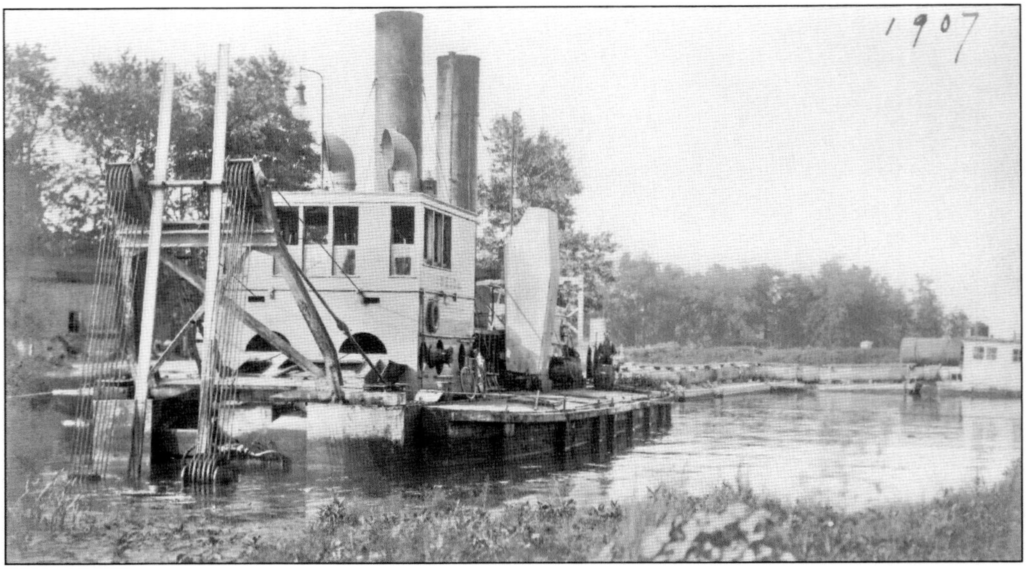

Maintenance of the canal included dredging the bottom. Here the *Oneida* steam dredge is at work in 1907.

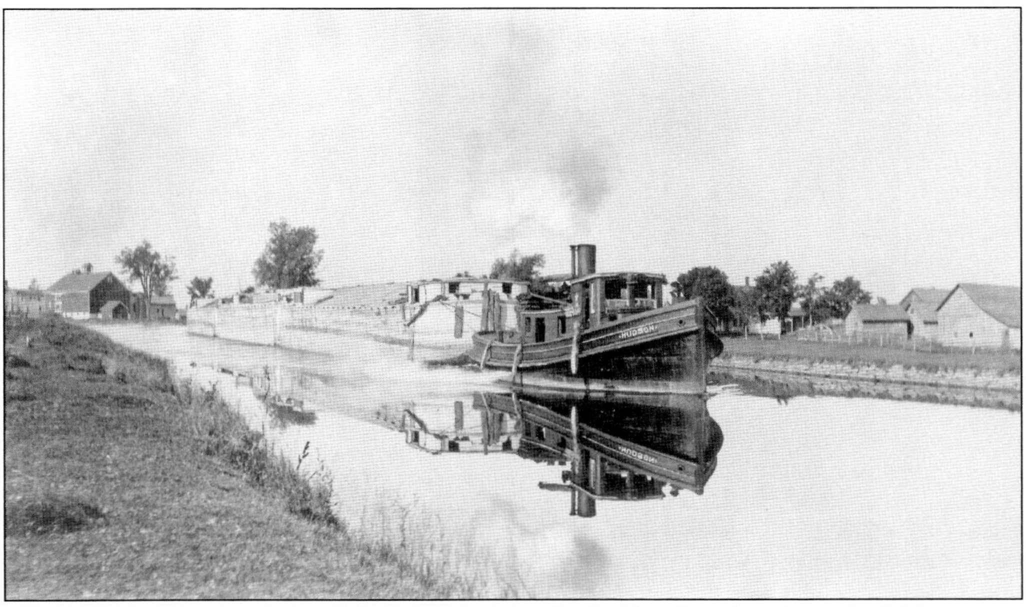

The *Hudson* tugboat was one of the last vessels to ply the Erie Canal in the early 1900s.

The home of Jerome Jackson was located at Paradise Hill on Happy Valley Road. Jackson was a farmer and active member and officer of the first Oneida County Pomona Grange.

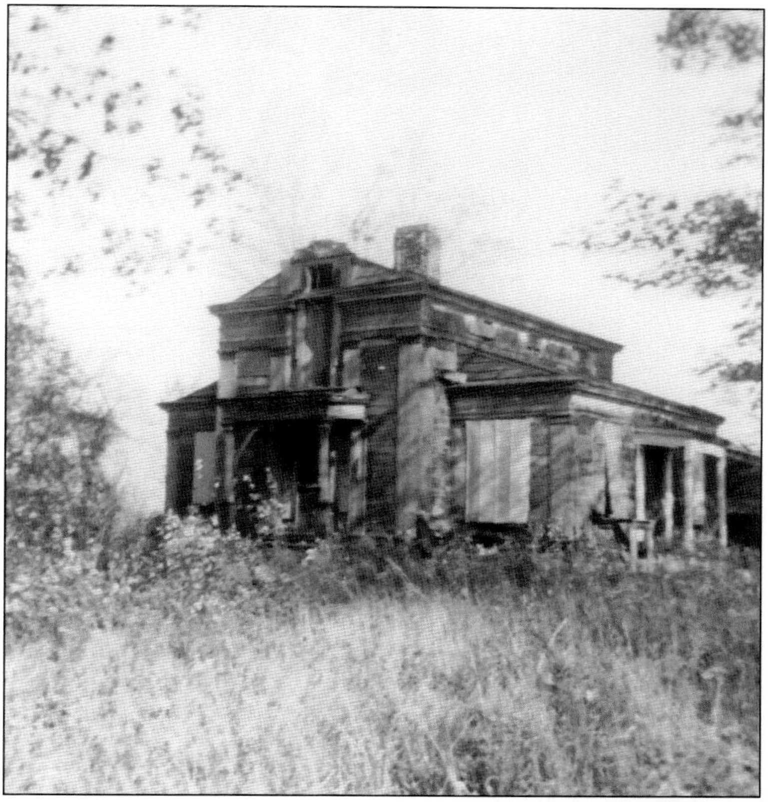

Paradise Hill School was another of the many one-room schoolhouses in the township. It was located on Germany Road near the Jackson farm. The building burned in the 1960s.

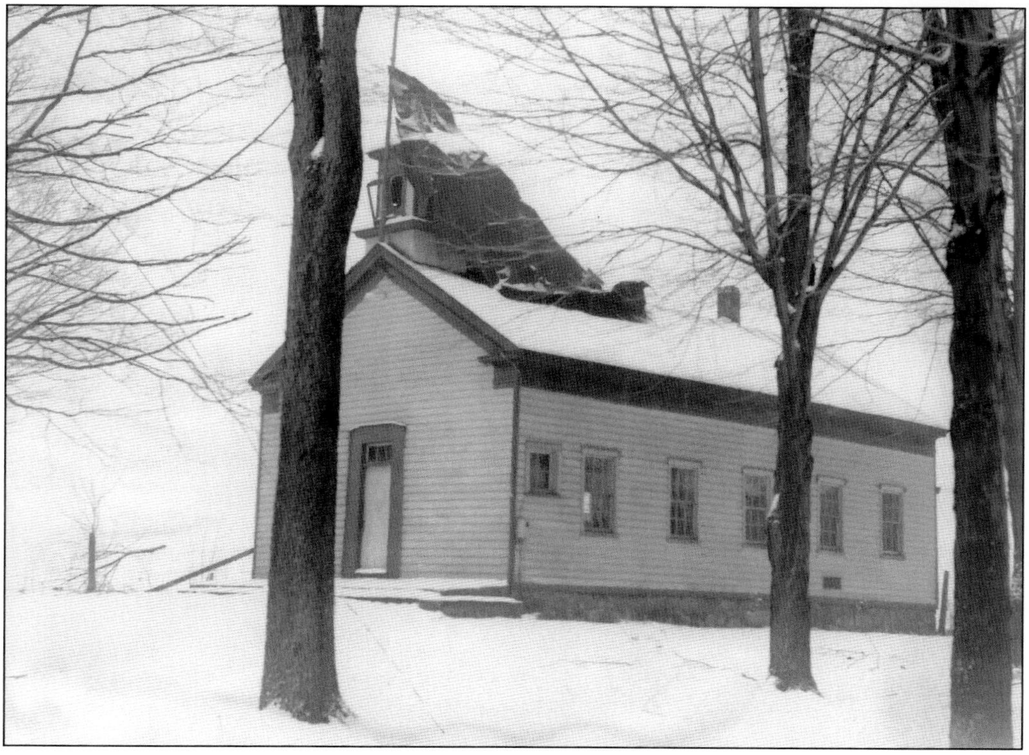

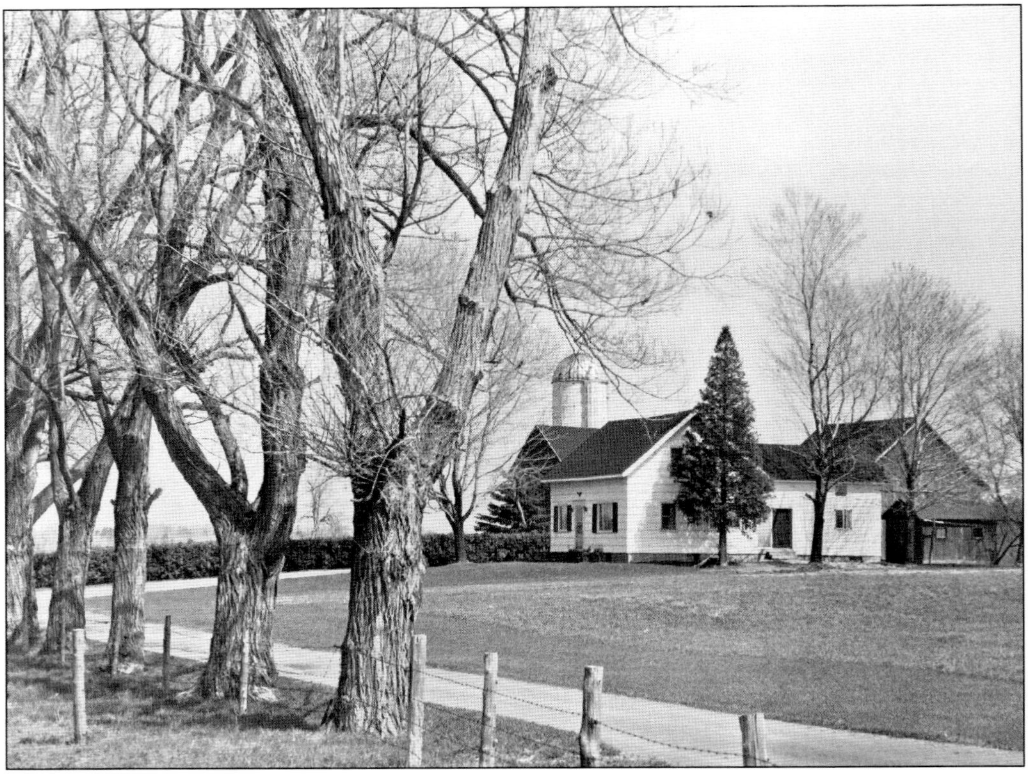

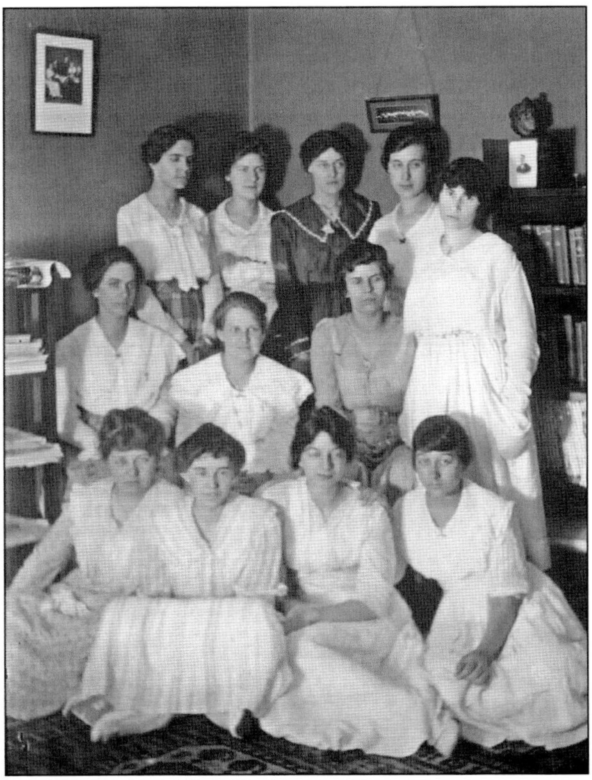

Pictured here is the farm of the Basil Trunko family. It was operated by Trunko and his family for many years and now is the private residence of Basil's son, Wesley, and his wife, Betty Trunko. Much of the land is now cultivated by the Van Lieshout family farm. (Photograph courtesy of the Wesley Trunko family.)

The photograph shows the ladies associated with the Dunbarton Glass Factory. The lady in the back, third from left, is Barney Tucker, daughter of John Cooper and his wife. Cooper was part owner of the factory after Munroe and Cowarden.

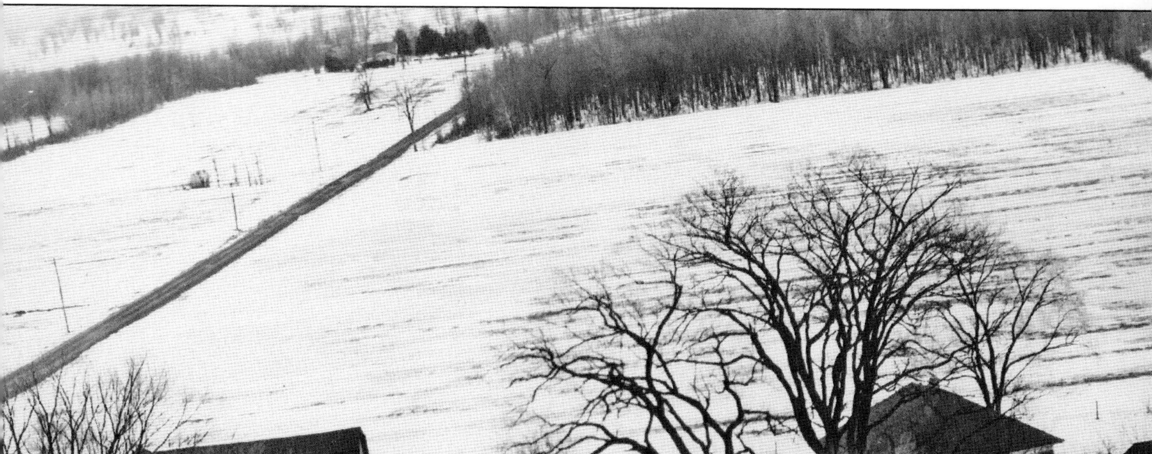

The Hojnacki farm is located on Side Cut Road in Higginsville. Frances Hojnacki and her husband, John Grot, purchased the 125-acre dairy farm in 1928, and her son, Walter Hojnacki, continued the operation until 1998. (Photograph courtesy of Walter and Betty Hojnacki.)

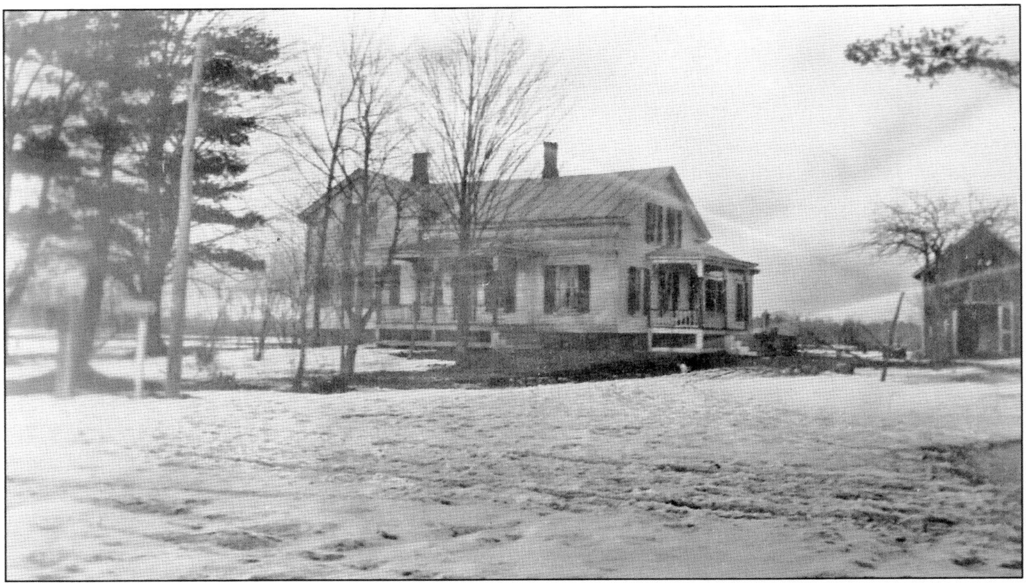

William and Angeline Williams Warner bought this homestead in the 1800s. The house passed down to Henry and Vie Newey Warner, who married in 1893, and then down to their son, Stanley Warner. It was located across the road from the Edgar Burdick farm near where the Barge Canal would later be built.

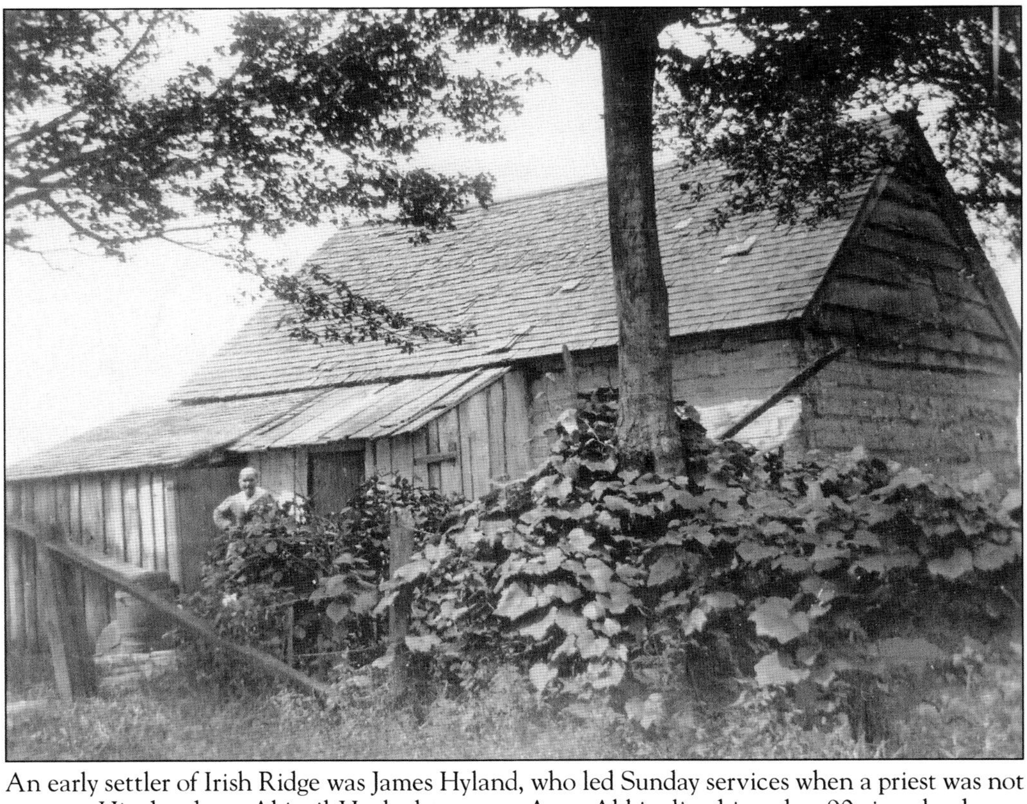

An early settler of Irish Ridge was James Hyland, who led Sunday services when a priest was not present. His daughter, Abigail Healy, known as Aunt Abbie, lived into her 90s in a log house directly across from St. Mary's Church.

Three

New London, Stacy Basin, Verona Mills, and Churchville

The northern end of the town of Verona contains the hamlets of New London, Stacy Basin, Verona Mills, and Churchville.

The largest of the hamlets at the peak of the Erie Canal was New London, located along the canal a few miles north of Durhamville. It was first settled in 1824 by Ambrose Jones. It became a bustling, busy commercial area complete with nice homes, tree-shaded streets, and two schools—one on each side of the canal. Lumbering and shipping were the main sources of industry here at the end of the 19th century, but dairy farms were numerous as well.

An interesting location just northwest of New London is Oak Orchard. It was a landmark for travelers along the Mohawk River and Wood Creek prior to the construction of the Erie Canal. Because navigation through here was difficult, the Western Inland Lock Navigation Canal Company constructed a small canal cut in 1793. Located here was a house owned by the company, a sawmill, and a cemetery, which contains the remains of some of the township's first settlers. A sign on the north side of Wood Creek Road marks the location of Oak Orchard, where headstones can still be seen.

Situated about midway in what was known as the "long level" of the Erie Canal is the small community of Stacy Basin. Located here were six stores, boatbuilding yards, dry docks, and three blacksmith shops. Similar to New London, the lumbering industry accounted for much of the commerce as lumber camps were located nearby. Cord wood was shipped by the canal to Syracuse for use in the salt industry. The Dunbarton and Durhamville Glass Factories also used the cord wood in the production of glass. Lumber was also milled and shipped for housing construction. The Empire State Canning Factory offered seasonal employment for local residents. It was consumed by a fire on February 13, 1957.

Nearby are the adjoining hamlets of Churchville and Verona Mills. The story is told that Churchville was named after two boys who first used it on a cardboard sign they posted on a stick, a reference to the several churches in the vicinity.

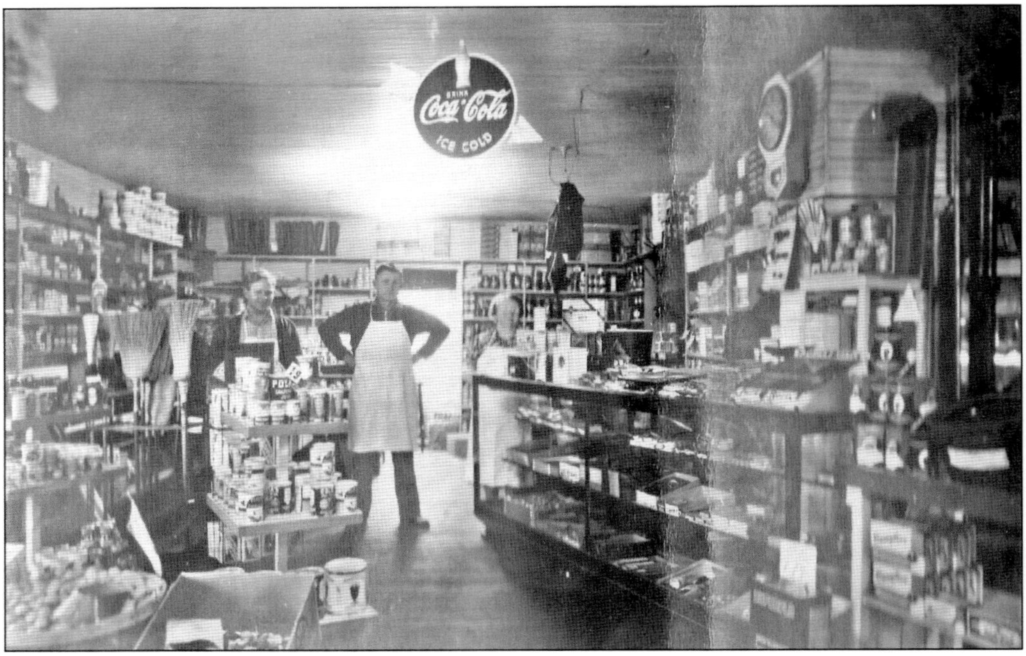

This store was located in Stacy Basin along the canal towpath. Here canal travelers and local residents could purchase their daily needs. The store was owned at different times by Ben Vaughn and the Yager family. Note the number of well-known products seen in the market.

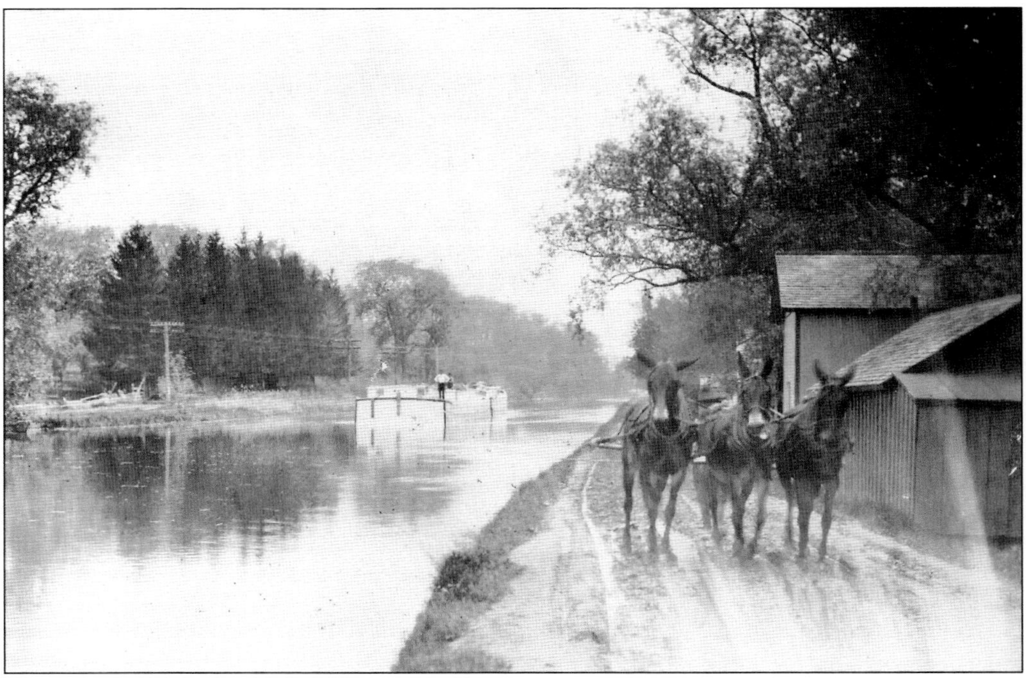

This photograph was taken along the Erie Canal at Stacy Basin. It shows a span of three mules towing a canal boat.

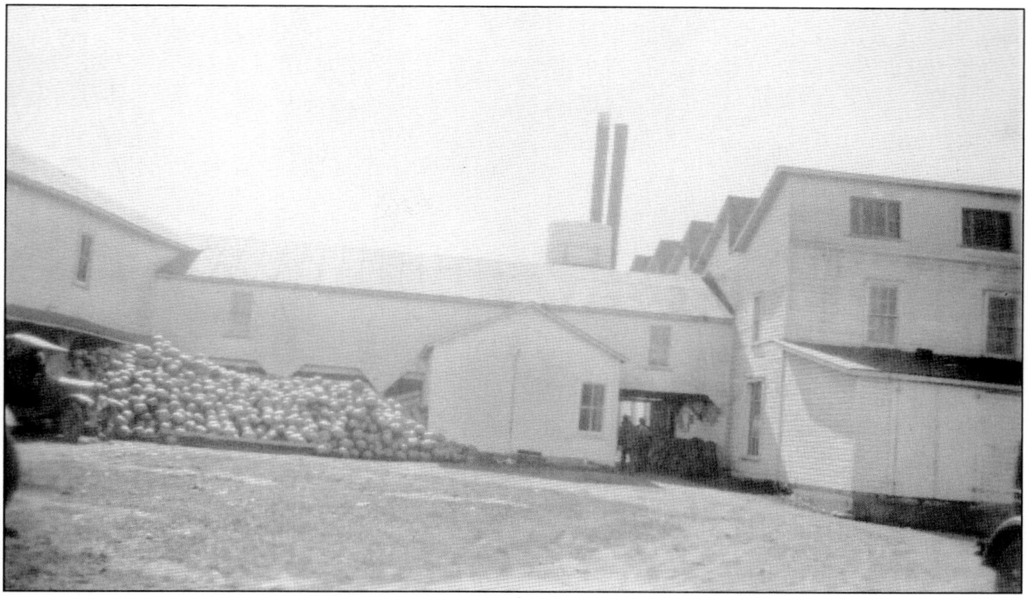

This is an aerial view of Stacy Basin and the Empire State Canning Factory. Crops were grown nearby for processing here, giving local residents seasonal employment. Organized in 1895 by Joseph H. Warren, as many as 175 local people worked during the harvest season. Volume reached 75,000 cans in 1899 and 600,000 cases by 1902, processing corn, beans, peas, succotash, and apples. In 1953, the equipment was sold, and the building burned in 1957. Below is a photograph of a label from a can of sweet corn processed at the Empire State Canning Factory. It was bright red with black lettering. (Above, photograph courtesy of Stuart Lohr.)

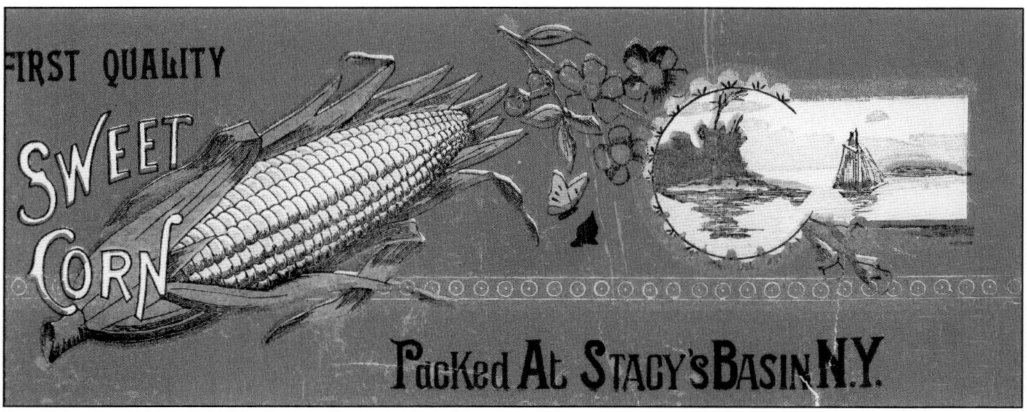

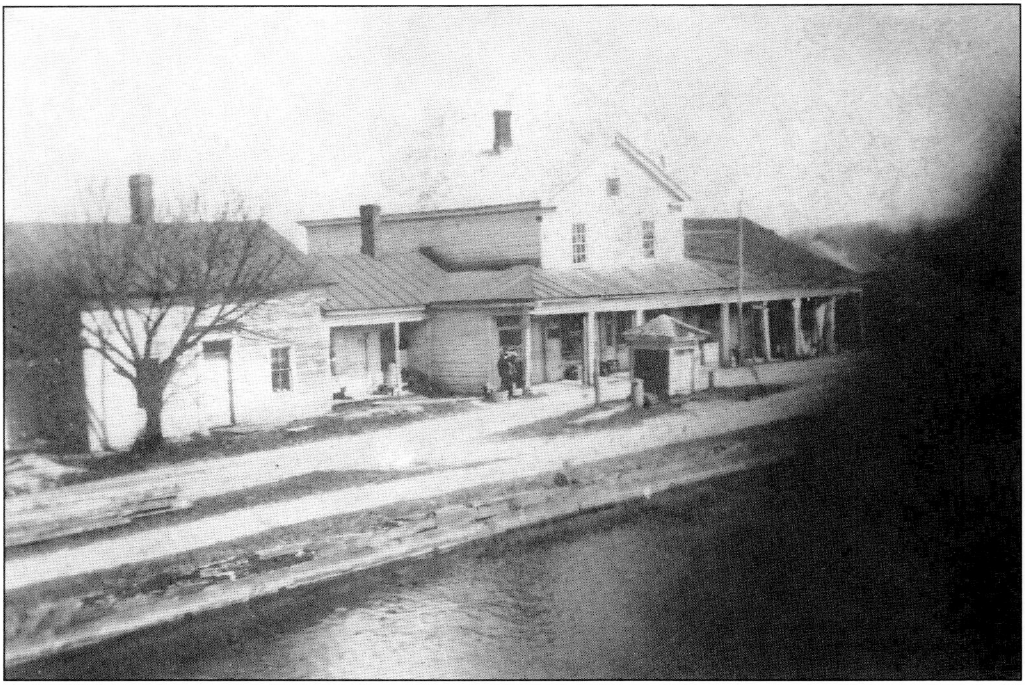

These photographs show the Weismantel store located between Stacy Basin and New London. Located along the canal, the shop provided for the needs of the canalers. Michael Schaller and Al Weismantel are pictured below in front of the shop at Grove Springs in July 1922. (Both photographs courtesy of Gloria Dunn Eddy.)

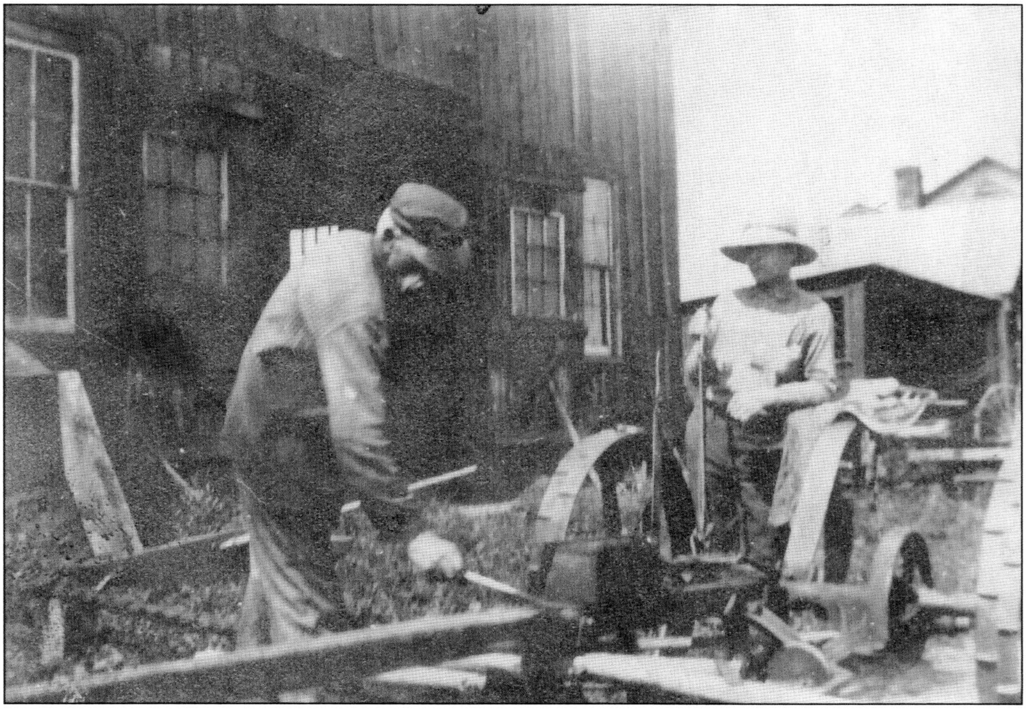

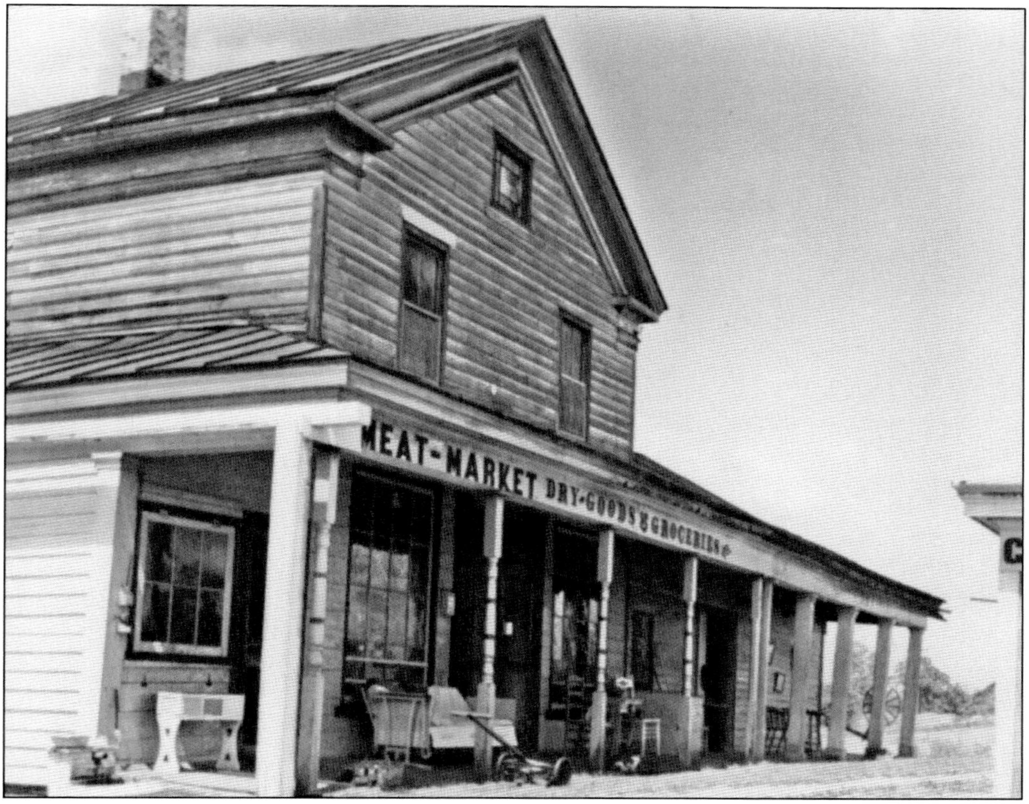

The Weismantel meat market, grocery, and dry goods store is shown in this photograph. The business at Grove Springs also contained a bar and a grainery for mule feed. The aerial photograph below shows the complex before the state of New York acquired the property, and the building was burned to accommodate the new Route 46. (Photographs courtesy of Gloria Dunn Eddy.)

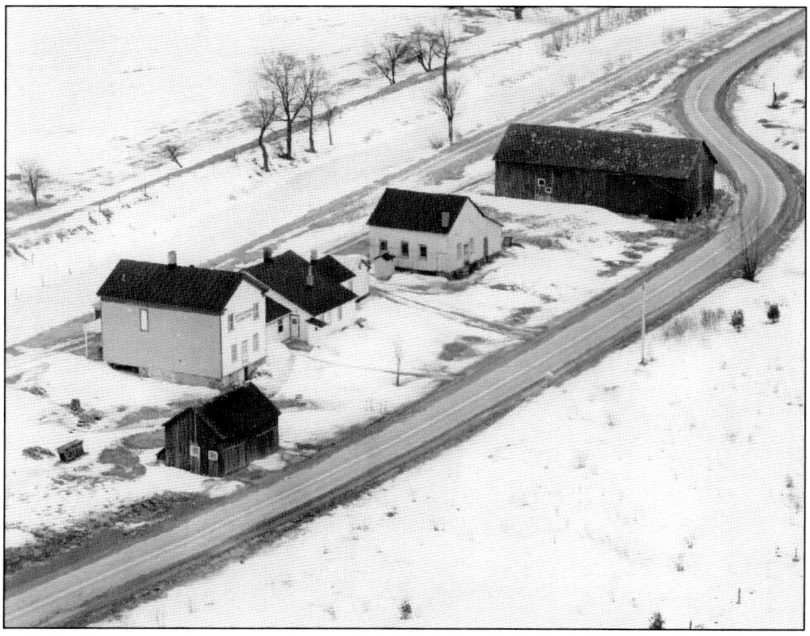

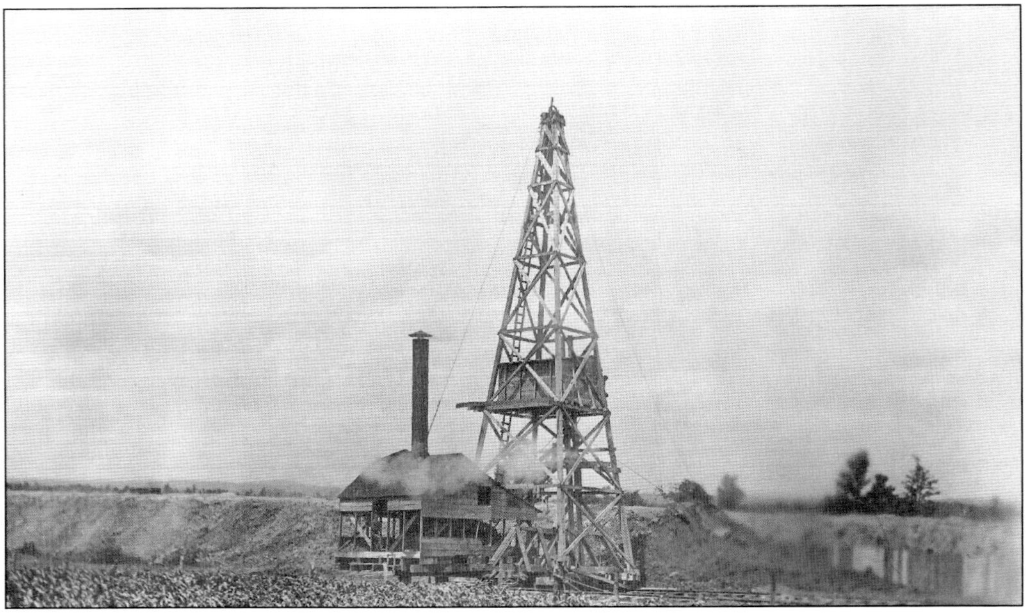

These 1911 photographs show the men with their machinery at work on the Barge Canal at Grove Springs. The Barge Canal replaced the Erie Canal, accommodating larger, swifter vessels.

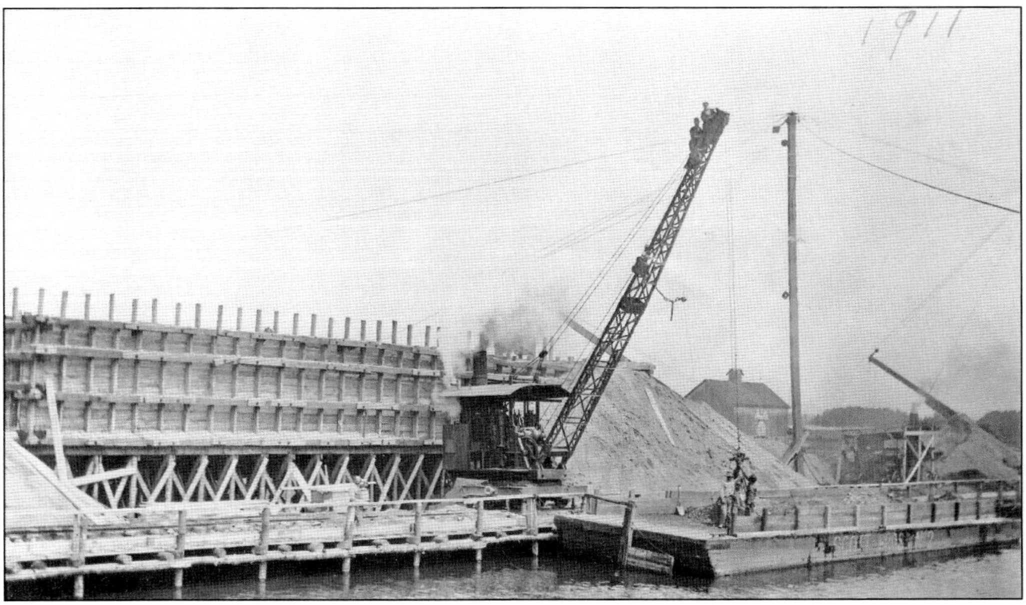

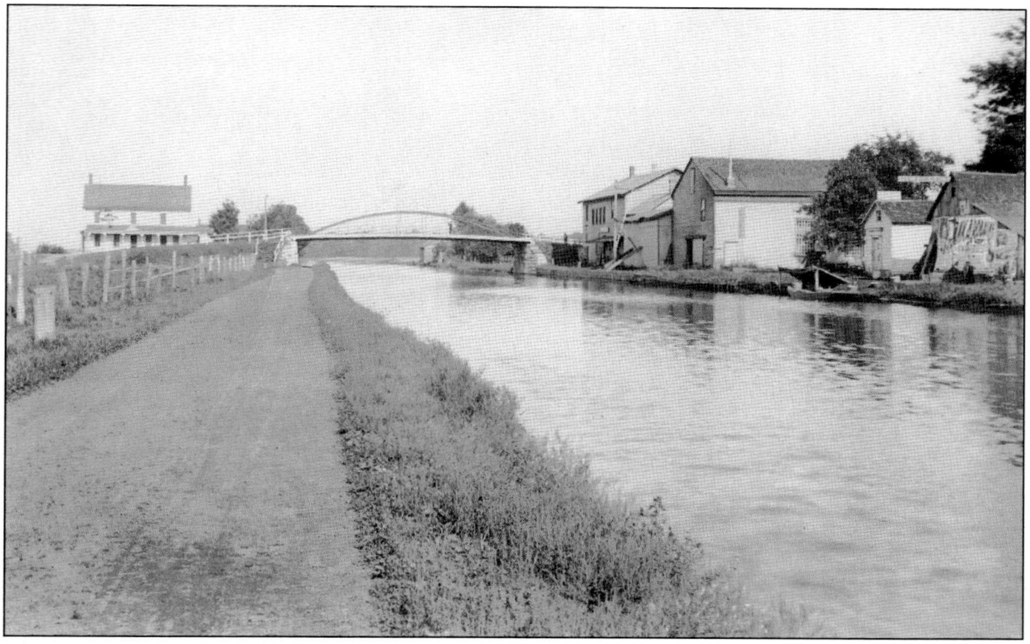

There were a number of businesses in New London. From this vantage point, George Wright's store and a hotel on the towpath side are shown in the photograph.

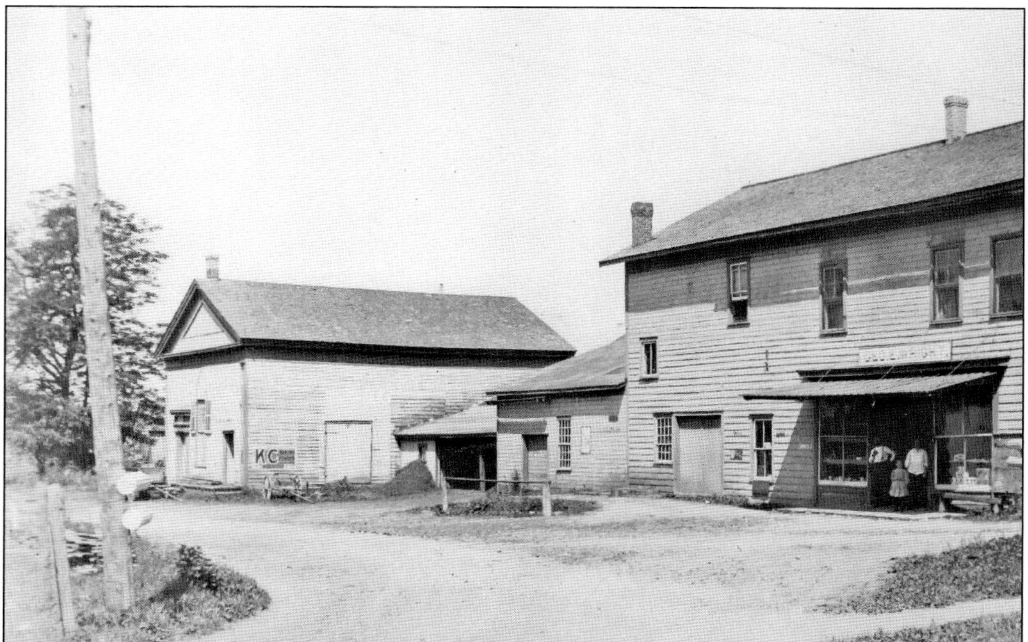

George E. Wright was the proprietor of the general store located in New London, pictured here. In all the canal side stores were available groceries and other sundries needed by canalers.

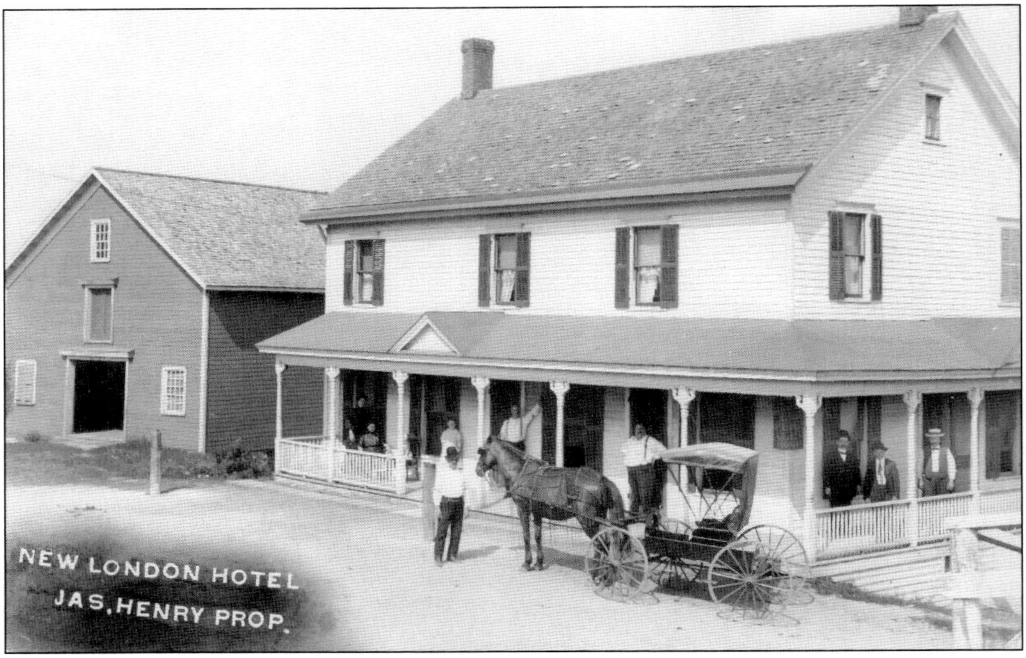

This hotel in New London was operated by James Henry. Note the horse and buggy, which was popular transportation for the day. This was a common place for neighbors and travelers to meet and pass the time.

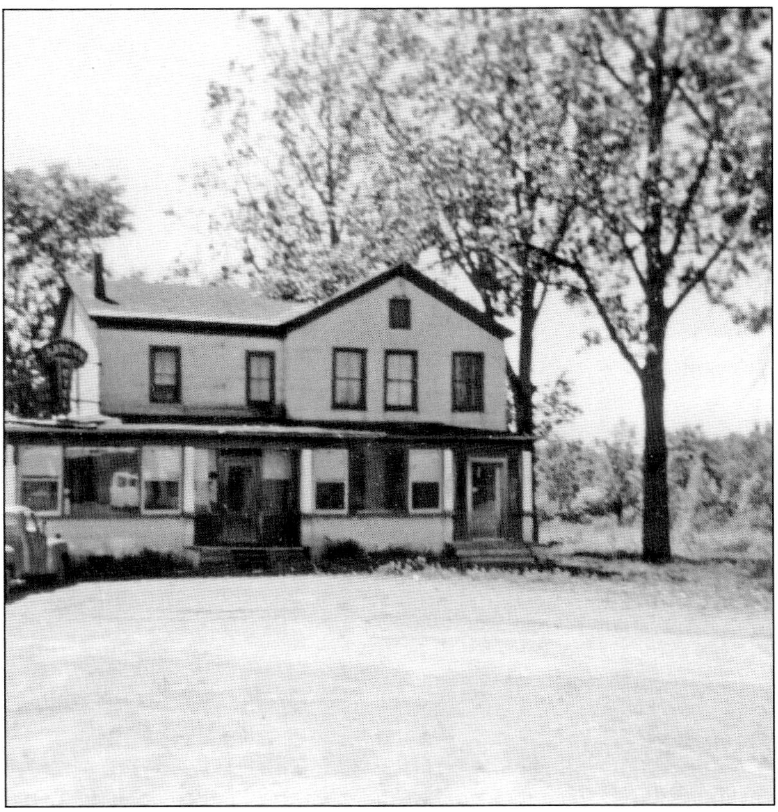

For many years, Satch's Hotel has stood as a landmark building in the hamlet of New London. Having had numerous owners through the years, it is currently in operation.

The New London Fire Company was organized in the late 1940s. Their early firefighting equipment was loaned from the U.S. government. (Photograph courtesy of Gene Carey.)

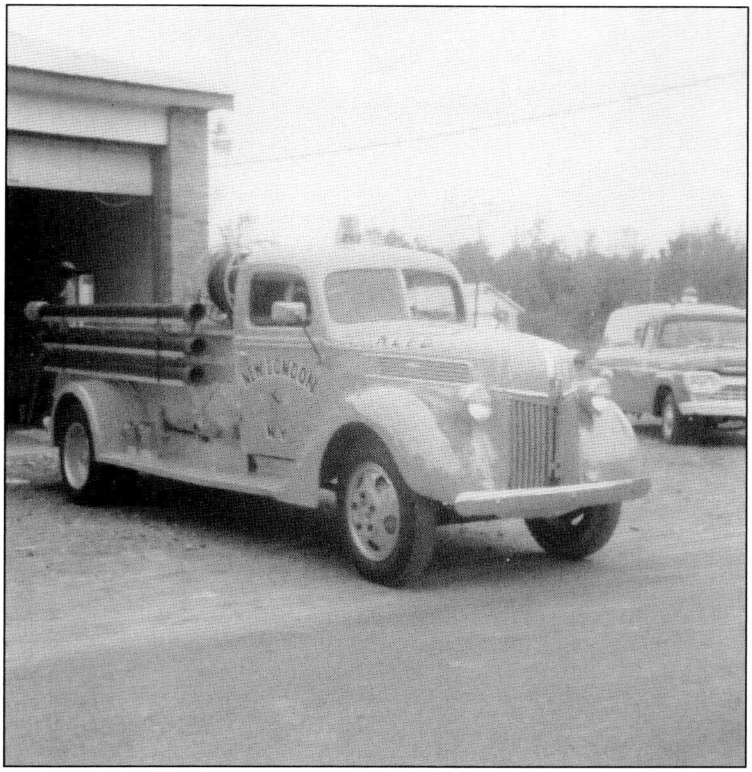

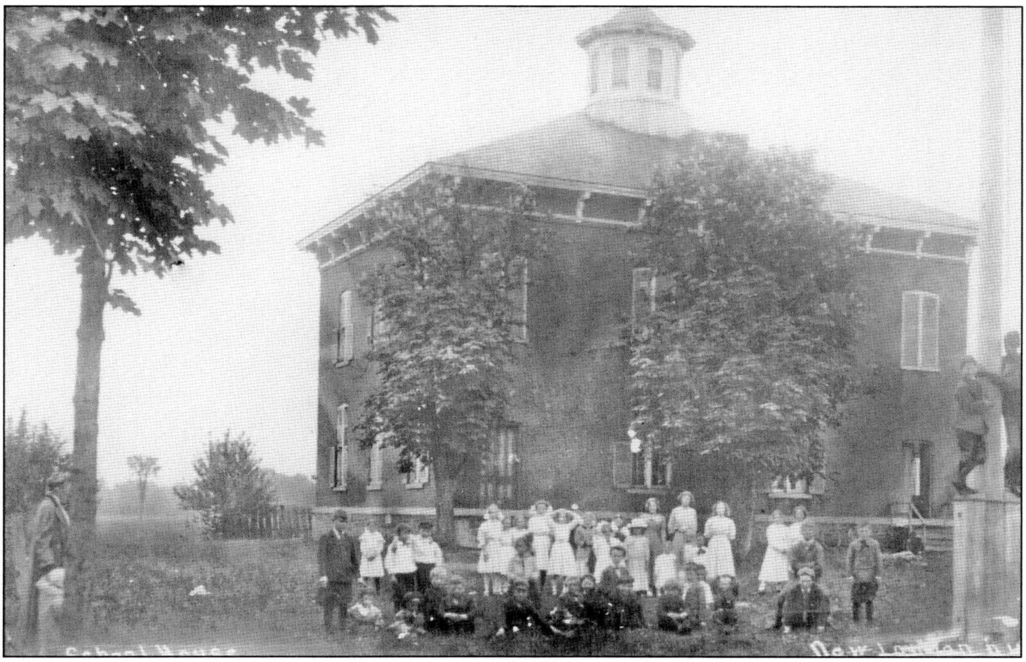

The New London school was the second largest school in the district of Verona. The brick building was constructed in 1863, provided learning for children of New London for many years, and closed when the district centralized. The building was demolished in 1967, and its bell made a part of a monument beside the Masonic temple.

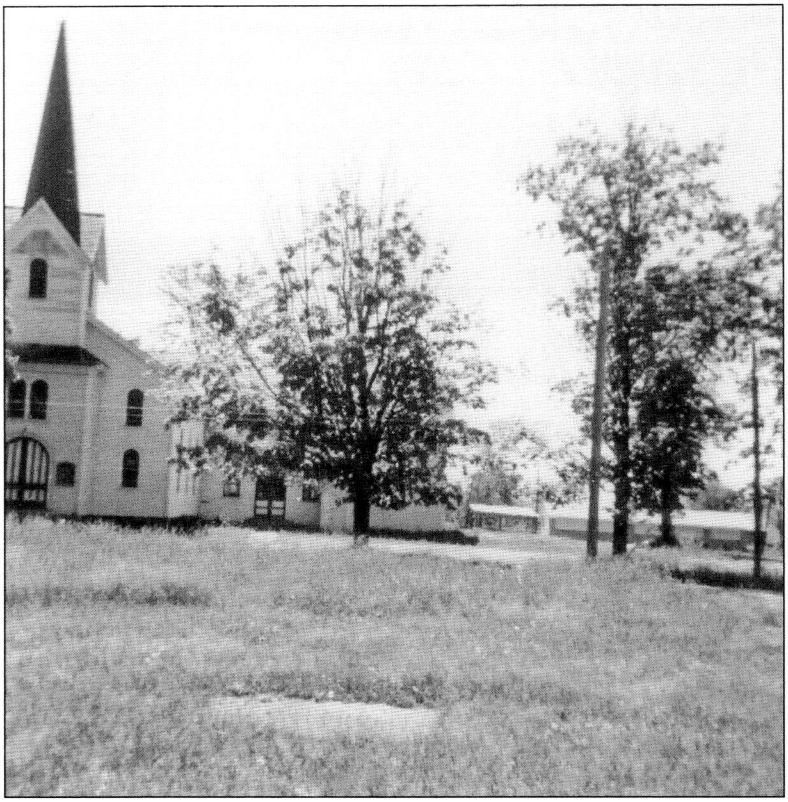

The First Methodist Church of New London was established prior to 1843 with a building they purchased from the German Lutheran Church. This building was later replaced and is currently active.

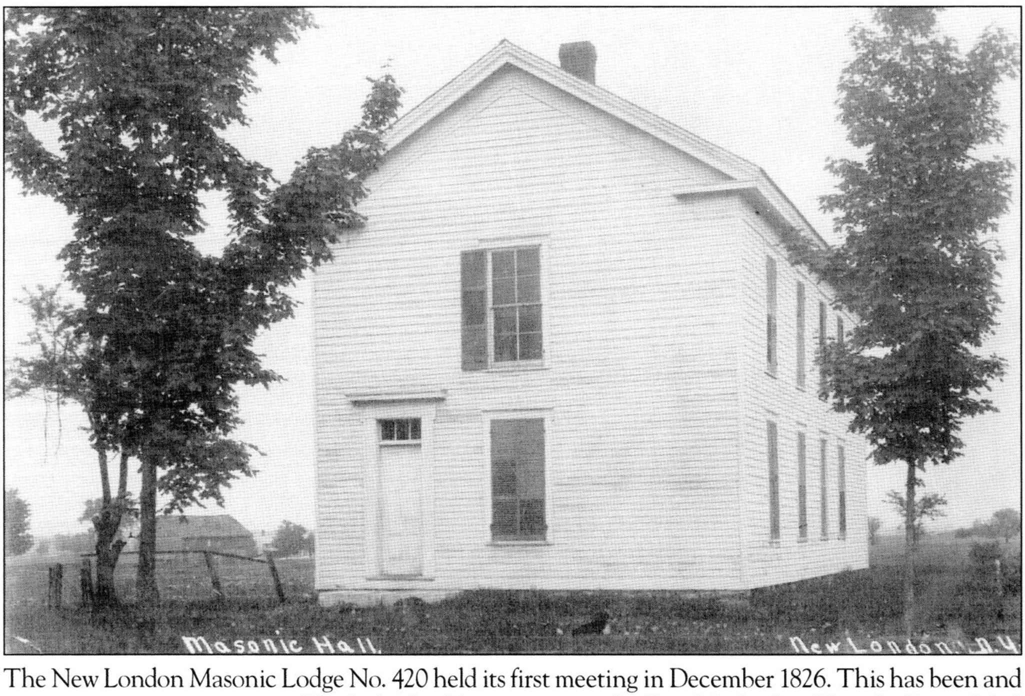

The New London Masonic Lodge No. 420 held its first meeting in December 1826. This has been and remains a very active group. The lodge building was once the Free Methodist Church. Remodeled and dedicated in 1898, the New London Masonic Temple is located on County Route 50.

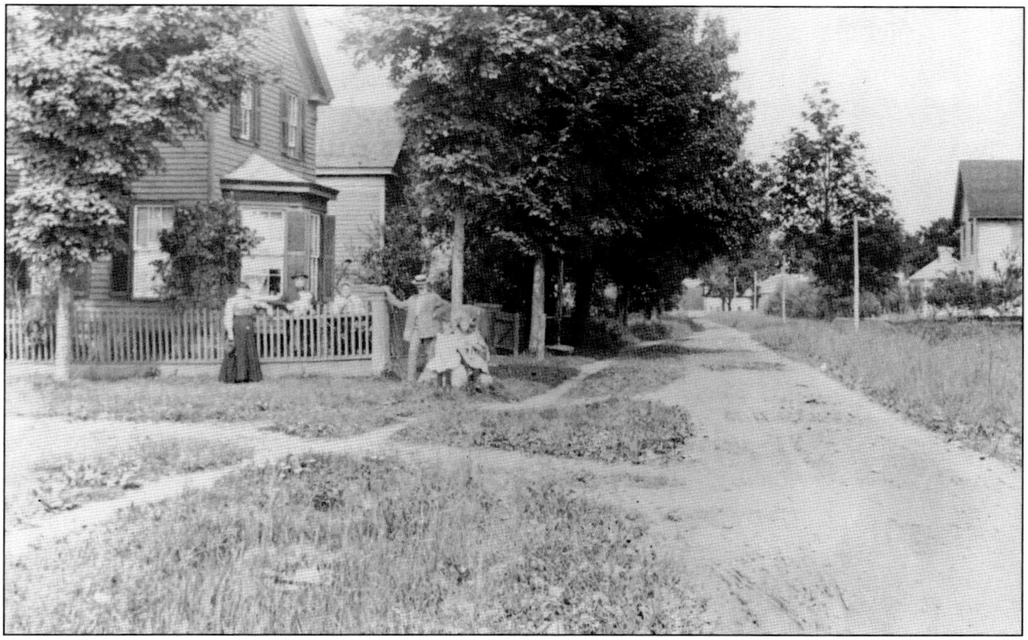

Looking down Cornell Street in New London, this photograph shows Ann Barton's house on the left and Dick Borst's house on the right. (Photograph courtesy of Gene Carey.)

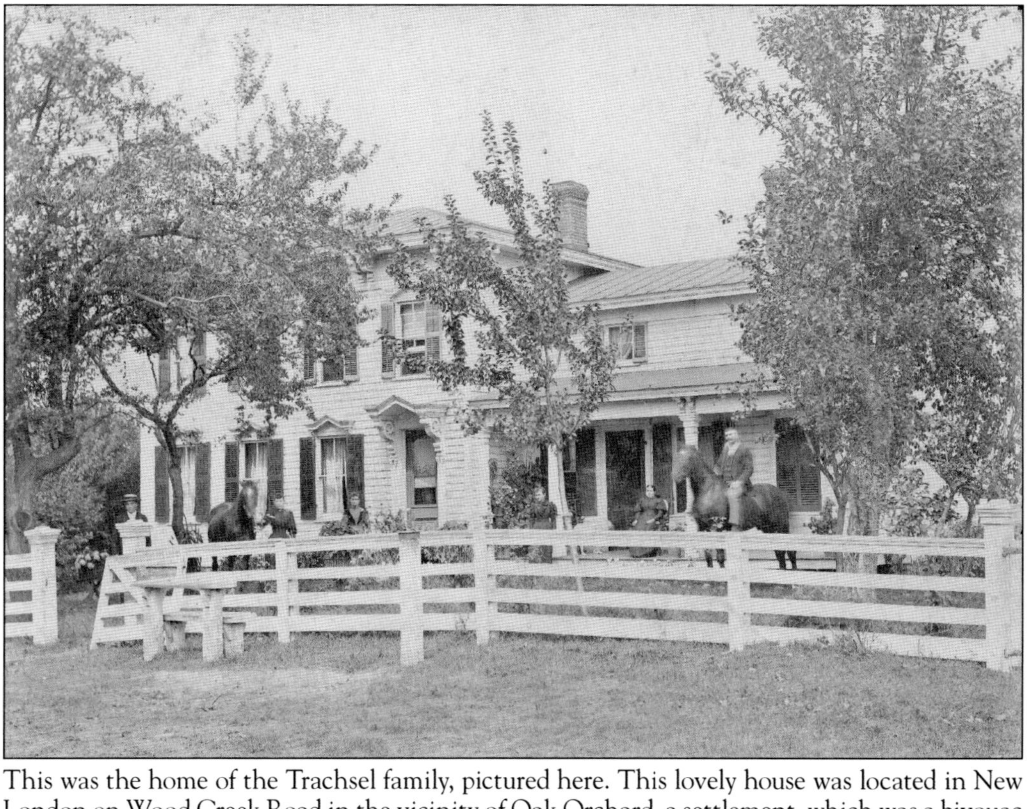

This was the home of the Trachsel family, pictured here. This lovely house was located in New London on Wood Creek Road in the vicinity of Oak Orchard, a settlement, which was a bivouac point during the Revolutionary War.

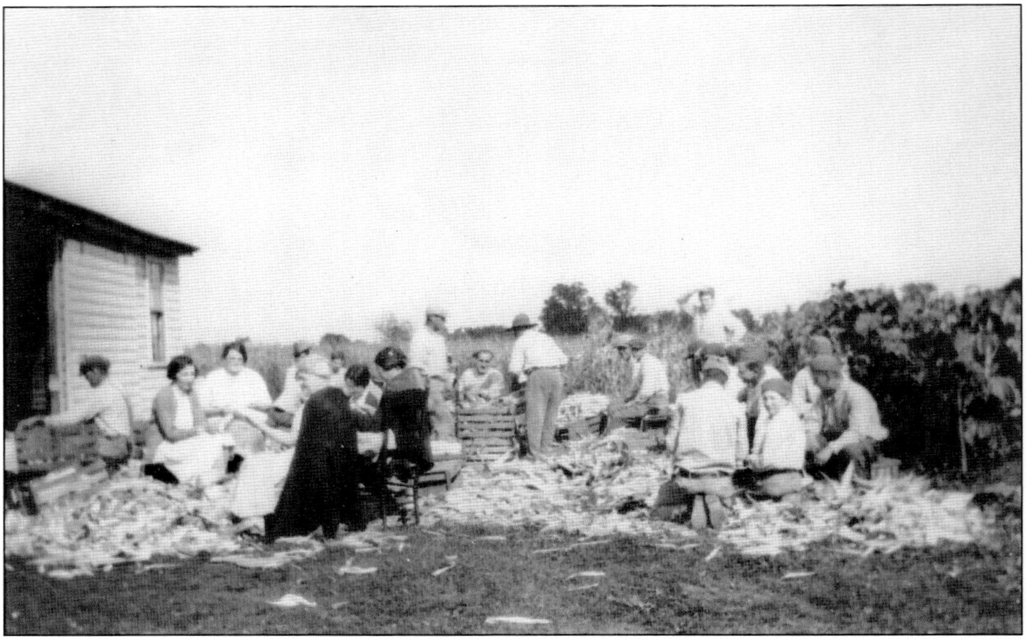

Pictured above are a group of local people employed by the Wilhelm Canning Factory at Verona Mills. They are husking corn to be processed in the factory. Pictured below, the workers gather to celebrate the end of the busy canning season.

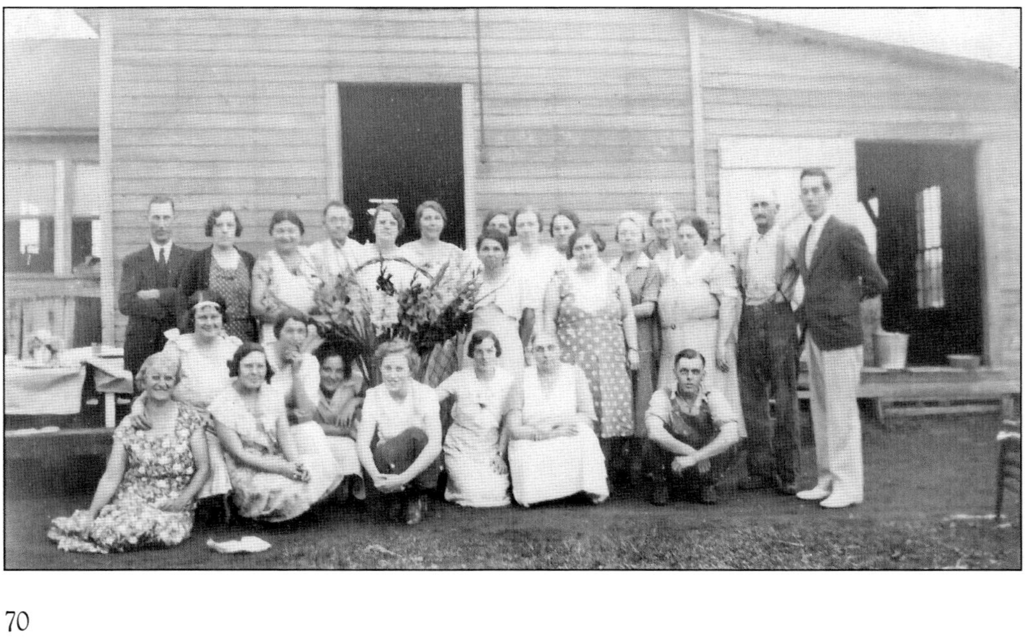

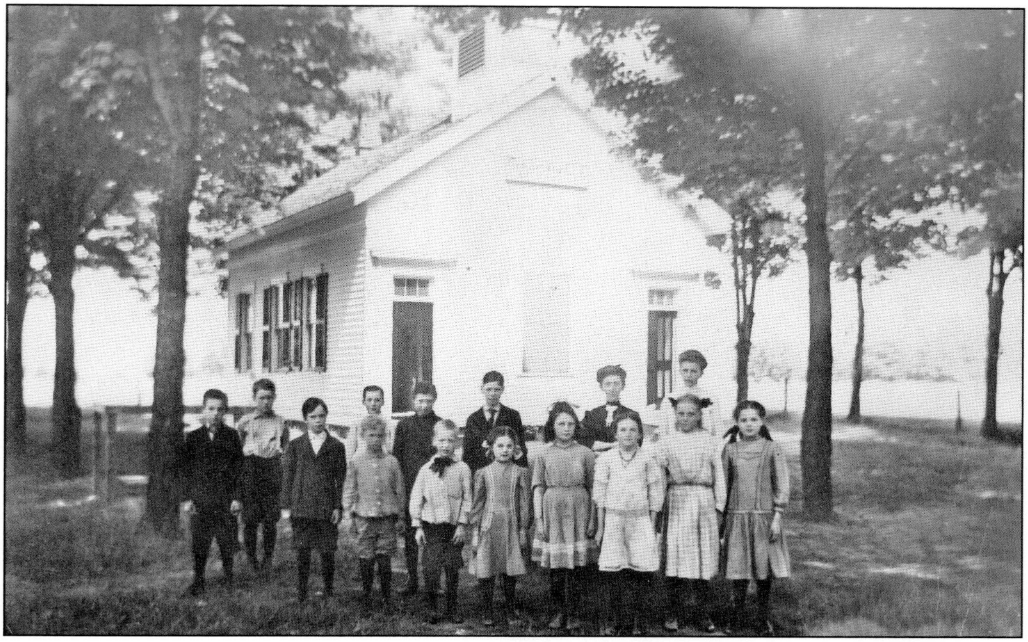

The Churchville School was located across the street from the Seventh Day Baptist Church. This photograph was taken in 1911, probably on the last day of school before summer break.

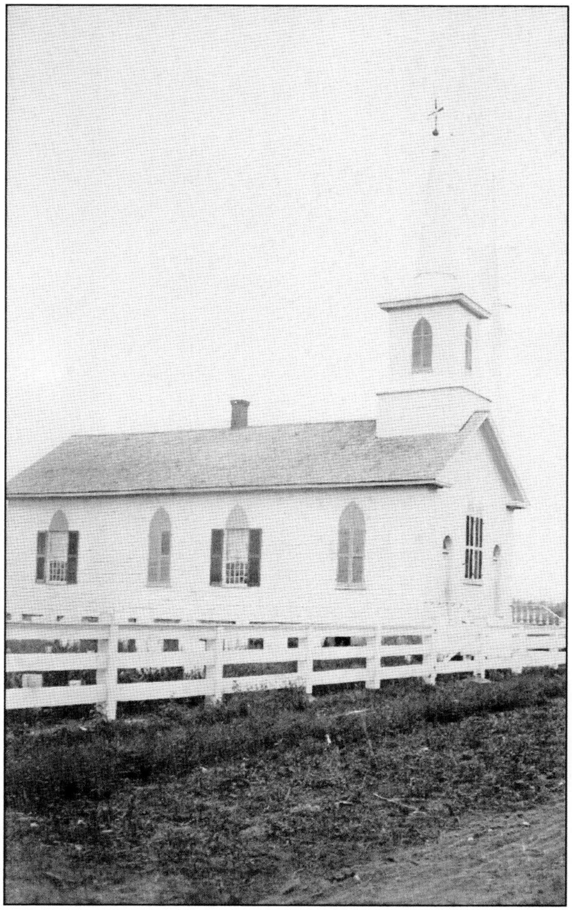

St. Peter's Lutheran Church, established in 1837, is pictured here around 1900 before the construction of two additions. The refurbished church was attended by Veronans who later voted to construct a larger, more spacious building in the 1990s on old Route 365 near the hamlet of Verona.

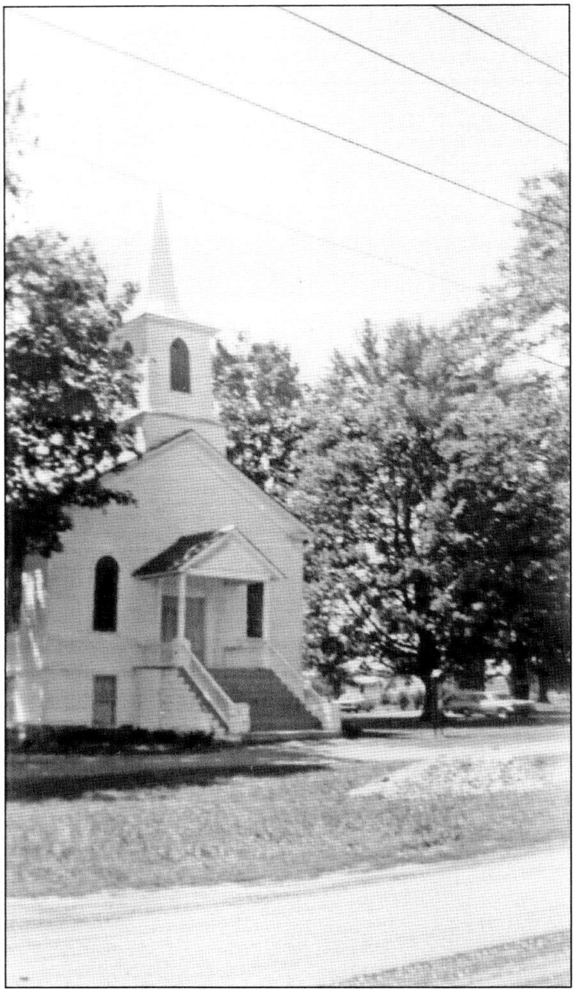

The Seventh Day Baptist Church was established in 1820 in Churchville at the corner of Blackman's Corners and Happy Valley Road. Around 1903, it was raised with a new higher foundation, permitting a kitchen and large room for church activities and Sunday school rooms.

The former parsonage of the Seventh Day Baptist Church, which is privately owned today, was located a distance away down the road.

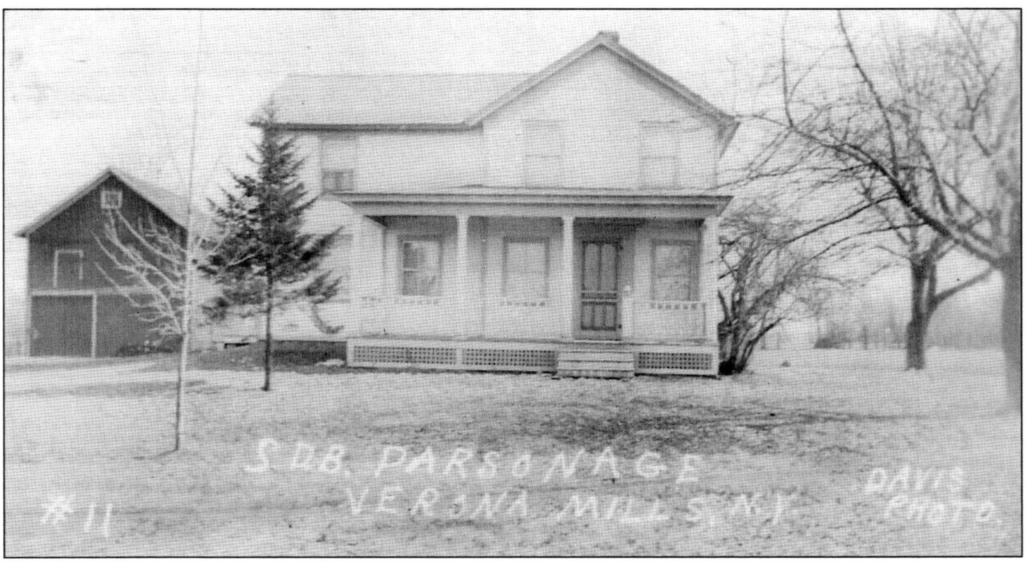

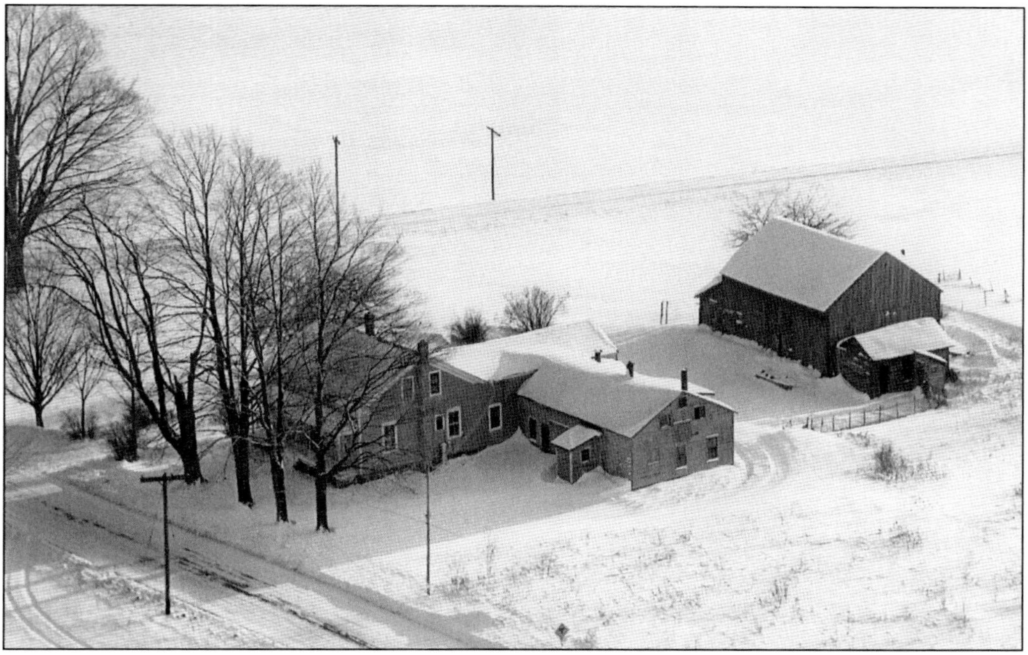

The Gottlieb Schallenberg home is one of the many sites in the town that made cheese. Many of these smaller operations went out of business when the Kraft Company expanded its mass production. The home is currently owned by the Burleigh family and is located at the corner of Senn Road and Happy Valley Road in Churchville.

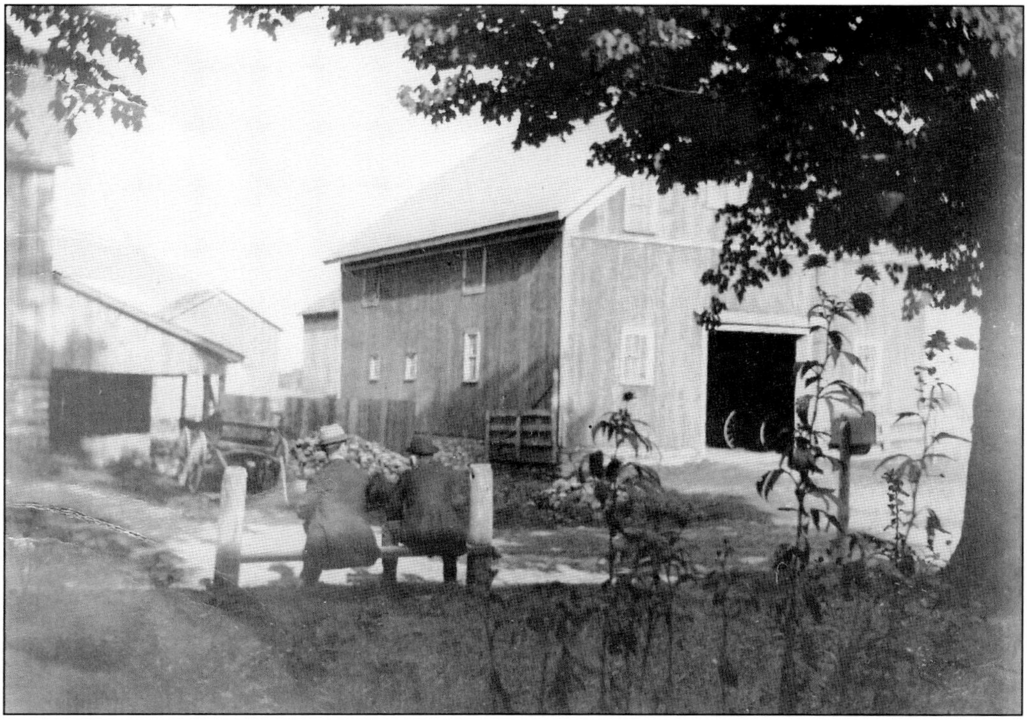

Pictured here are Fred Leichty and a neighbor discussing matters of the day at the Leichty farm in Churchville.

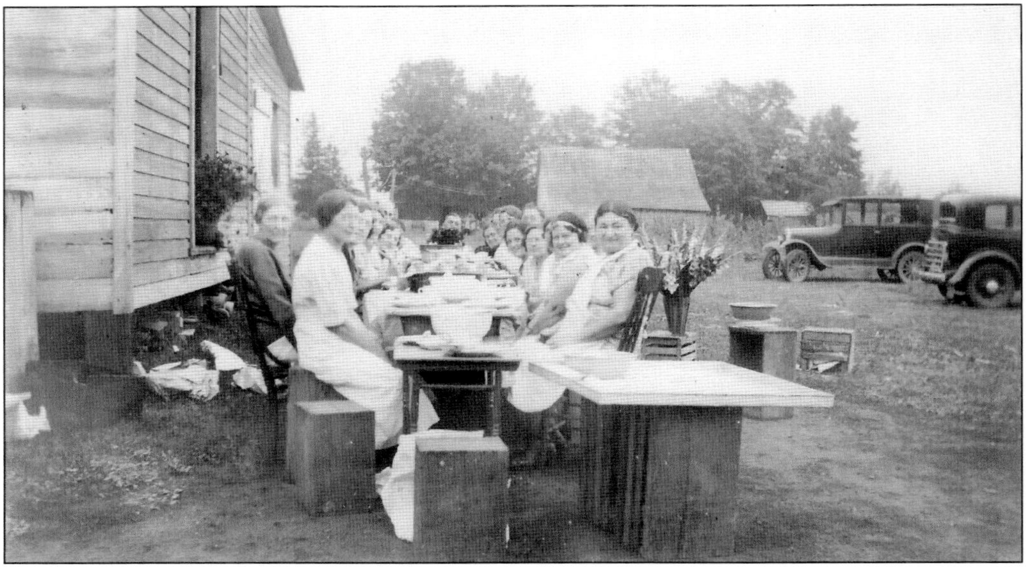

The ladies of the area found seasonal employment at the Wilhelm Canning Factory at Verona Mills. Pictured here are a group of ladies enjoying a picnic during a respite from their factory labor.

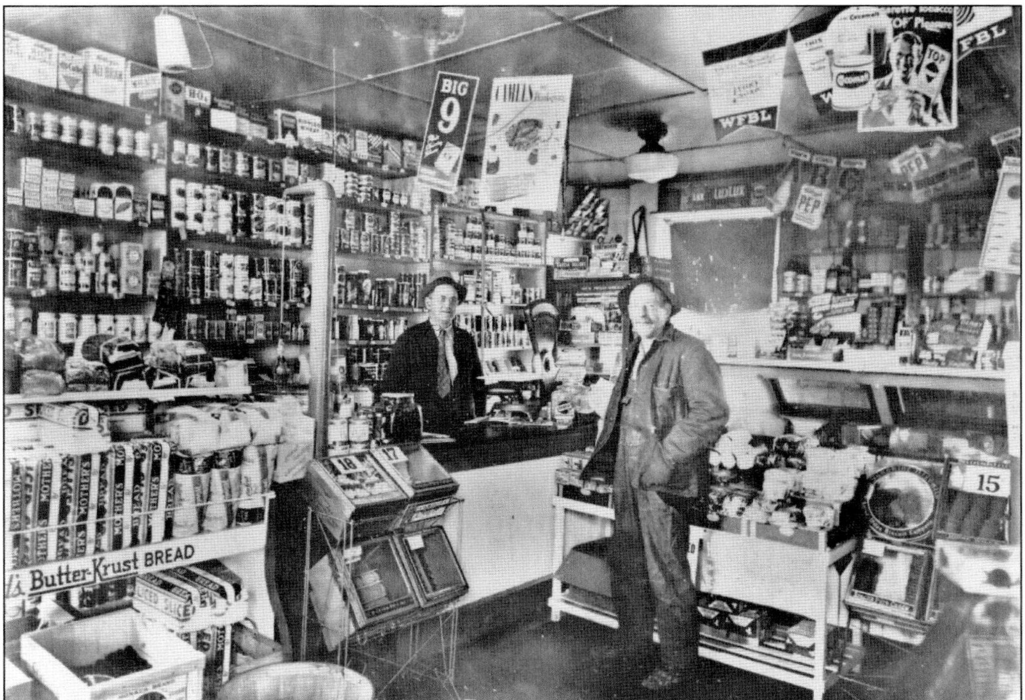

Ben Vaughn's store was located in Stacy Basin along the canal towpath. Both canalers and locals could purchase their daily needs from Mrs. Vaughn or other helpers, like the ones pictured here. How many present-day brand names can be spotted?

Four

SCONONDOA

Scononda is a small area along the creek of the same name in the southwest corner of the township. The land was first purchased in 1824 from the Oneida Indians by Samuel L. Breese. He and his family were one of the first to permanently settle here.

Originally know as Oneida Castleton, the property was renamed Scononda in honor of the Native American chief who signed the property deed and with whom the Breese family had a cordial relationship. The Oneida Indians operated a sawmill and gristmill here that was also used by early white settlers.

The Breese Mansion was built in 1813. The well-educated patriarch, Samuel L. Breese, constructed and operated a prosperous cotton mill until 1845. He was a cousin to Samuel Finley Breese Morse, the inventor of the telegraph. Breese's son, Samuel S. Breese, first gained business experience in his father's cotton mill before building a sawmill here in 1840. He later became vice president of the Oneida Valley National Bank.

In ensuing years, other families moved to this area. Among them included the Abraham Randel family who came here from Albany around 1813. He and his wife, Rebecca Harrison Randel, built a three-story house for their family, like those found in the state's capital. Rebecca was a cousin to Pres. William Henry Harrison. Abraham received a patent in 1840 for designing the first workable farm mowing machine.

Another notable of the township is Russell Sage. Born in 1816, he grew up on his father's farm near the intersection of Kotary and Sand Hill Roads. He attended the local one-room school and worked on the farm with his father. As a young man, he moved to Troy, New York, and established a Hudson River shipping company. He also amassed a fortune investing in railroad companies in the later 19th century. After his death in 1916, his wife used his fortune to establish Russell Sage College, in Troy.

Throughout its history, Scononda remained a mostly agricultural and residential area as business development stayed in nearby Durhamville, Verona Hamlet, and the city of Oneida. The landscape changed significantly when the Oneida Indian Nation purchased the Davis farm on Patrick Road and built the Turning Stone Casino, hotels, and golf courses in the 1990s. This has resulted in a considerable increase in tourism traffic and related economic development.

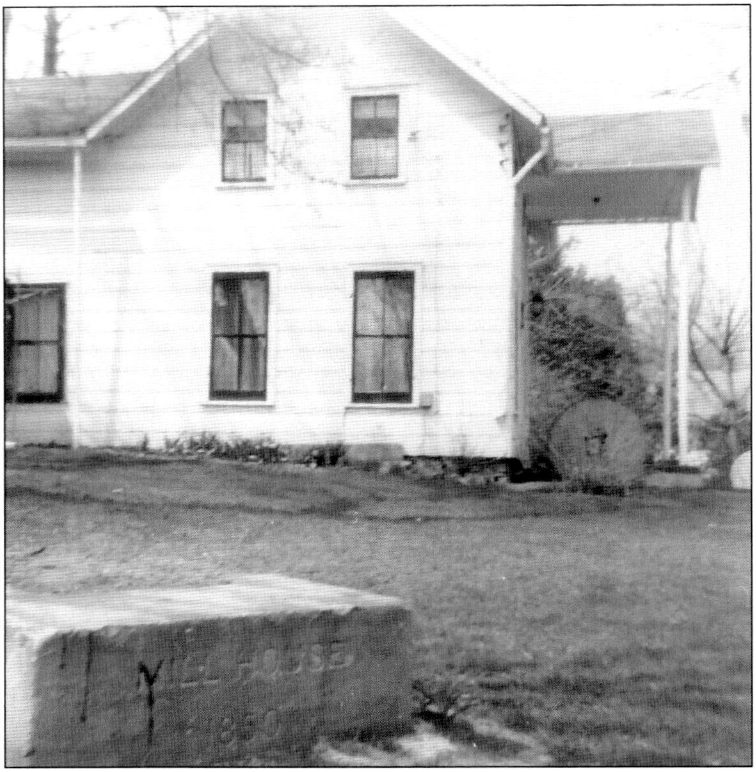

The Mill House of Scononodoa was located on Mason Road. The view at left shows the stepping stone with the date of 1850. This stone was used for people stepping out of carriages and wagons. The view below shows millstones on the porch. These stones were from the flouring mill located nearby.

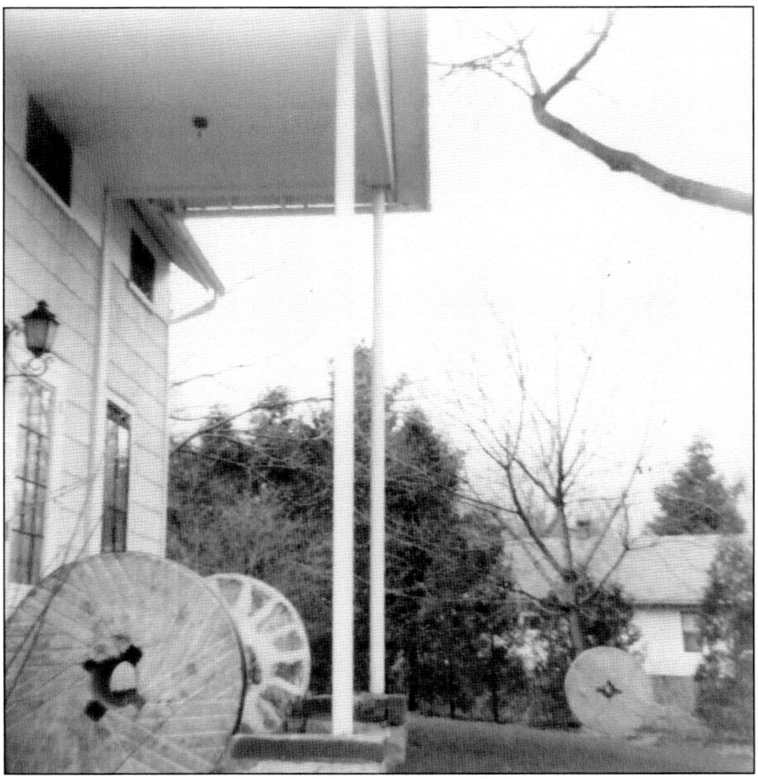

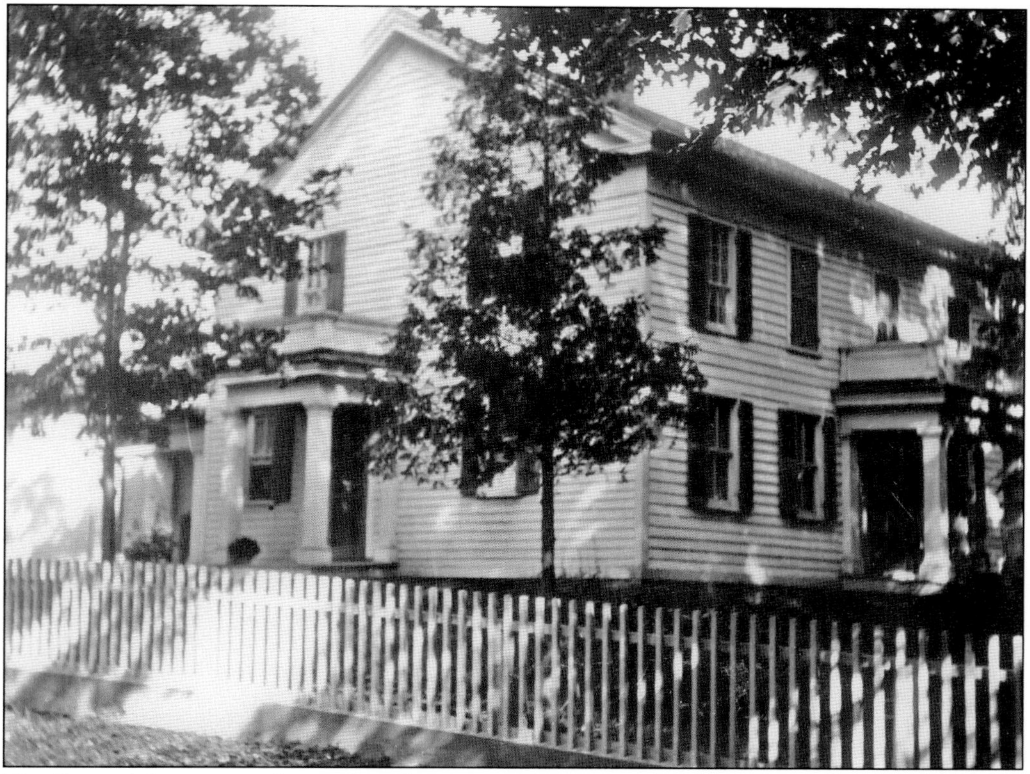

The Breese Mansion was located on the corner of Sconondoa Street and Route 365. Built in 1813, the house was owned by Samuel and Helena Burrows Breese. The main part of the house has 11 large rooms, 4 small rooms, and 6 fireplaces and 2 cisterns for collecting rainwater. One of several additions was a carriage house built in 1880. The front door still locks with a key that measures 5- to 6-inches in length. The mansion is now Charlotte's Creekside Manor.

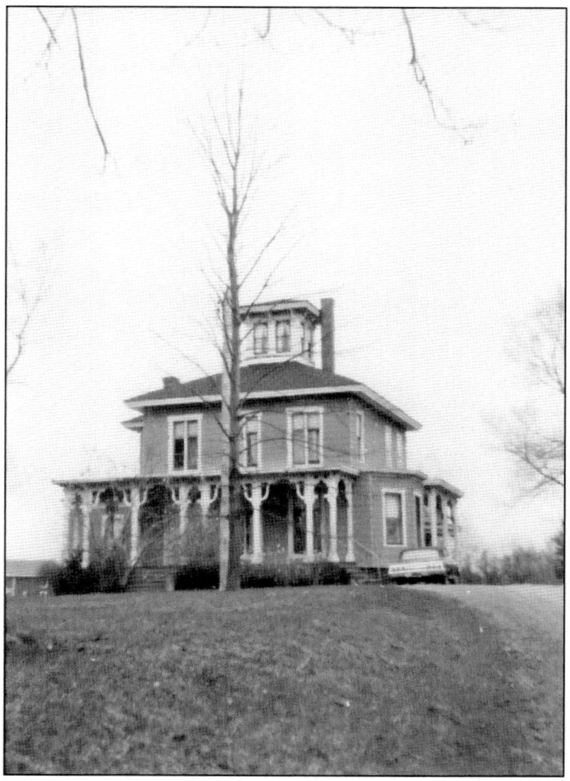

The home of George and Helen Breese Sanford had windows made of plate glass. The huge ornate rugs were cleaned by fastening them to whiffletrees rods that connected a wagon to the harness, and the team of horses then pulled the rugs over the snowy fields in winter to remove the dust and dirt.

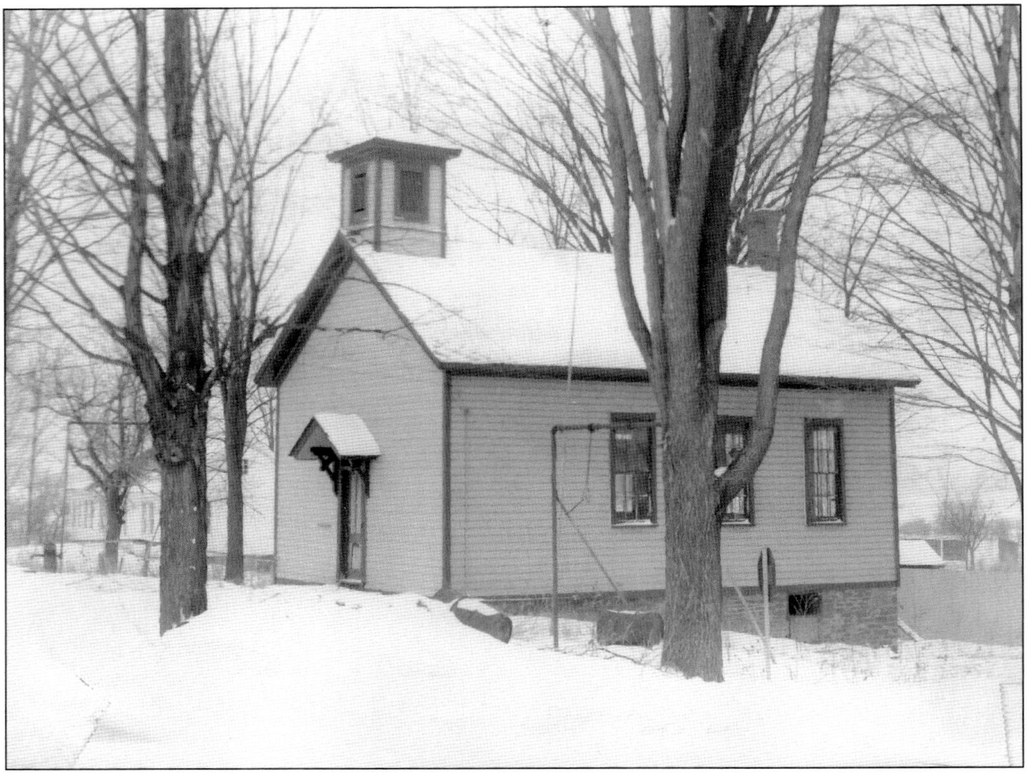

Willow Valley School, designated as District No. 15 and located in the area of Route 365 and Hill Road, educated many students in the 1900s.

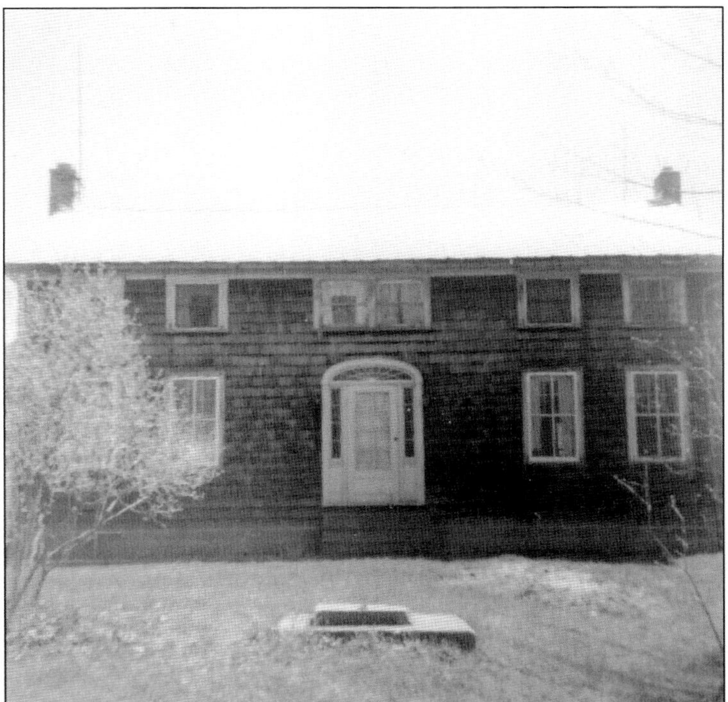

The Old Butterfield Hotel was the home of Frank Morrow. It is on the Verona town line in Sconondoa. For a while it served as a place for the care of animals and is now a home.

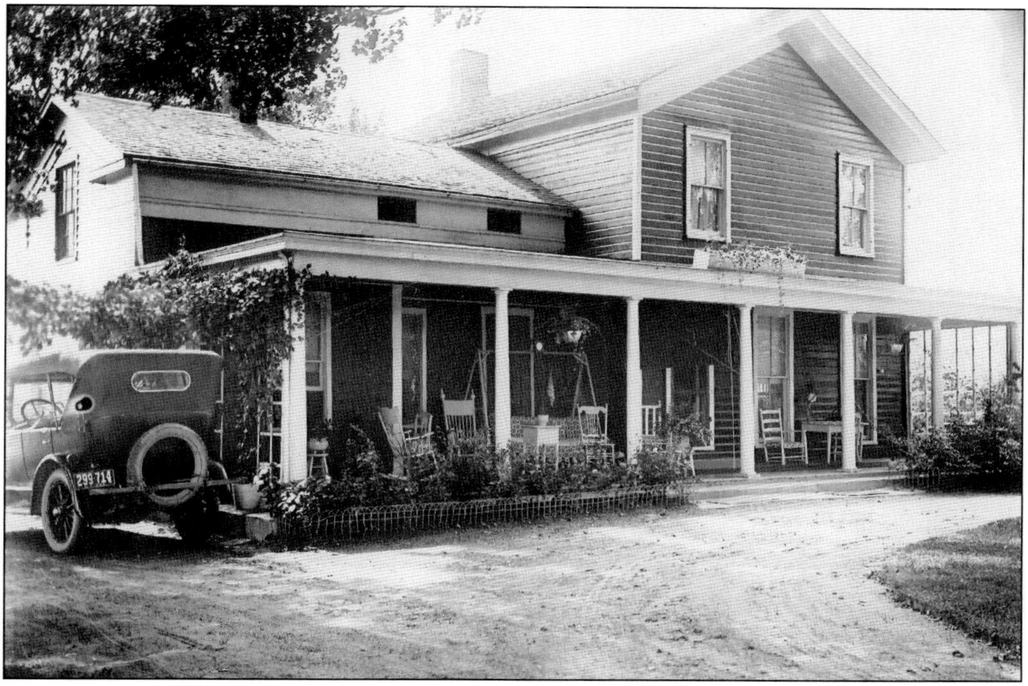

John Randel Jr., a surveyor of the Erie Canal, moved to Sconondoa from Albany and built this homestead in 1813, named the "Cottage in the Woods." The structure was originally three stories, later reduced to two stories by Abraham Randal, whose wife, Rebecca, planted the notable grove of maple trees, where the Native Americans had a camping ground and borrowed utensils and the big iron kettle from the Randel family to prepare for their feasts. In 1854, the New York Central Railroad gained right-of-way through the Randel property, granting the family a life pass on the railroad. The house remained in the family for many years but was eventually demolished. The automobile in the yard dates this photograph in the 1920s.

The home of Jon J. Loomis is located on Sconondoa Road in Sconondoa and appears very much the same today. Loomis was a successful farmer who engaged in growing hops.

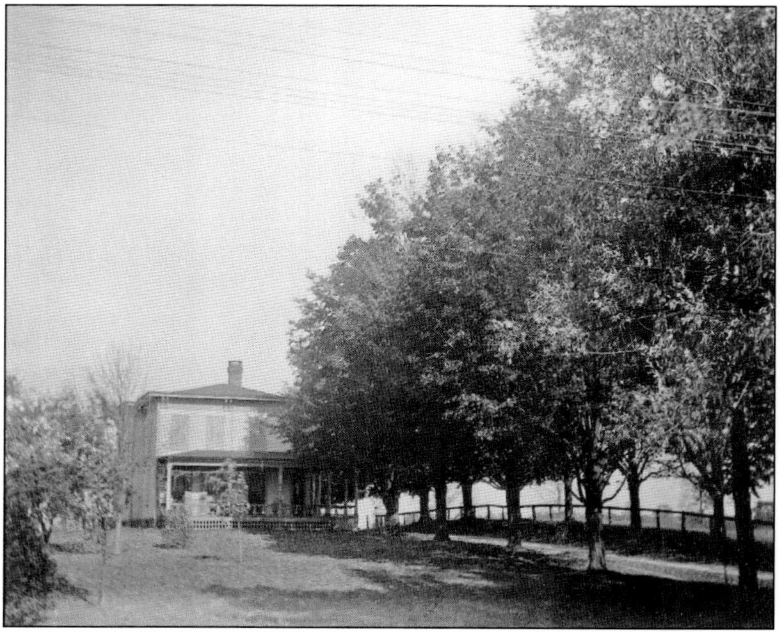

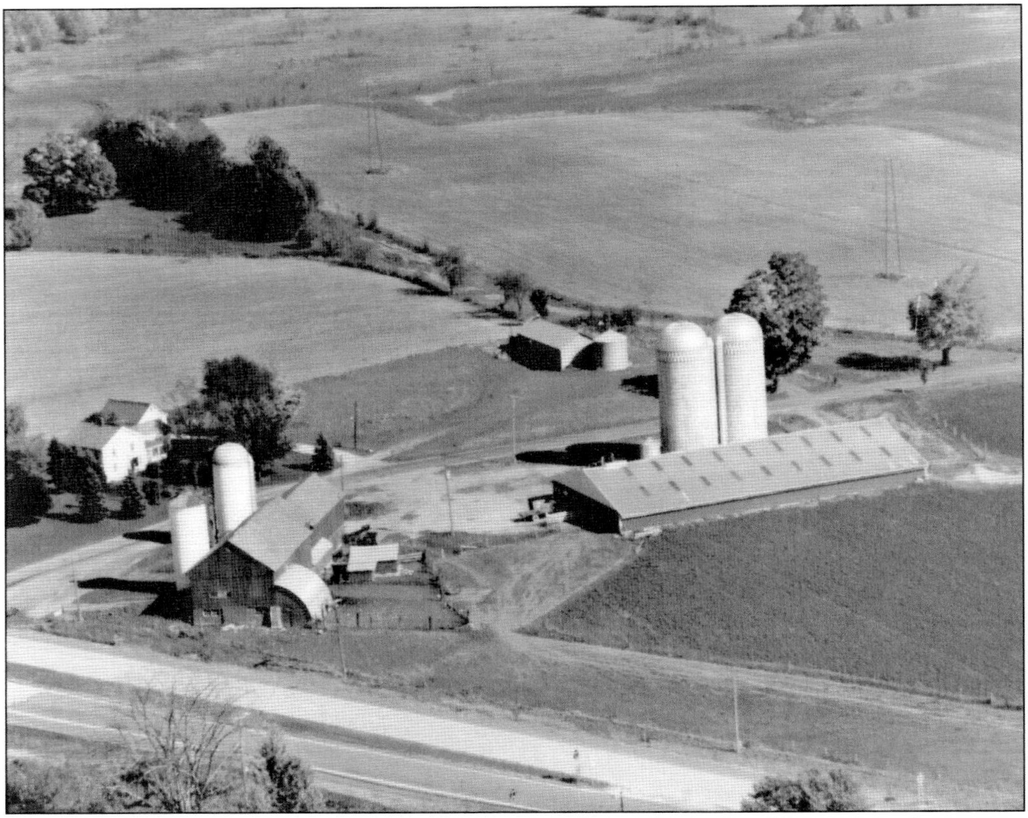

The LaVerne Davis farm was located on the corner of Patrick Road and Route 365, the current site of the Oneida Nation Casino.

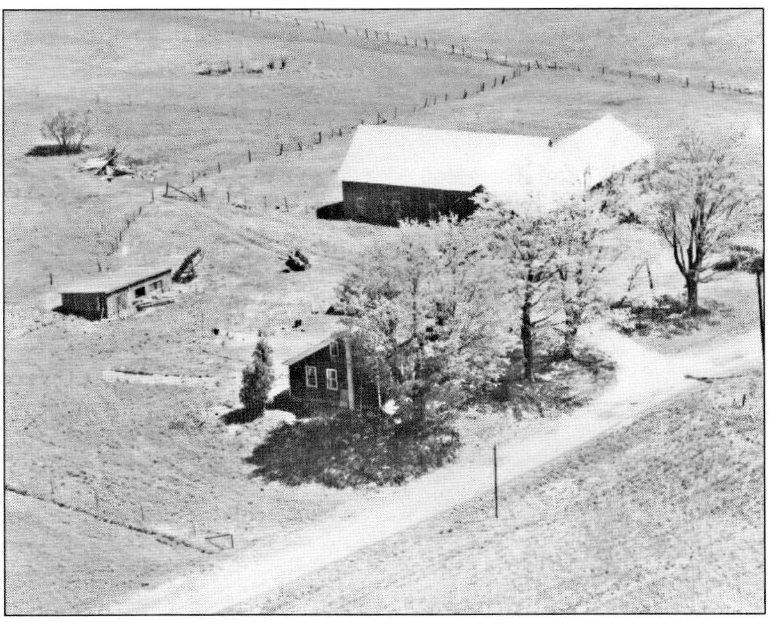

The Dela Ridge farm, owned by the Lake family, was located on Stoney Brook Road. It was converted into a popular nine-hole golf course named Pleasant Knolls, frequently known as Peter's Patch.

Five

Verona, Verona Station, and Verona Springs

Known today as the Verona Hamlet, this area in the southern region was once large enough to encompass three distinct settlements: Verona Station, Verona Springs, and Main Street, Verona.

Verona Station earned its name from a stop on the New York Central Railroad. In addition to the train station and adjoined freight house was a store, hotel, milk station, gristmill, post office, and other commercial enterprises, which made this a busy location. The gristmill and coal yard were destroyed by fire, and many other buildings were either dismantled or removed when a new bridge was constructed over the railroad tracks.

Verona Springs gained popularity for the natural mineral waters first discovered by Native Americans. The Verona Springs Hotel was a popular destination in the late 1800s for tourists who wanted to take advantage of the curative powers of the water. Onsite were a well house, bathhouse, and a 62-room hotel, which had all of the modern conveniences of the day. It was struck by lightening in 1916 and burned to the ground.

Main Street, Verona, is a tree-shaded street along which are located private homes, churches, and the elementary school. It was once the main route between the cities of Rome and Oneida, making it an ideal location for the stores and local businesses. It has since been bypassed by State Route 365. Since the demise of Verona Springs and Verona Station, the vicinity of Main Street is recognized as Verona Hamlet.

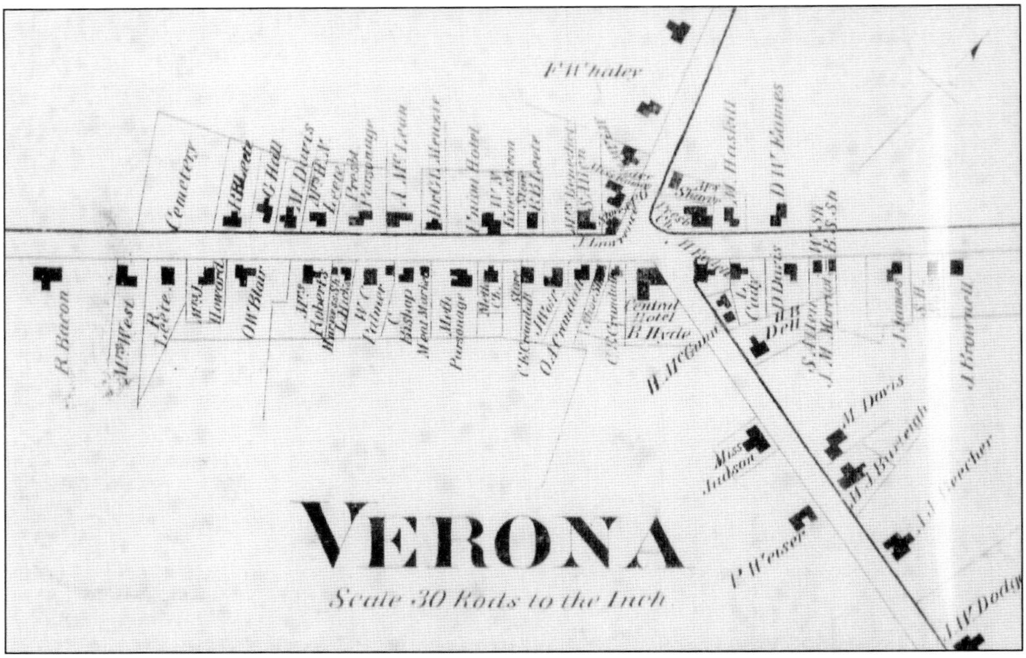

This 1874 map of the hamlet of Verona shows churches, businesses, and homes that existed on Main Street, Rock Road, and Spring Road.

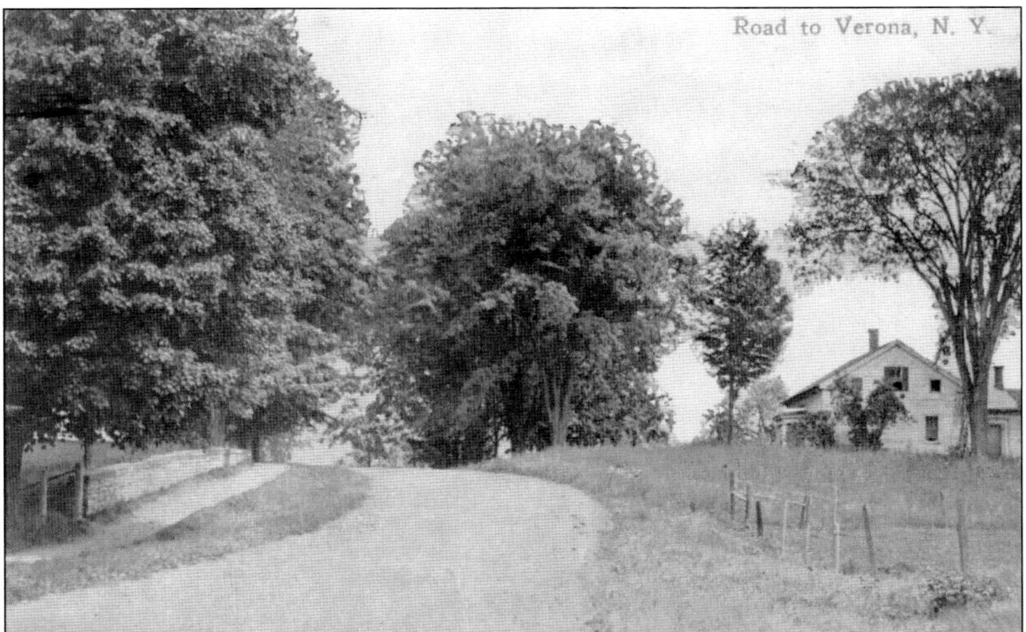

This postcard depicts the road traveling east up the hill on West Main Street. The Cook house is located on the right side of the road.

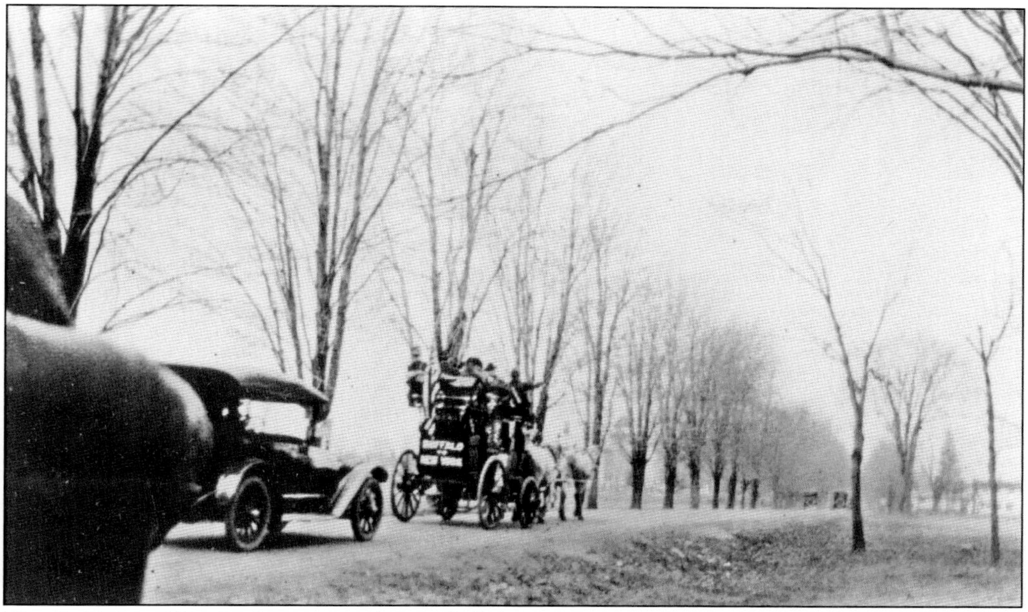

The Buffalo-to-New York stagecoach traveled through Verona during the late 19th and early 20th centuries. This photograph was taken to observe the last run of the stage.

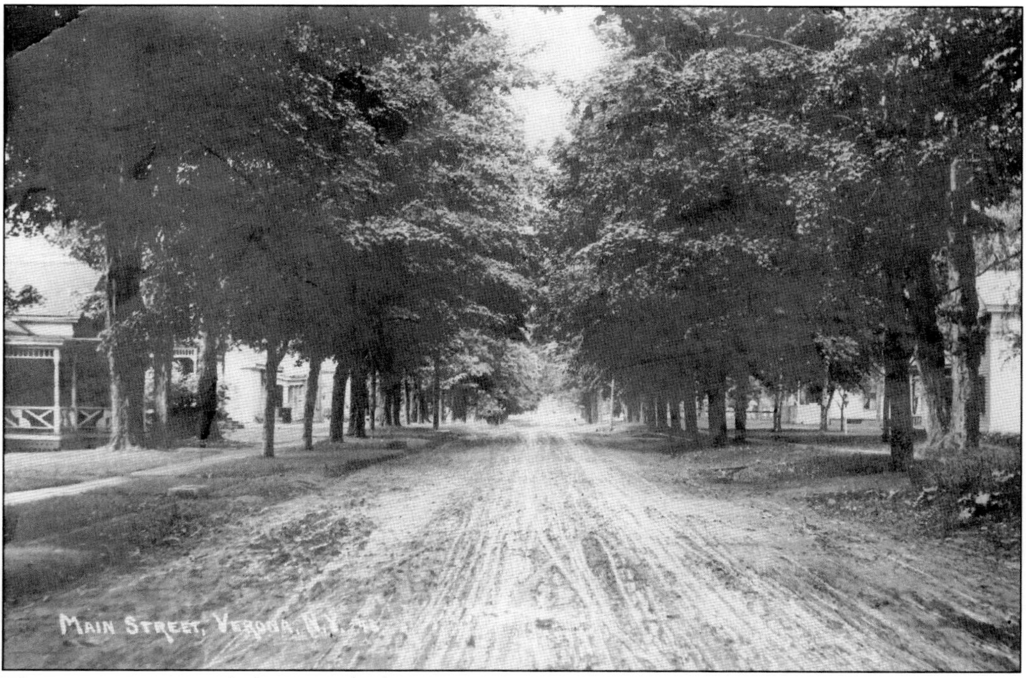

This vintage postcard photograph shows West Main Street in Verona.

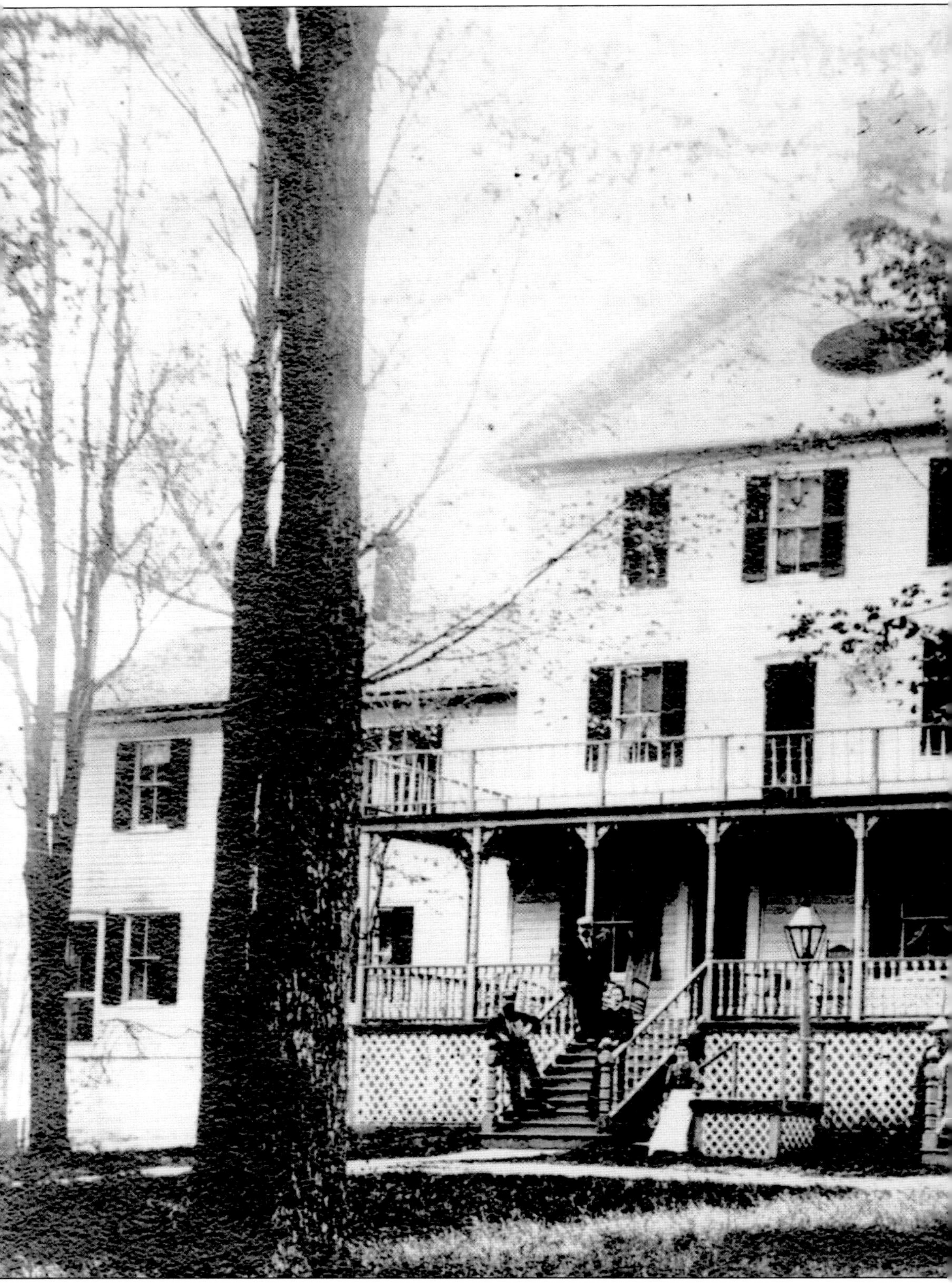

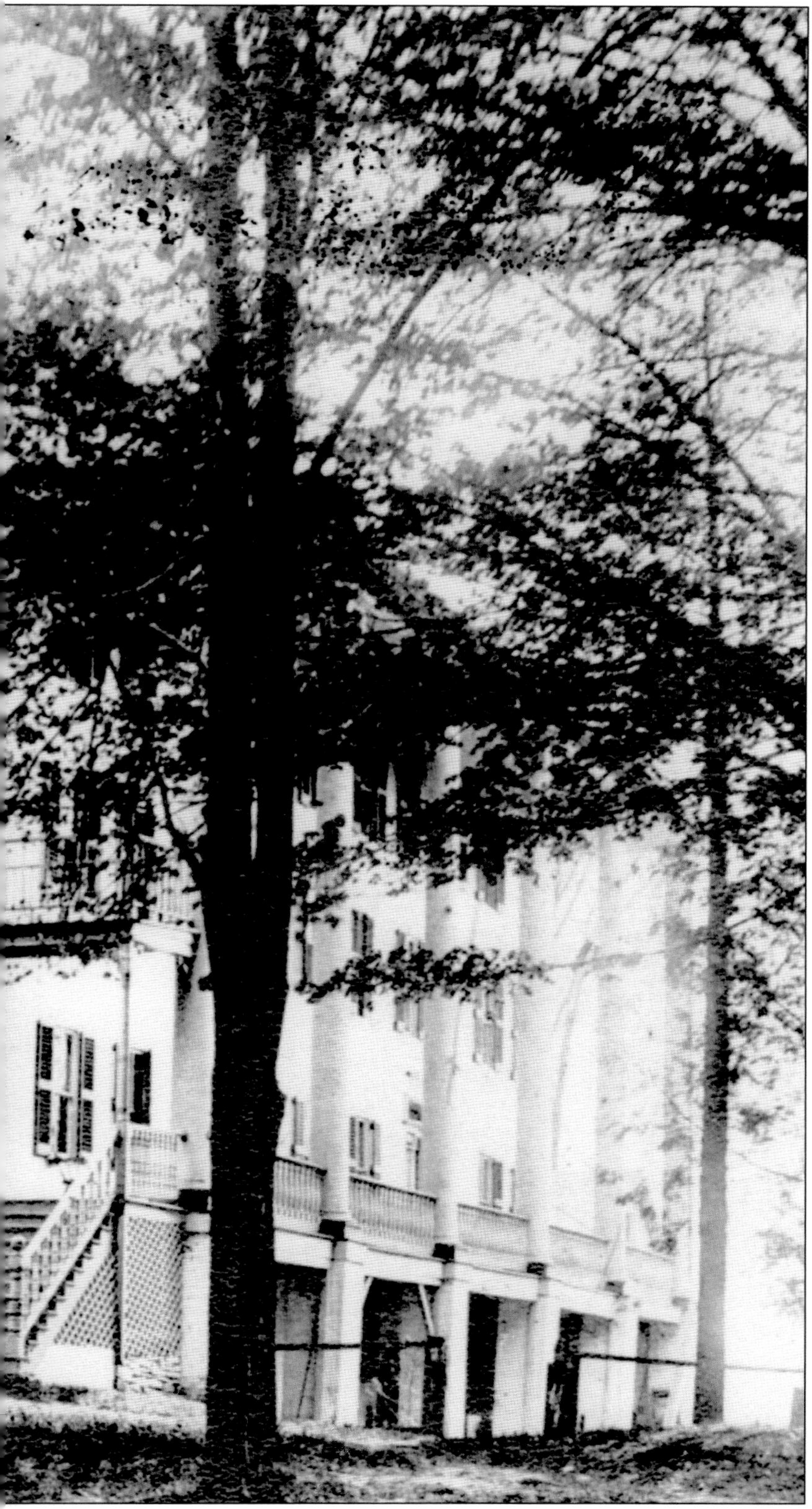

The Verona Springs Hotel property was bought in 1853 by Charles Wardwell and Dr. Seymour Curtiss, who established a water cure. It was sold in 1858 to Dr. Nelson Hunt and his wife, Dr. Angennette Hunt, one of the first women granted a medical degree in the country. The 62-room hotel was a very imposing structure, one of the most admired in Oneida County in its day. In 1905, it burned to the ground as a result of an overturned oil lamp. In 1906, a new hotel was erected; this building also burned in 1916, ending the era of the spring and house.

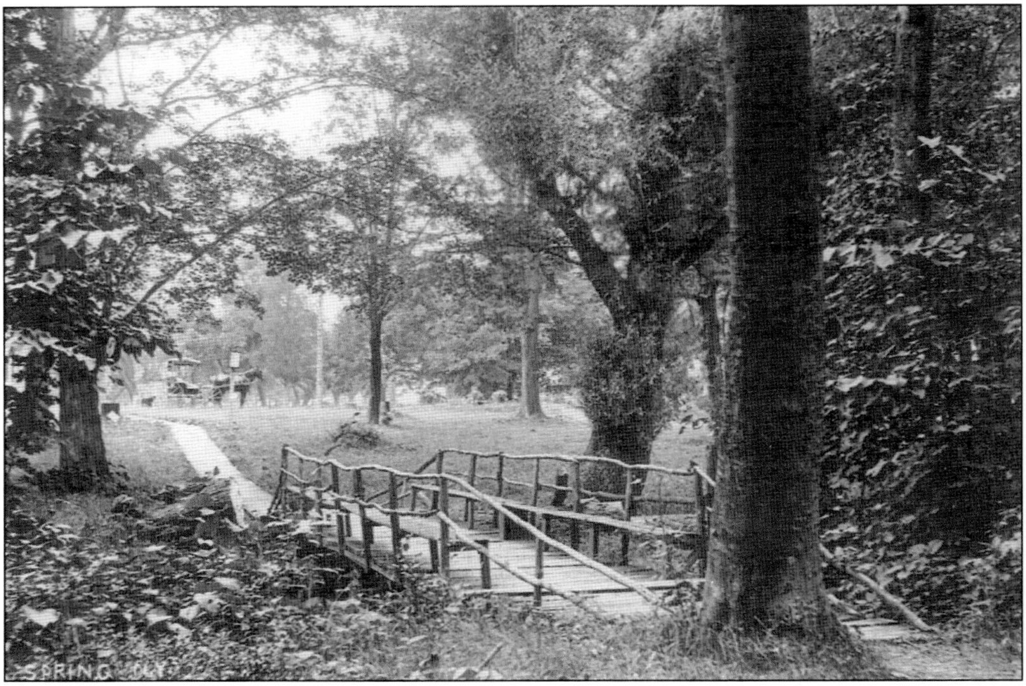

The bridge at Verona Springs was in the gardens over a rivulet.

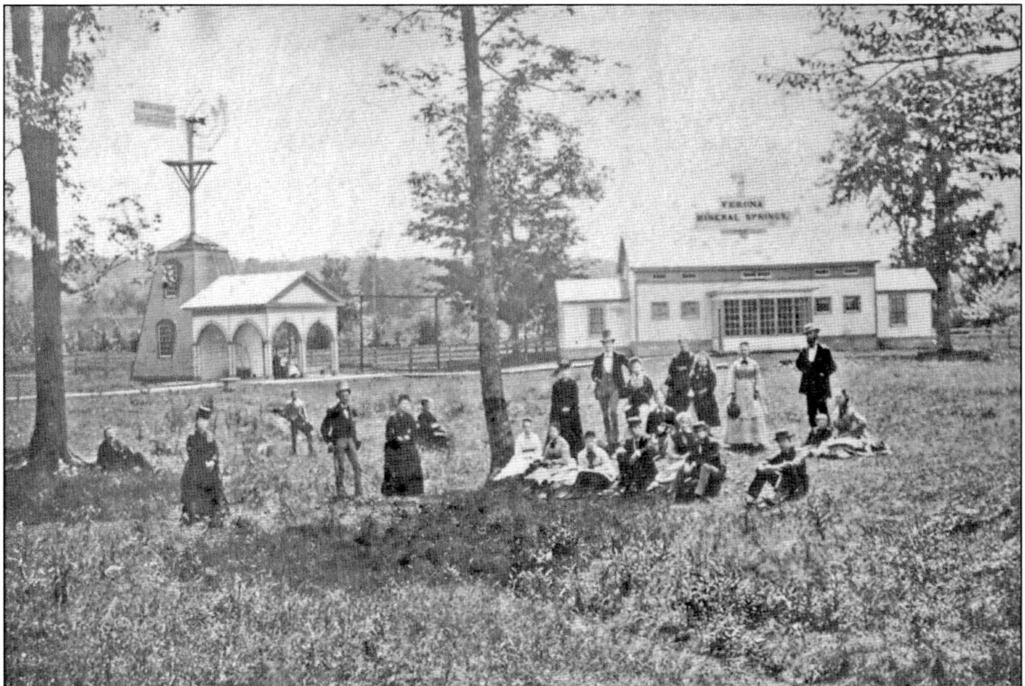

This photograph shows guests at Verona Mineral Springs. It was said that the springs could cure skin diseases, rheumatism, kidney, liver, and stomach troubles. Patrons included notables from other countries, as well as many businessmen seeking respite. (Photograph courtesy of Oneida County Historical Society.)

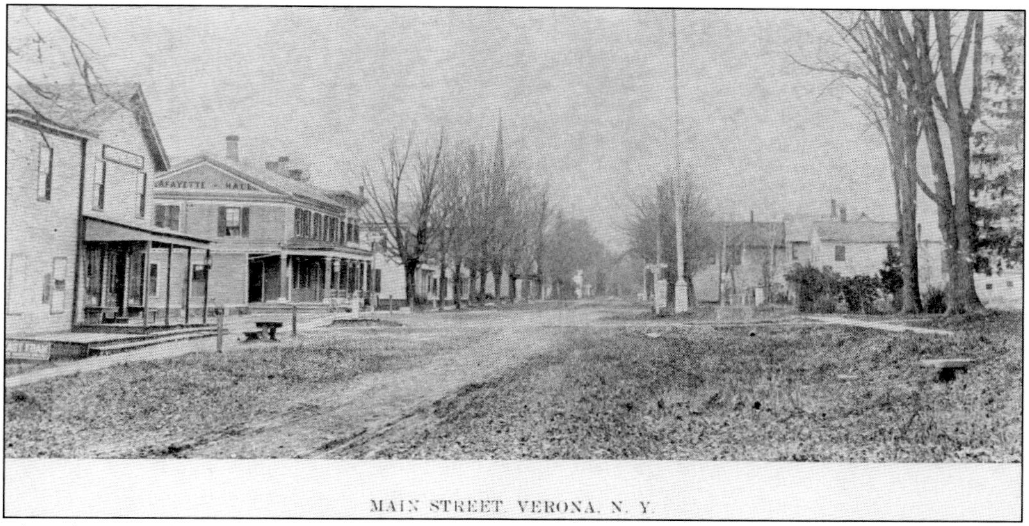

This photograph of Main Street in Verona shows a well-traveled rutty dirt road looking west. On the right side are two liberty poles. On the left are Joseph Felts's store and the Lafayette Hall, and further down the street the spire of the Methodist church is visible above the trees.

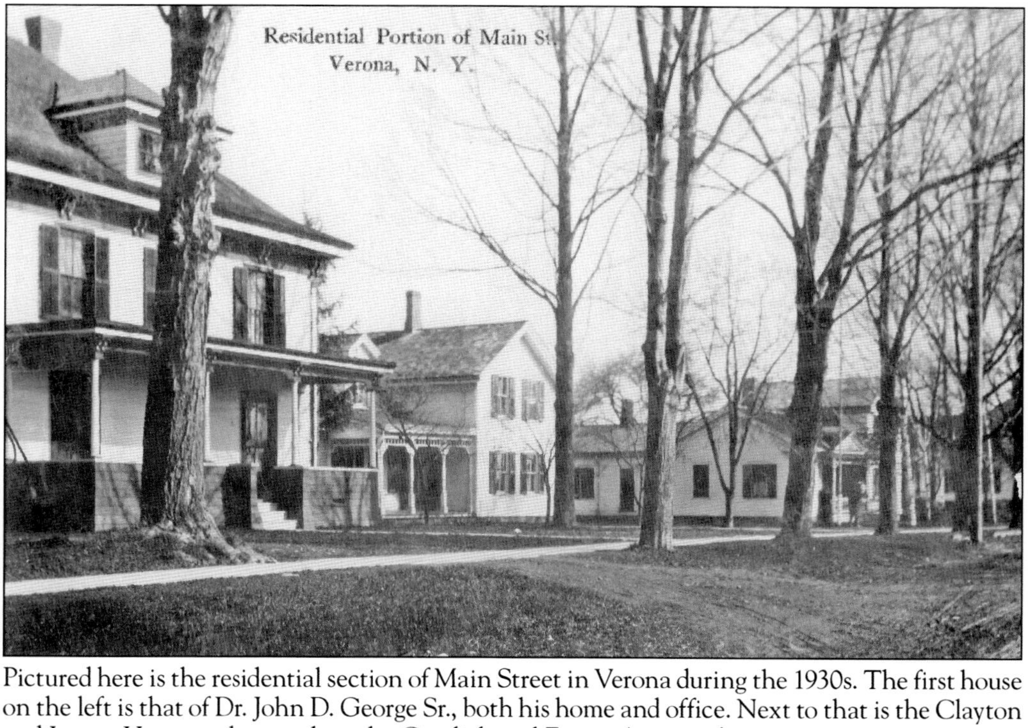

Pictured here is the residential section of Main Street in Verona during the 1930s. The first house on the left is that of Dr. John D. George Sr., both his home and office. Next to that is the Clayton and Leona Hartman home, then the Gottlieb and Fanny Aegerter house.

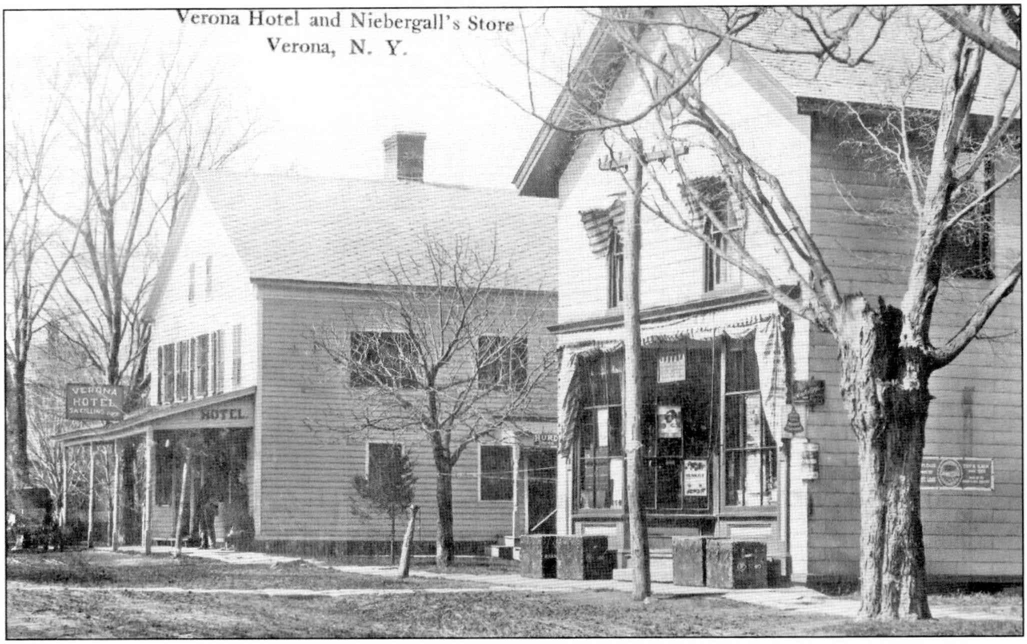

Charles and Celeste Neibergall's store was located on Main Street in Verona, next to the Verona Hotel with the Grange hall upstairs. The store flourished in the late 1800s but later burned.

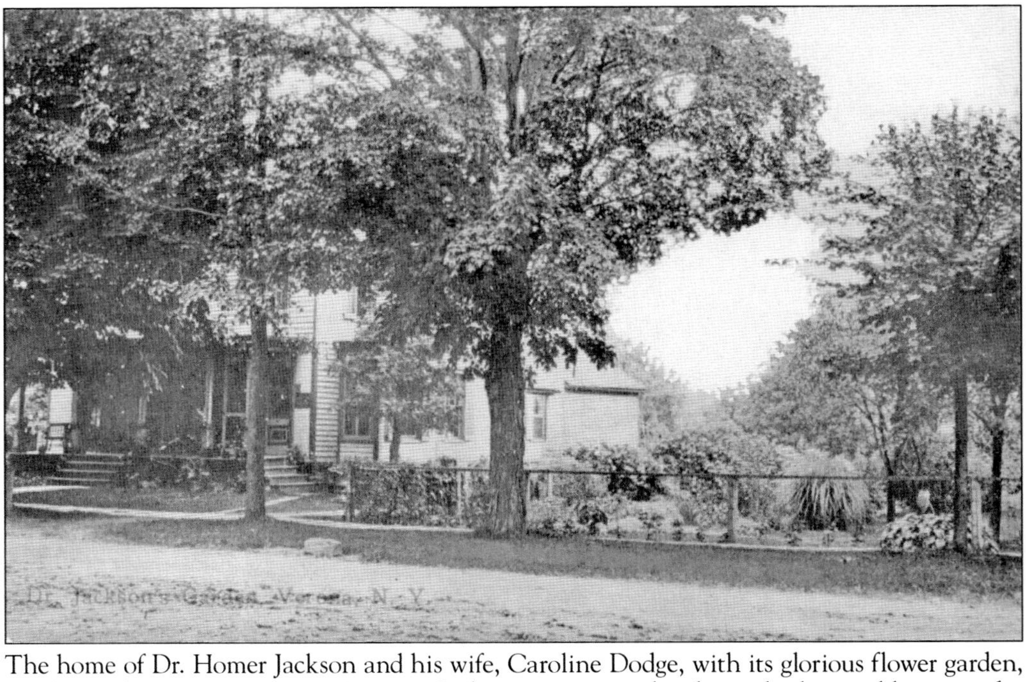

The home of Dr. Homer Jackson and his wife, Caroline Dodge, with its glorious flower garden, was located on Main Street in Verona. Jackson was reputed to have the largest library in the village. The house was later owned by the Cobb and Finnerty families. In the 1990s, the house burned. Today there is a parking lot for the Methodist church and also a road, Volunteer Avenue, leading to the volunteer firehouse.

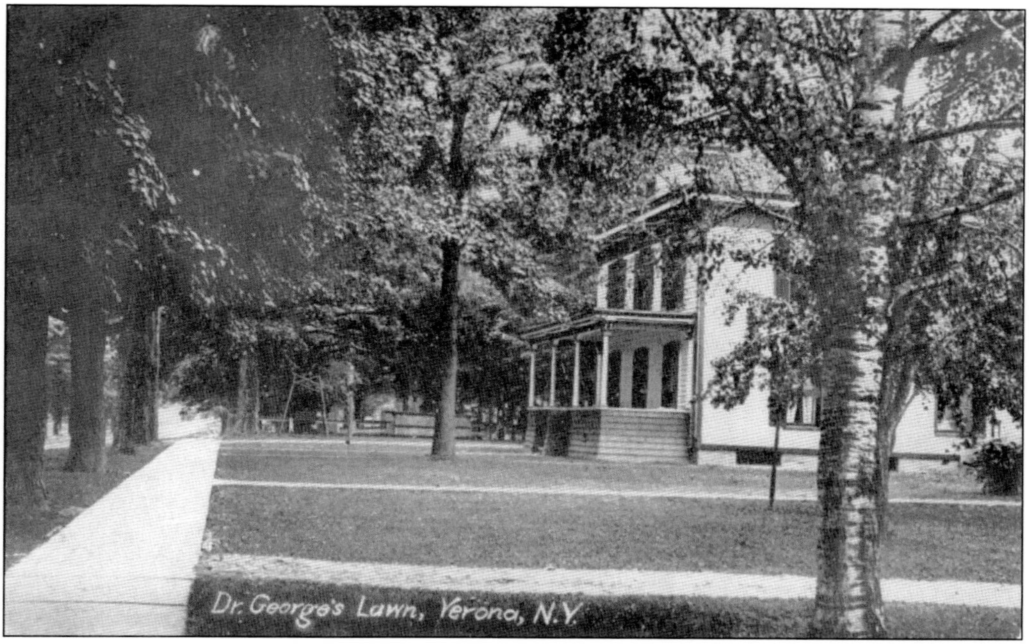

Dr. John D. George Sr. lived on Main Street in Verona. This house served as his home as well as his office. He had this snowmobile built from a Model T Ford in order to do winter house calls.

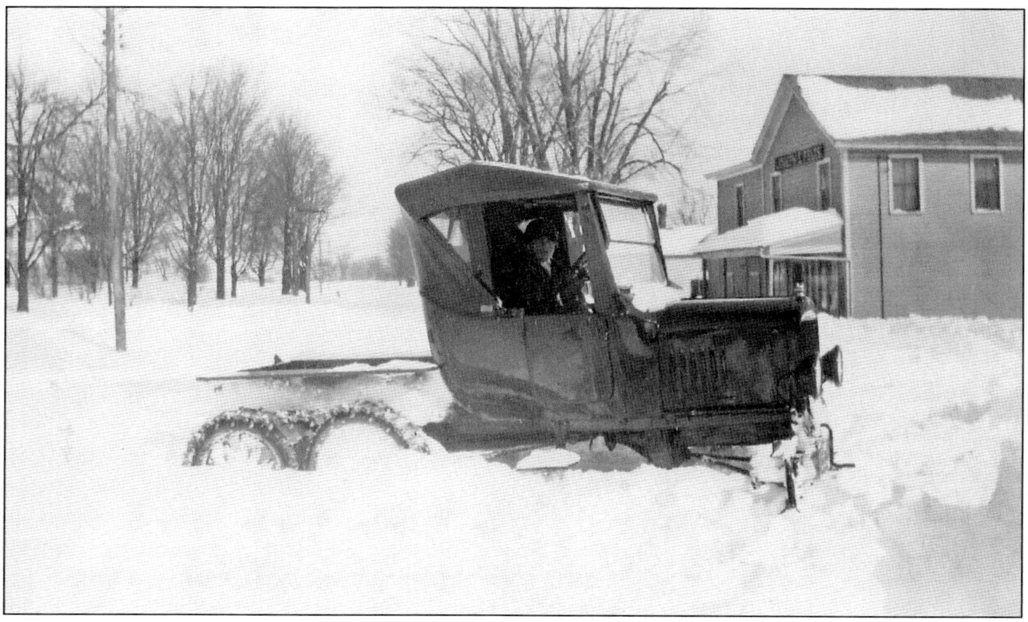

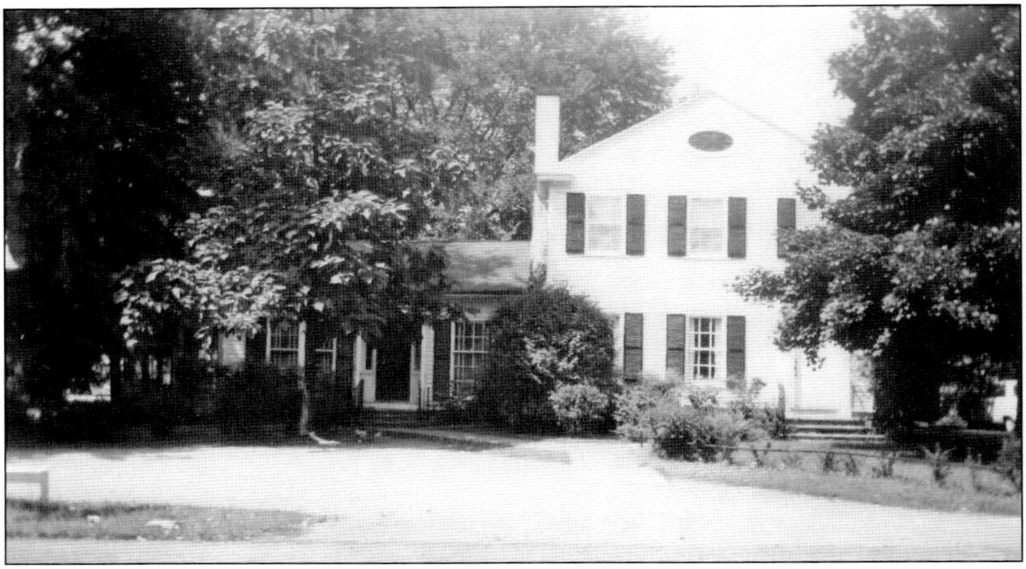

Margaret Cheney's store on Main Street was a popular place with students in the 1930s and 1940s. At the store, they could buy candy and ice cream as well as school supplies.

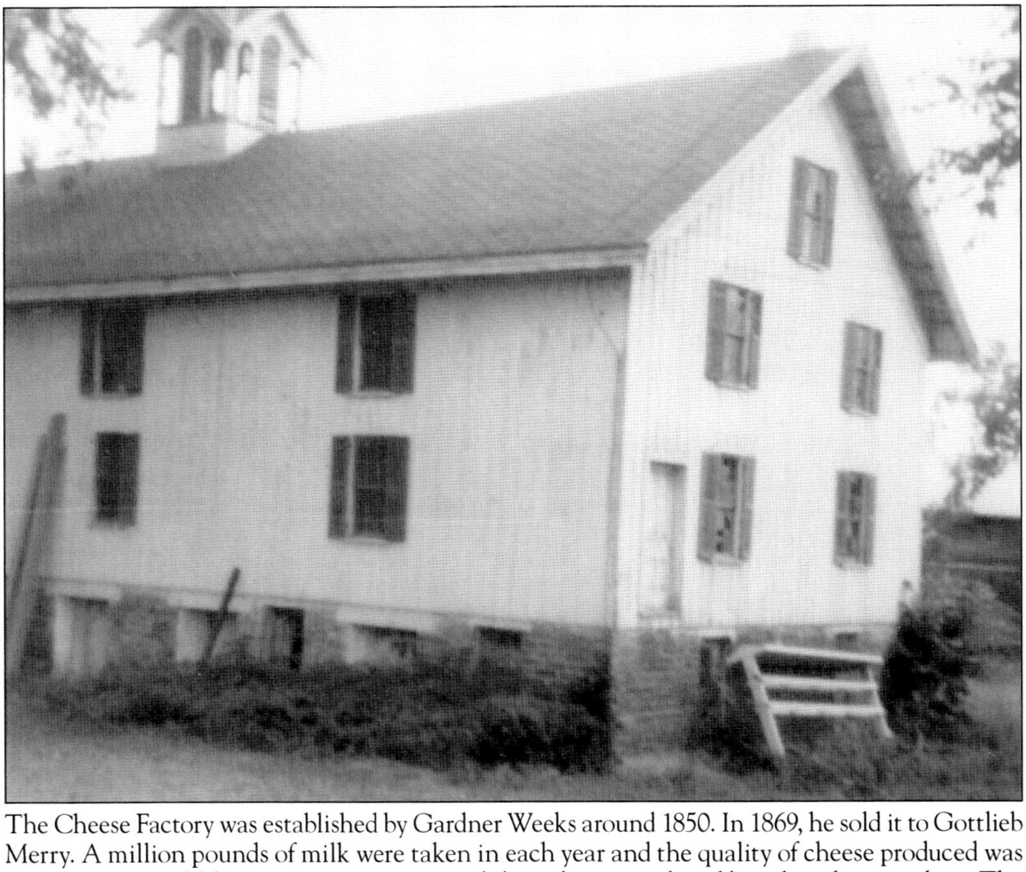

The Cheese Factory was established by Gardner Weeks around 1850. In 1869, he sold it to Gottlieb Merry. A million pounds of milk were taken in each year and the quality of cheese produced was so good that it sold for 1 to 2¢ more per pound than cheese produced by other cheesemakers. The factory was moved to Erie Canal Village in Rome.

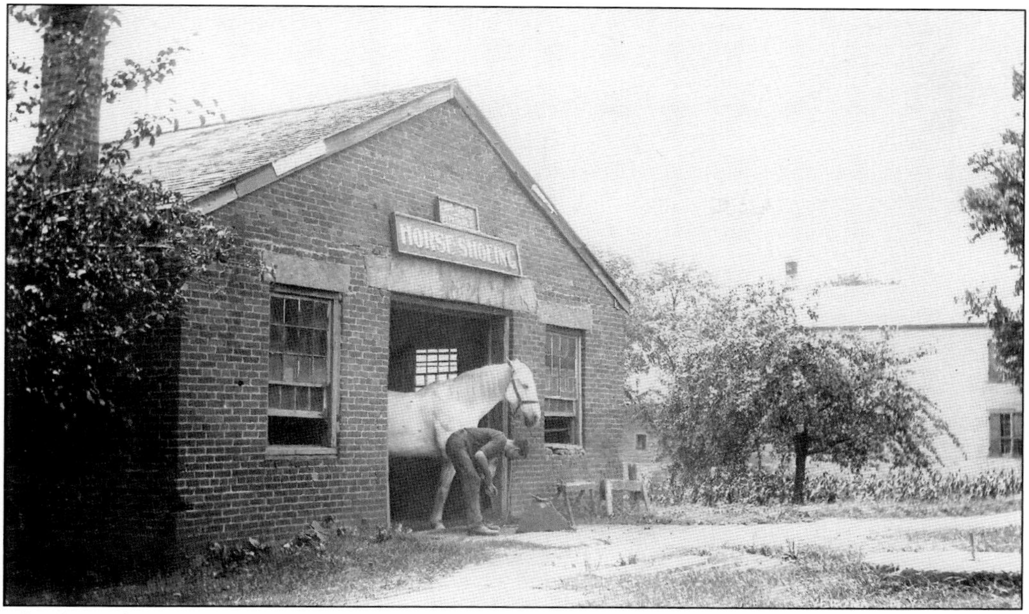

Charles Fuhs, a native of Bavaria, operated a blacksmith shop on Main Street in Verona for 43 years, until 1931.

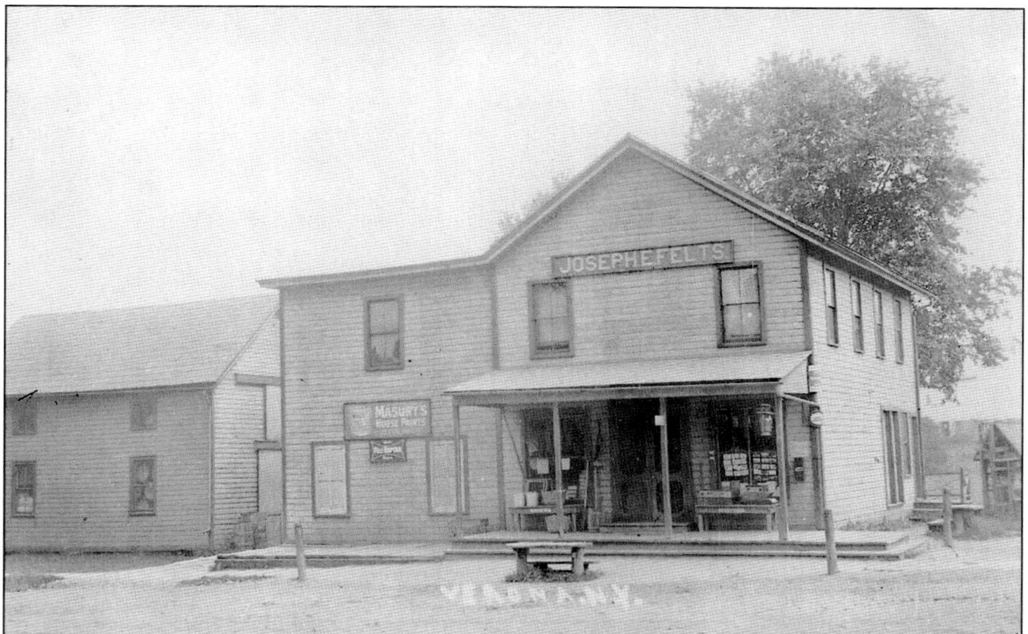

Joseph Felts came to Verona from Buffalo, New York, in 1876. He opened a general store with George Cagwin and later operated it with his brother, Charles. Felts later sold the store to Arthur Ketter. Today it is an apartment house.

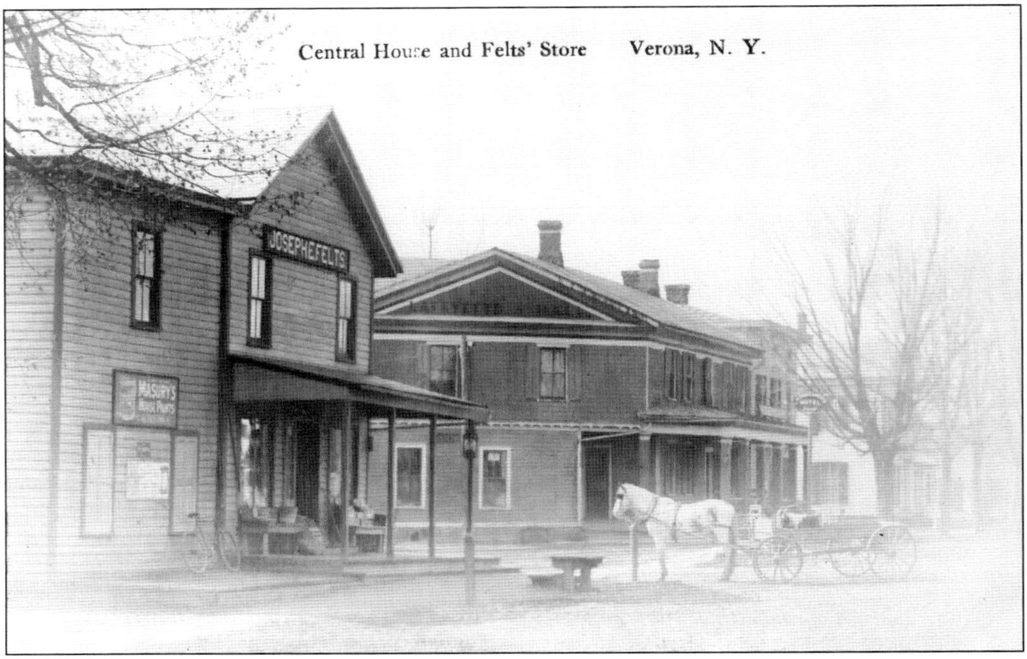

The Central House, later called the Lafayette Hall, and Felts's store were located at the intersection of Spring and Main Streets in Verona. On February 28, 1914, an explosion and ensuing fire destroyed the buildings in spite of valiant efforts by many firefighters.

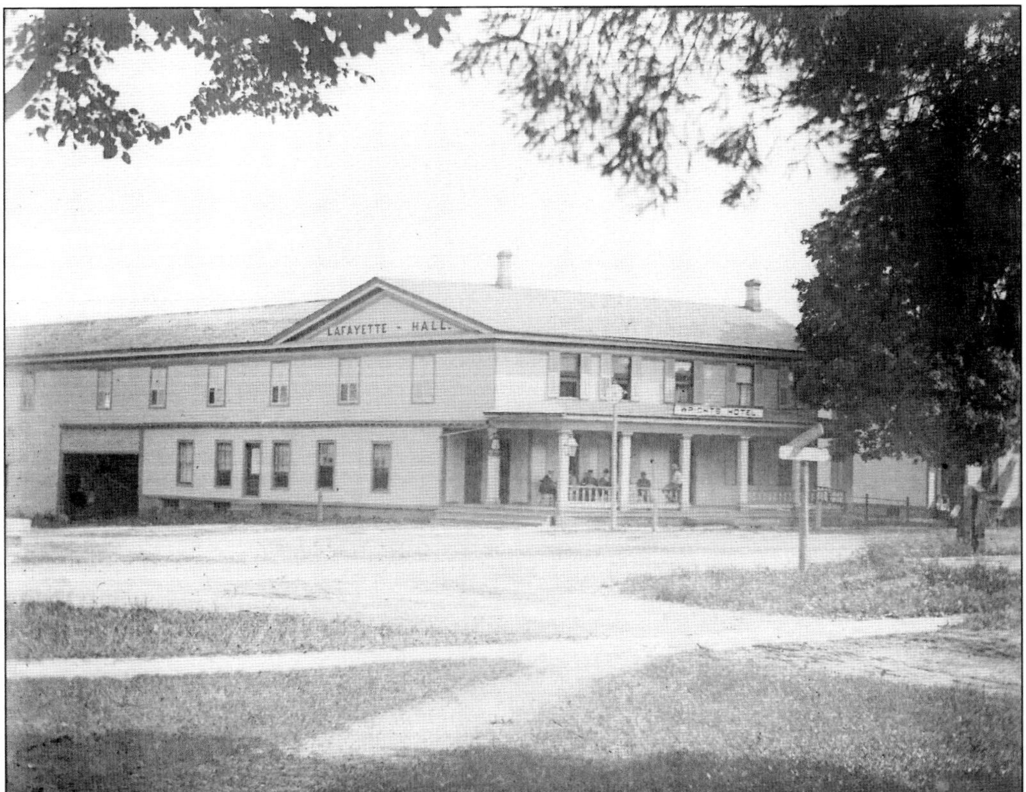

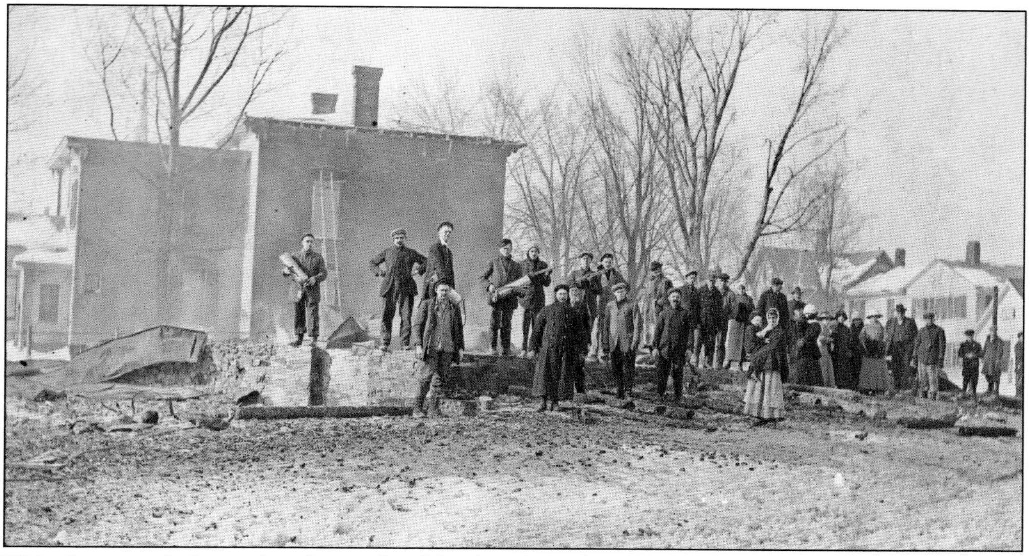

This photograph shows the aftermath of the disastrous fire of 1914, which consumed the Lafayette Hall and Felts's store. Wet blankets were hung to contain the fire from spreading to adjoining buildings as civilians and Oneida firefighters battled the blaze. Today it is the site of the Veteran's Memorial Park.

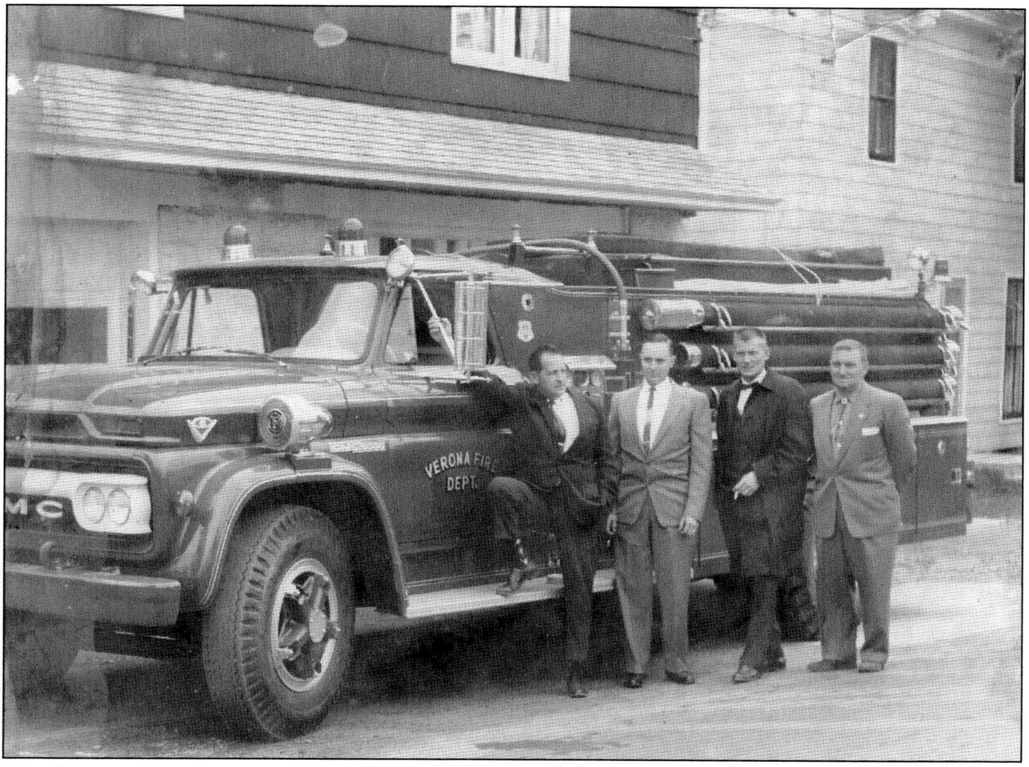

The Verona Fire Department was organized shortly after the devastating fire of the Central Hotel in 1914. Fund-raisers and contributions made possible the construction of a firehouse and purchase of equipment. Pictured is a fire truck from the middle of the 20th century. (Photograph courtesy of Verona Fire Department.)

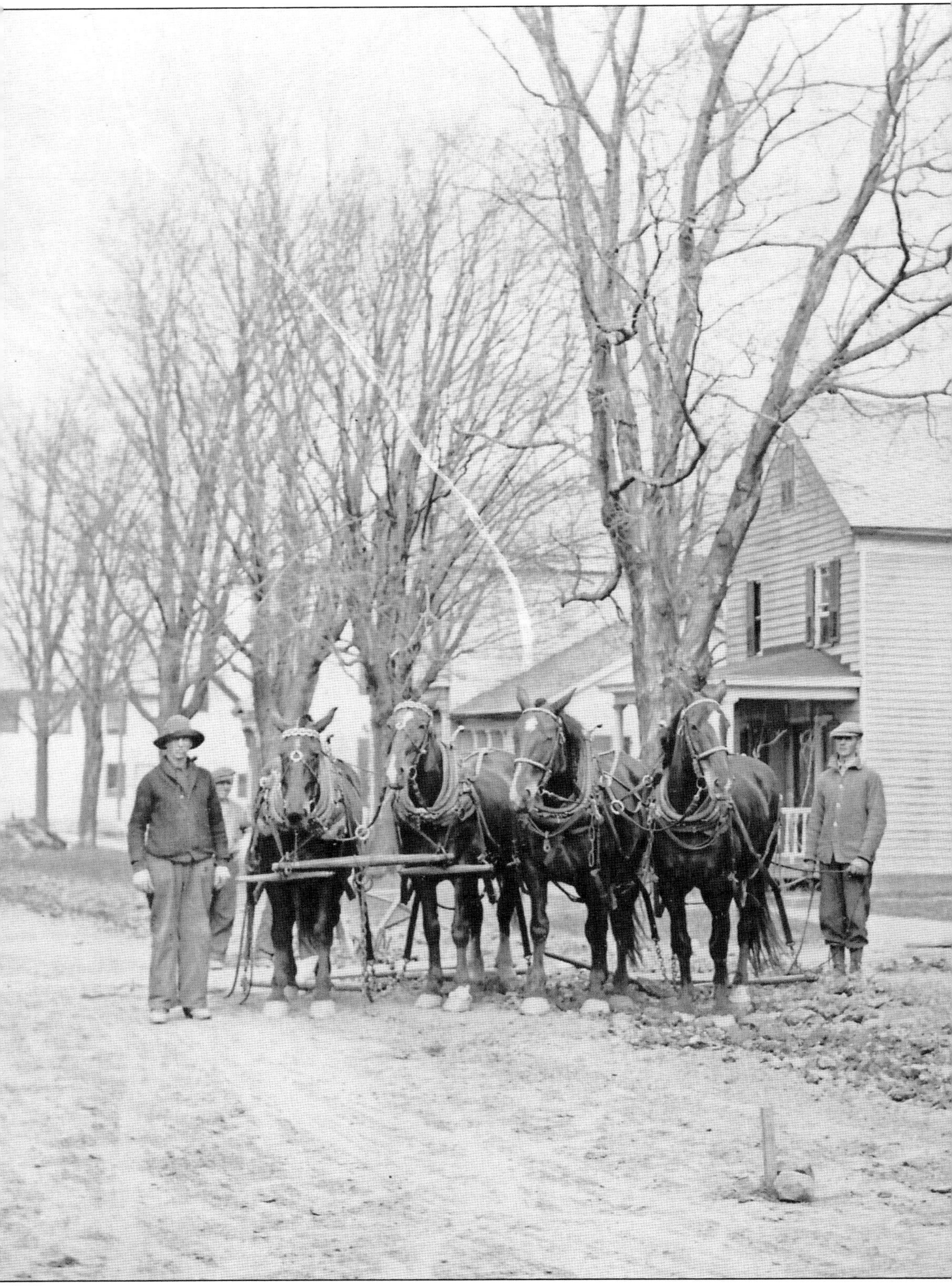

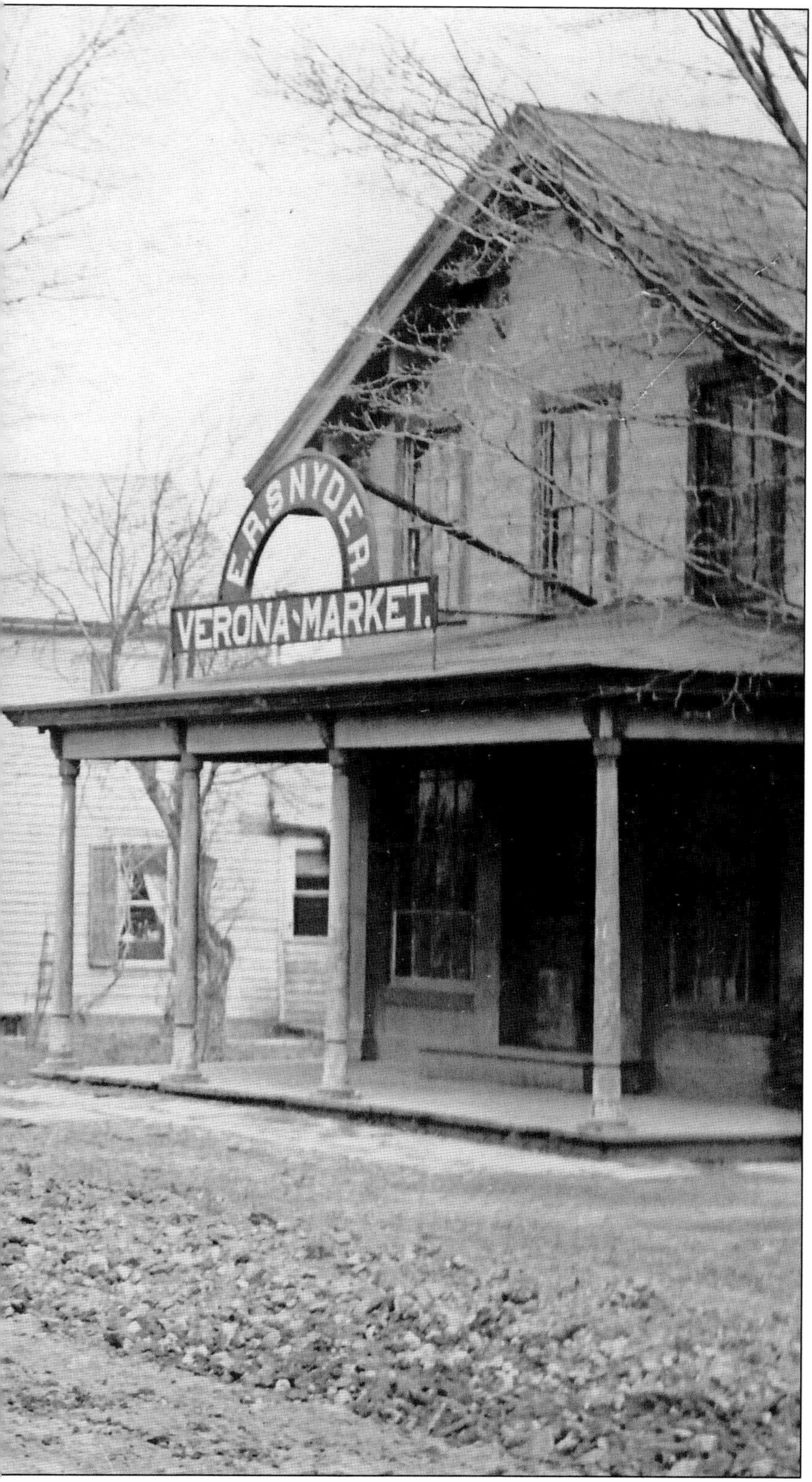

Snyder's Market was located on Main Street in Verona. Pictured is a four-horse team and drivers ready for a day's work.

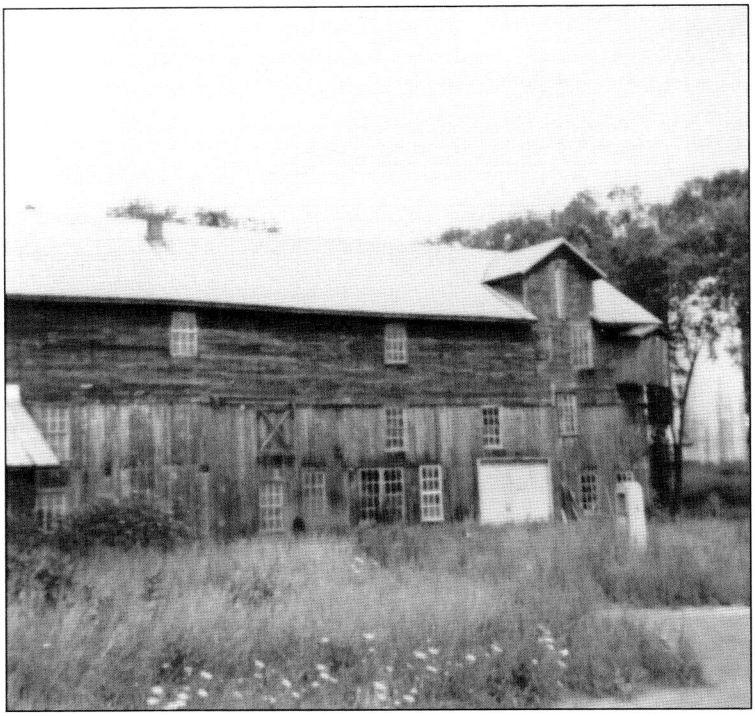

The Oneida canning factory was on Merry Street. It was started between 1882 and 1883 with Nash Peckham as president and Gottleib Merry as manager and superintendent. The factory, as the only one in the hamlet of Verona, processed local fruit and vegetable produce. Later owned by Marvin Bentley, it was used for the storage of boats and camping trailers.

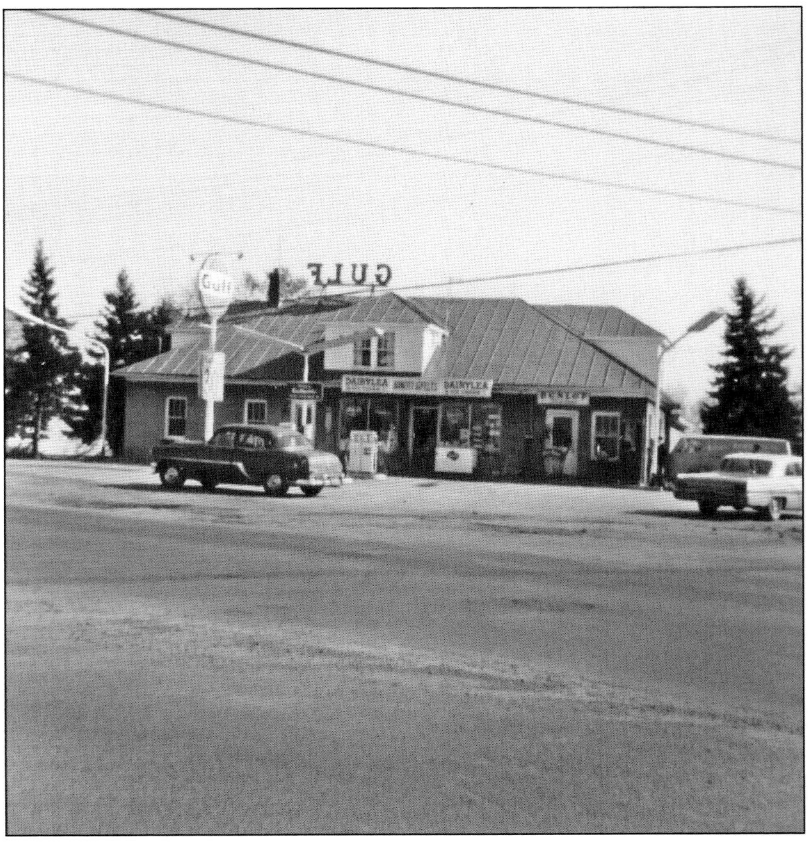

This photograph was taken in the 1950s of the building known as Arnott's Store. Recently closed, it was previously owned by Tom Ray, Bub Arnott, and Charles Felts and most recently owned by Bob and Theresa Arnott.

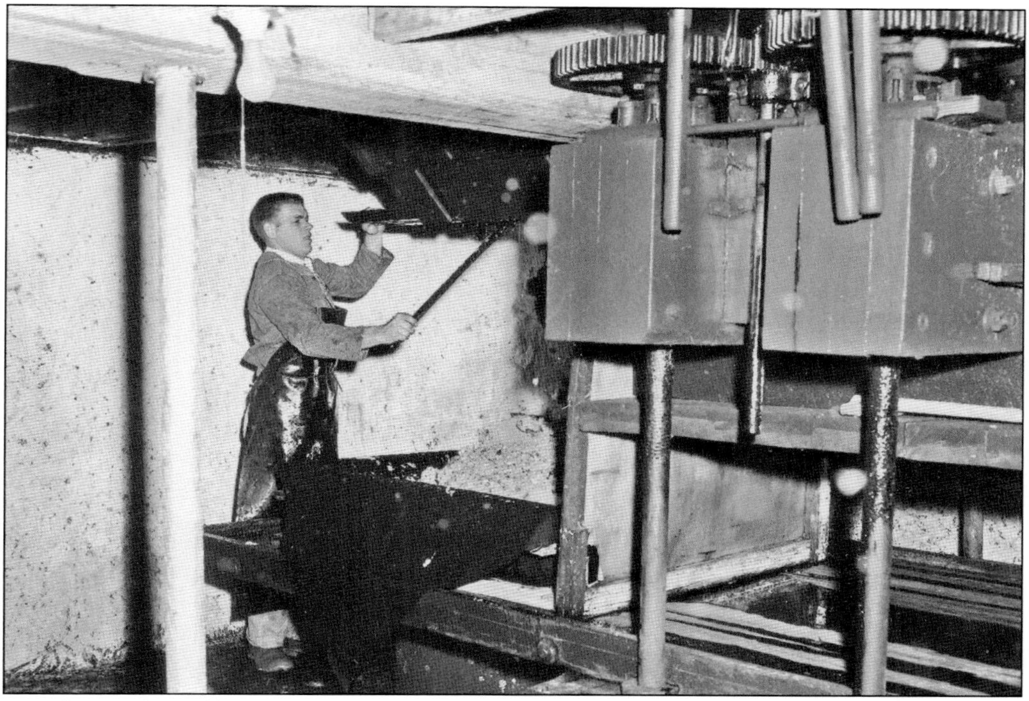

Murphy's Cider Mill was established by Charles Dam and John Murphy, when they purchased a sawmill that had been moved from Oatman Road to Main Street. Originally run as a farm, they converted it to a cider mill. For over 80 years, three generations of the Murphy family provided the Verona area with fresh cider. Folks stopped in every autumn to sample the cider and then fill their jugs with some that was fresh squeezed daily in the old-fashioned technique. Pictured above is Ted Murphy, and below is Gertrude Dam.

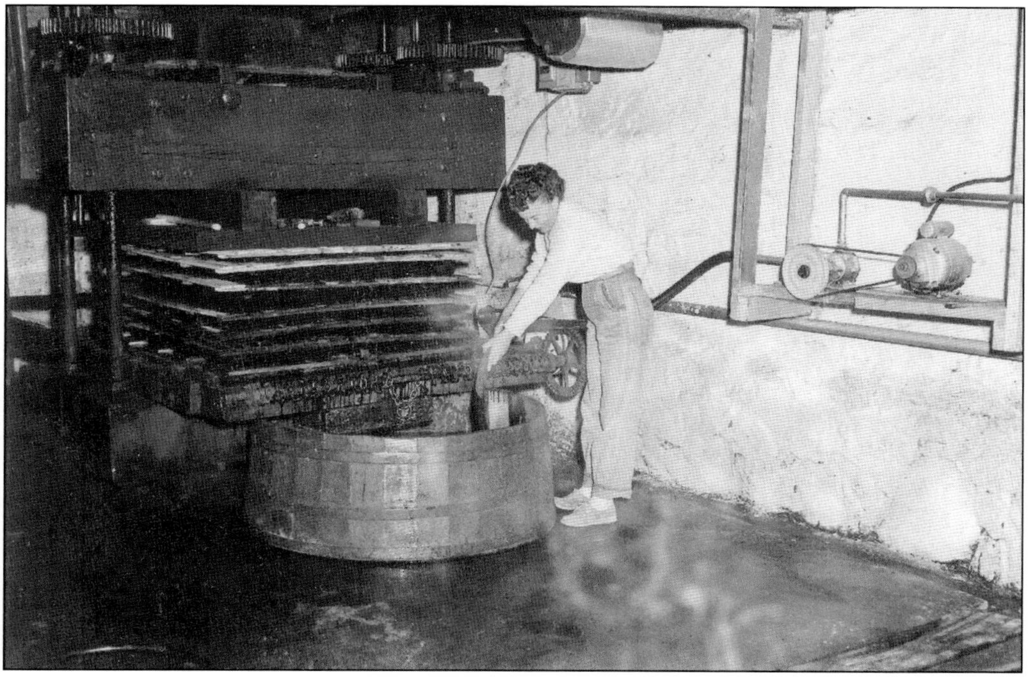

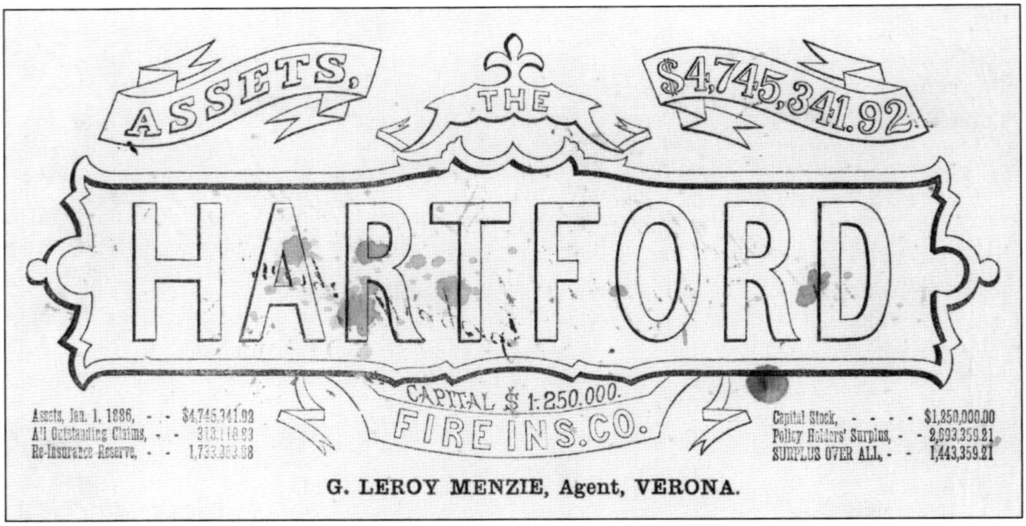

This photograph of an ink blotter dated 1886 reveals the nature and financial status of Hartford Insurance fire insurance business. George Leroy Menzie was the Verona agent.

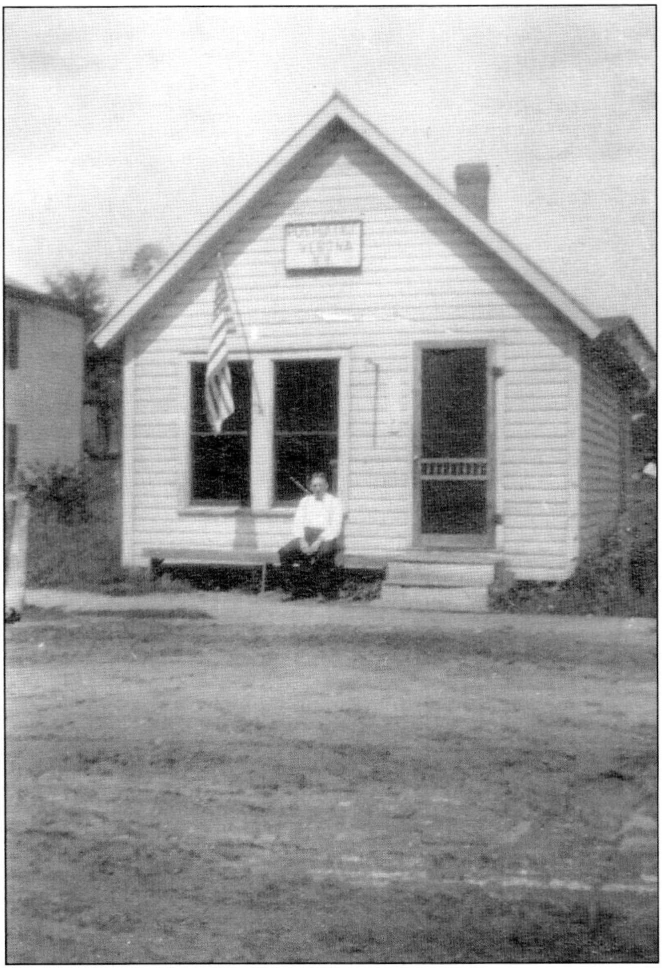

The old Verona Post Office still stands on the corner of Rock Road and Main Street. The postmaster pictured in this 1935 photograph is Harry D. Beaver.

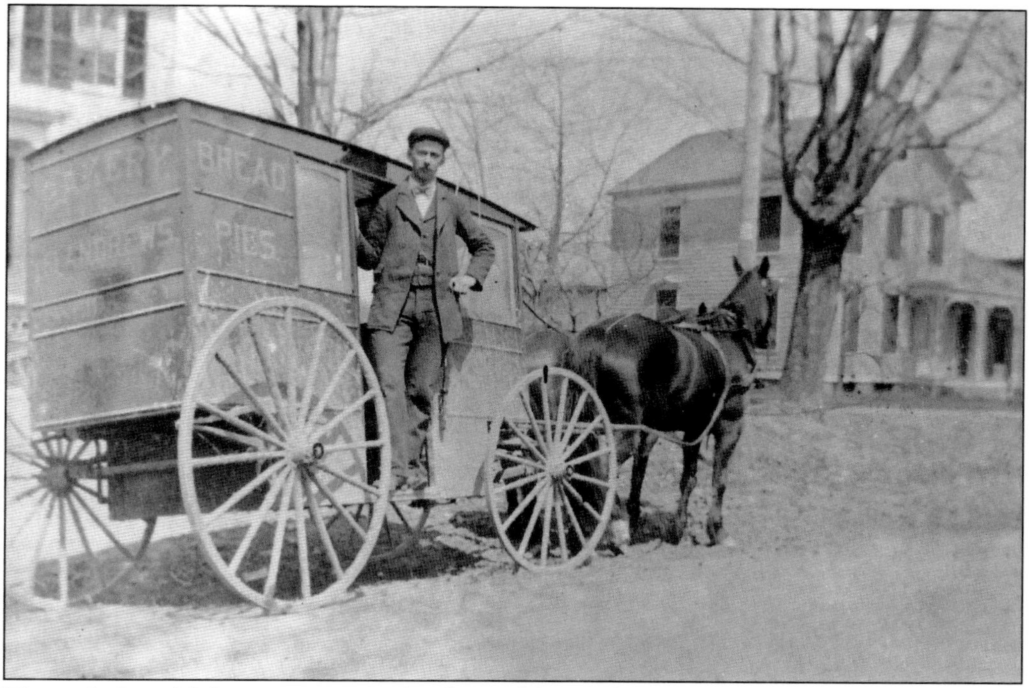

This is the bread delivery van pictured in front of the Presbyterian manse. The wagon was horse-drawn, delivering goods from the F. Andrews bakery in Verona.

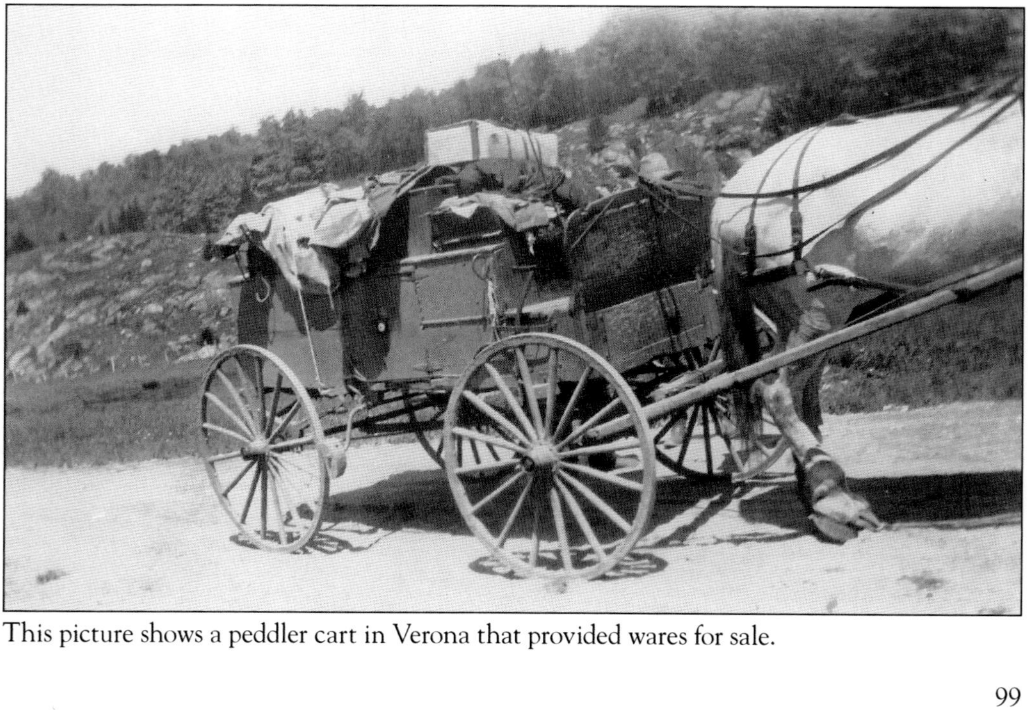

This picture shows a peddler cart in Verona that provided wares for sale.

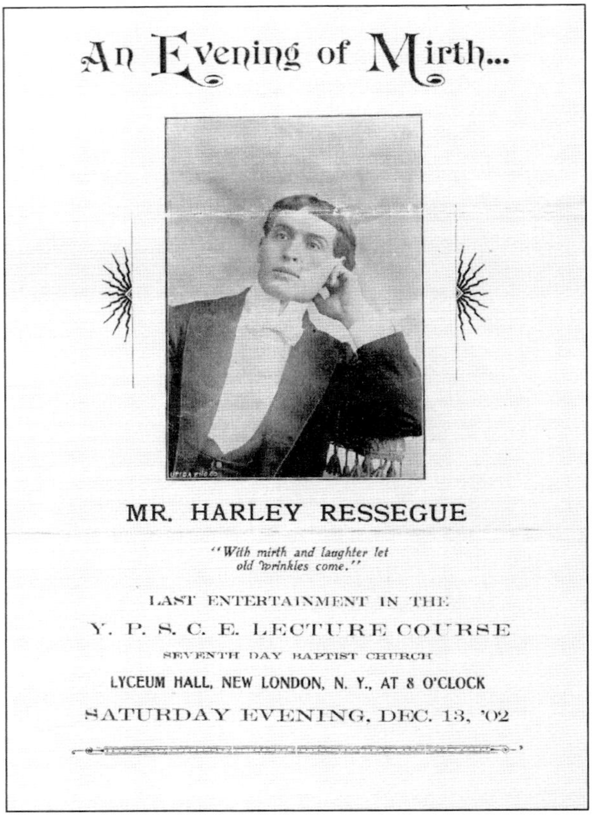

Harley Ressegue was a well-known reader and famous impersonator, having experience in Shakespearian plays as he traveled through the south and west. Ressegue was received across a broad section and assisted many local entertainments. His life was cut short by typhoid fever.

The Verona Cornet Band is pictured in the early 1900s. Members are, from left to right, (first row) Frank Hawley, Howard Goff, Irving Wilson, Mitt Green, Joe Johnson, and Fred Snyder; (second row) Fred Pittock, Alden Hatch, Ernest Cole, Fred Phelps, Herman Cole, Benjamin Wilson, and Dick Everett; (third row) Herbert Wilson, Frank Cagwin, George Cagwin, Julian Tafft, Vaughan Chandler, Gary Cooley, Dr. John D. George, Sr., Charles Tafft, and Harry D. Beaver Sr. Records reveal that the band was organized as early as 1880.

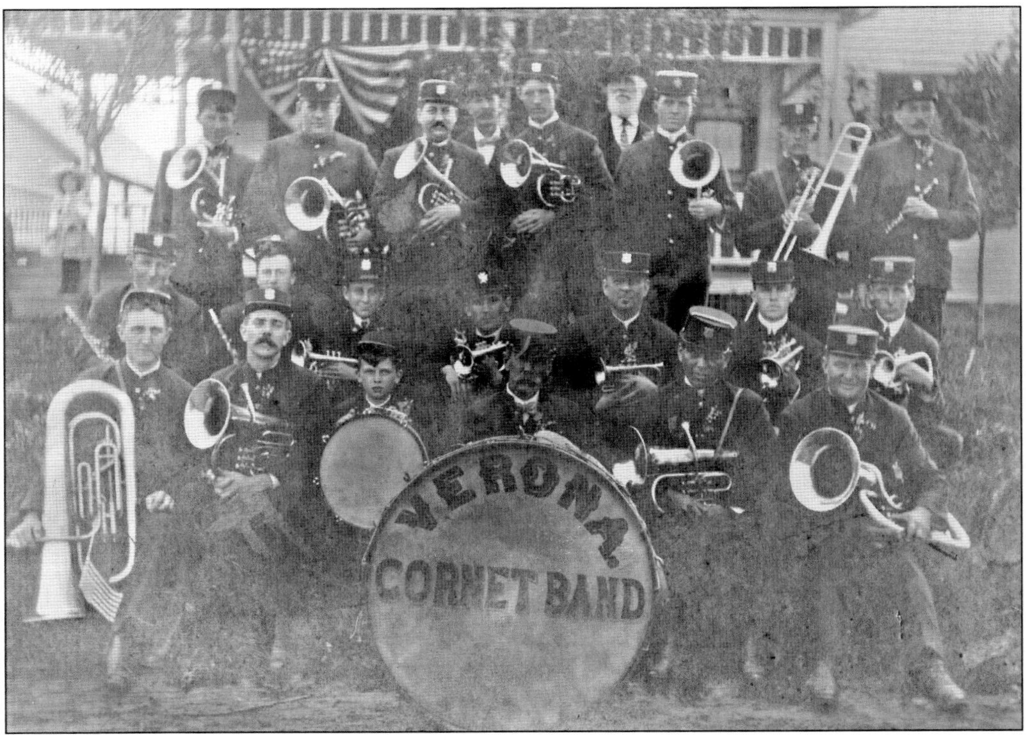

The barbershop, located on Main Street in Verona, still exists as a small home today. Complete with shaving mugs and tools of the trade, a shave and a haircut was the order of the day.

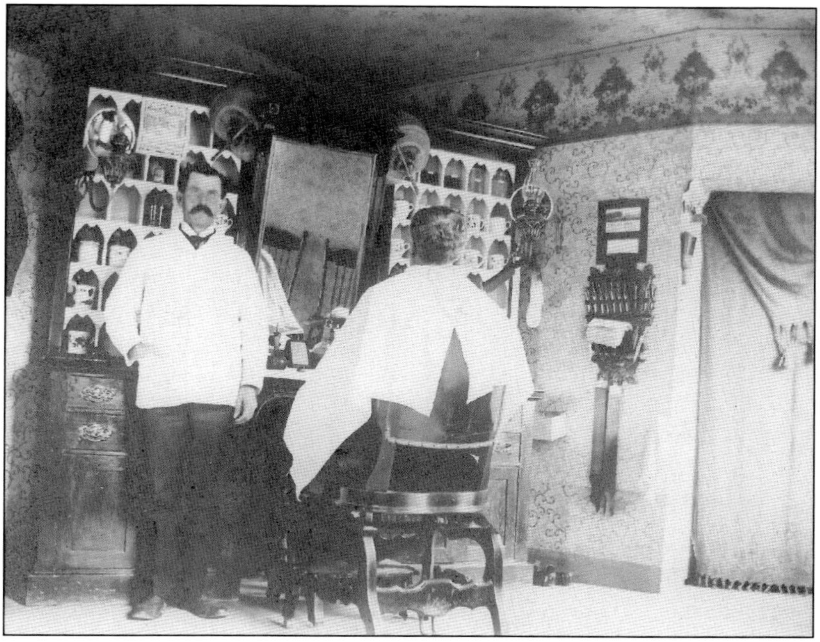

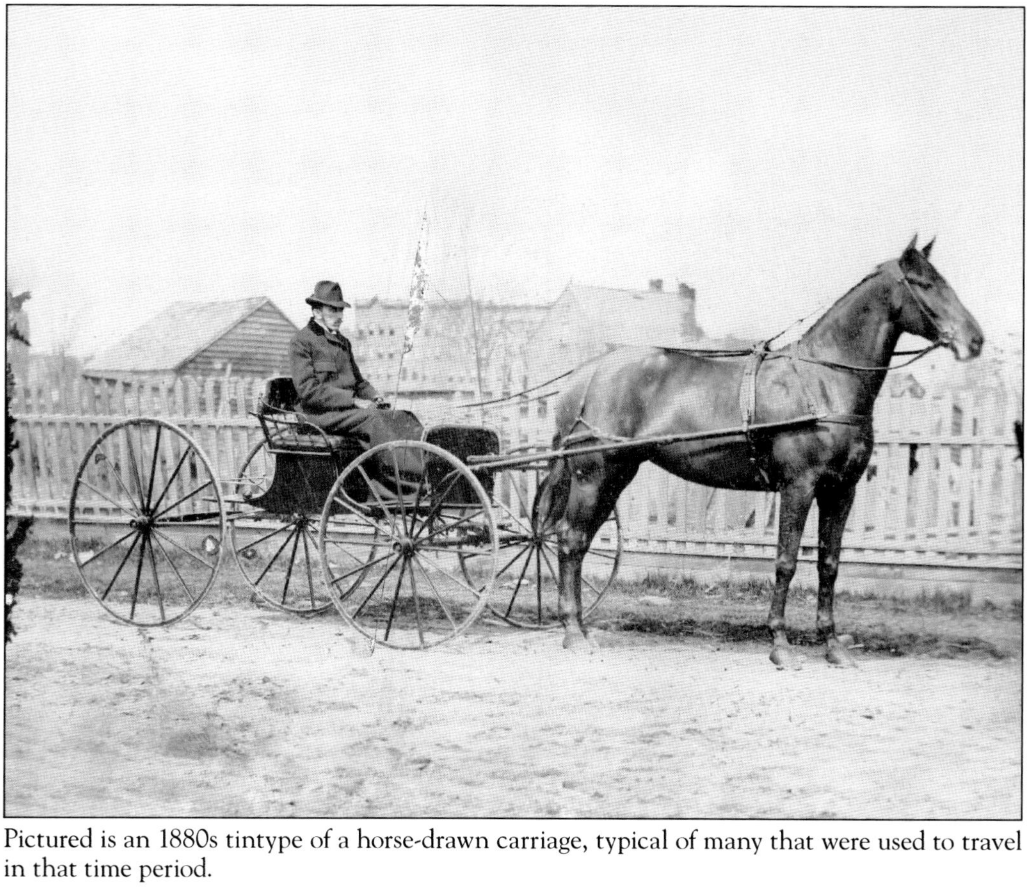

Pictured is an 1880s tintype of a horse-drawn carriage, typical of many that were used to travel in that time period.

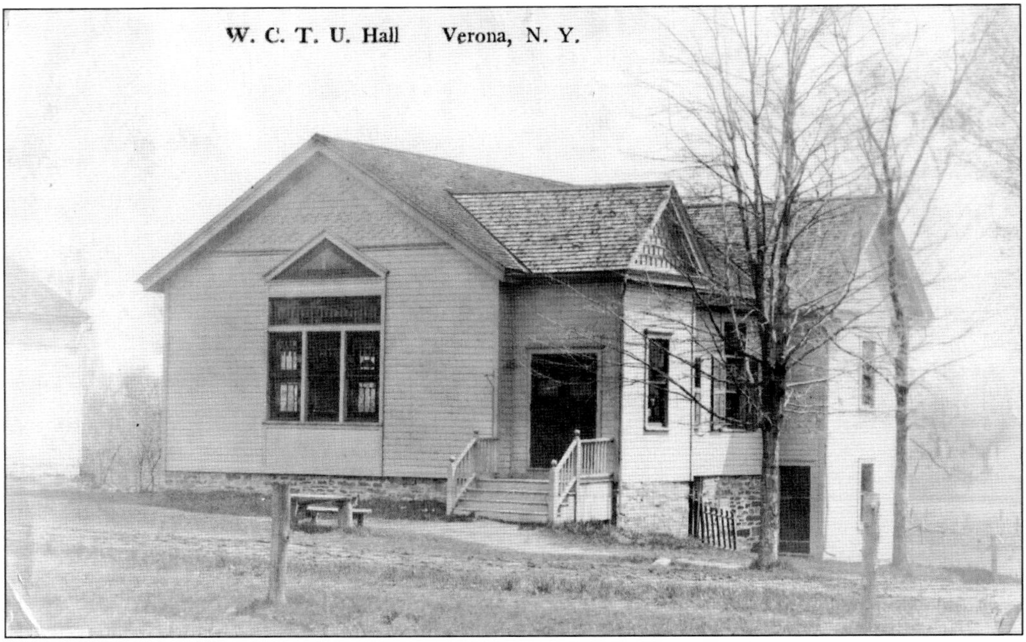

The Women's Christian Temperance Union (WCTU) Hall was built on East Main Street in Verona. Many organizations used the hall for meetings, as well as the Verona Union School for sports.

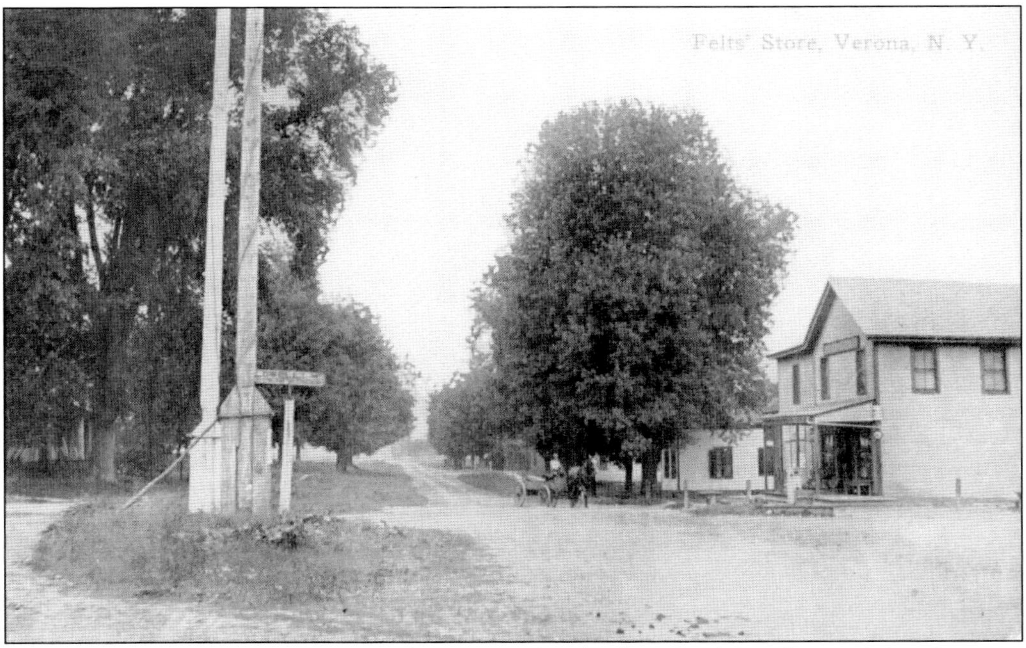

This scene shows the liberty poles at the memorial park where Rock Road meets Main Street in Verona. There is one liberty pole for Republicans and another for Democrats.

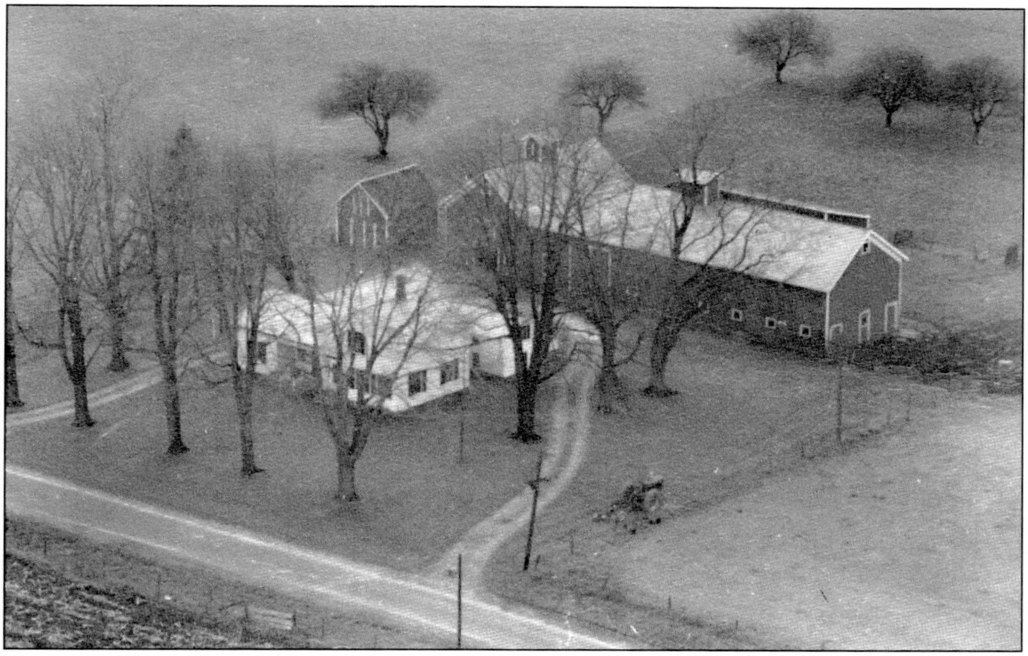

Known in the 1930s as the Bittner farm, later the Bittner's daughter, Doris, and husband, Albert Anderegg, occupied the property. In more recent times, the farm was purchased by the Stephanik family and run as a popular pumpkin farm during the fall season.

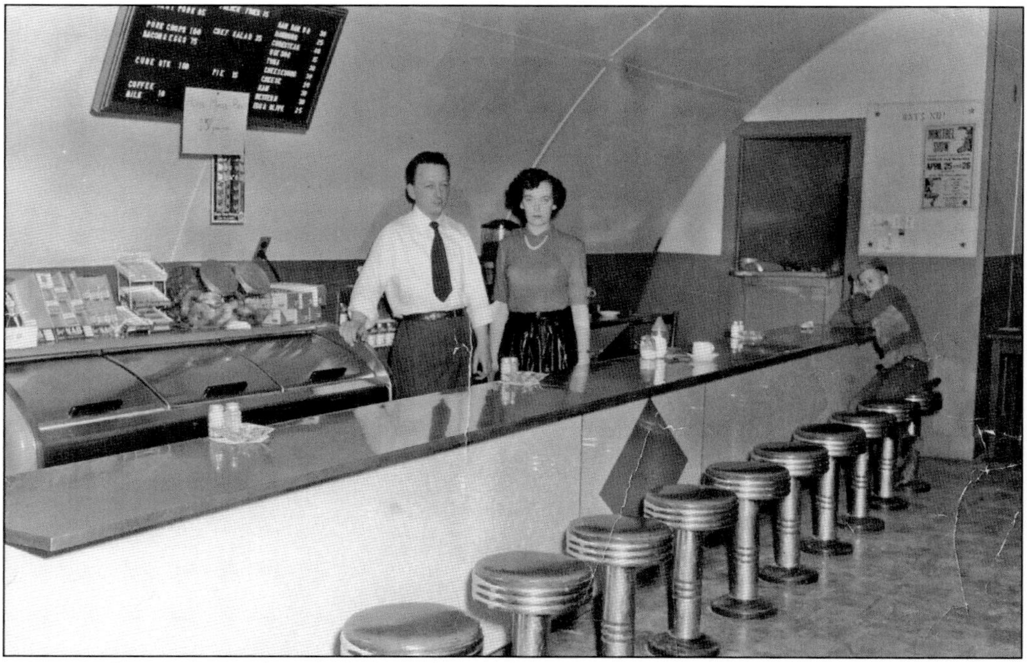

Henry and Margaret Bednarski built and owned this Quonset hut–style restaurant in 1951, next to the old Verona High School. The restaurant was sold in 1971. The menu at that time included pork chops or cube steak with meal for $1, bacon and eggs for 75¢, hamburgers for 25¢, milk and coffee for 10¢ per cup, soda for 15¢, and homemade pie for 15¢ per large slice. (Photograph courtesy of Henry Bednarski.)

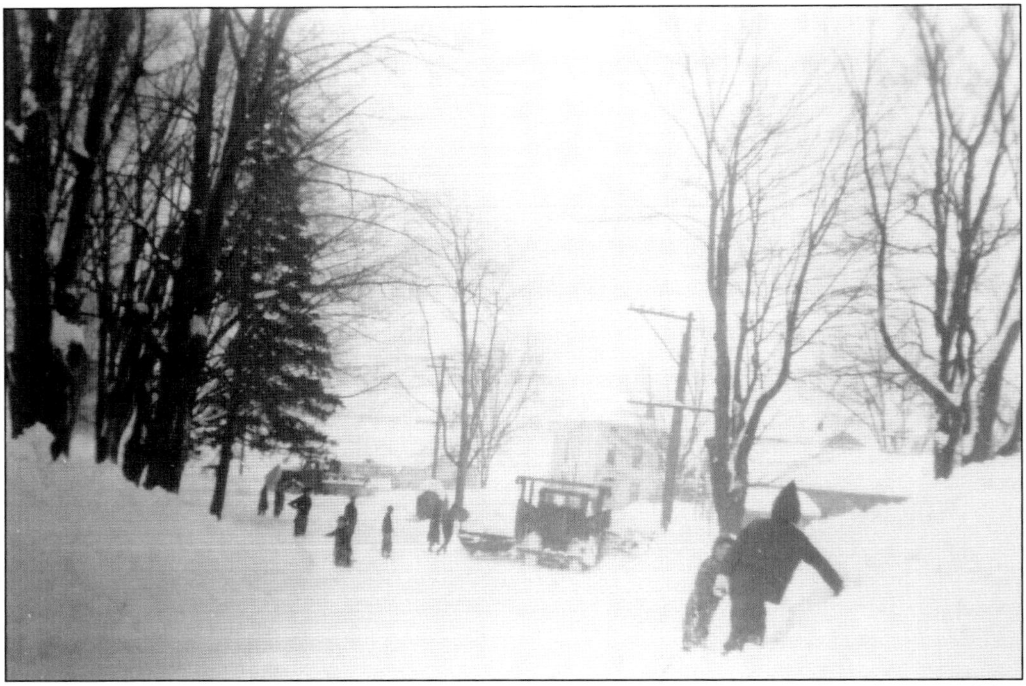

This photograph shows the scene of the big snowstorms of 1936. Four-foot drifts hampered fire department travel and mail delivery with all main roads in Verona closed. Many students spent a night in private homes in Verona, and school closed for the week. Shovelers were employed at State Bridge to assist railroad plows to keep the tracks open. In March, the town bought a Caterpillar snowplow costing $7,800. (Photograph courtesy of Elizabeth Kenfield.)

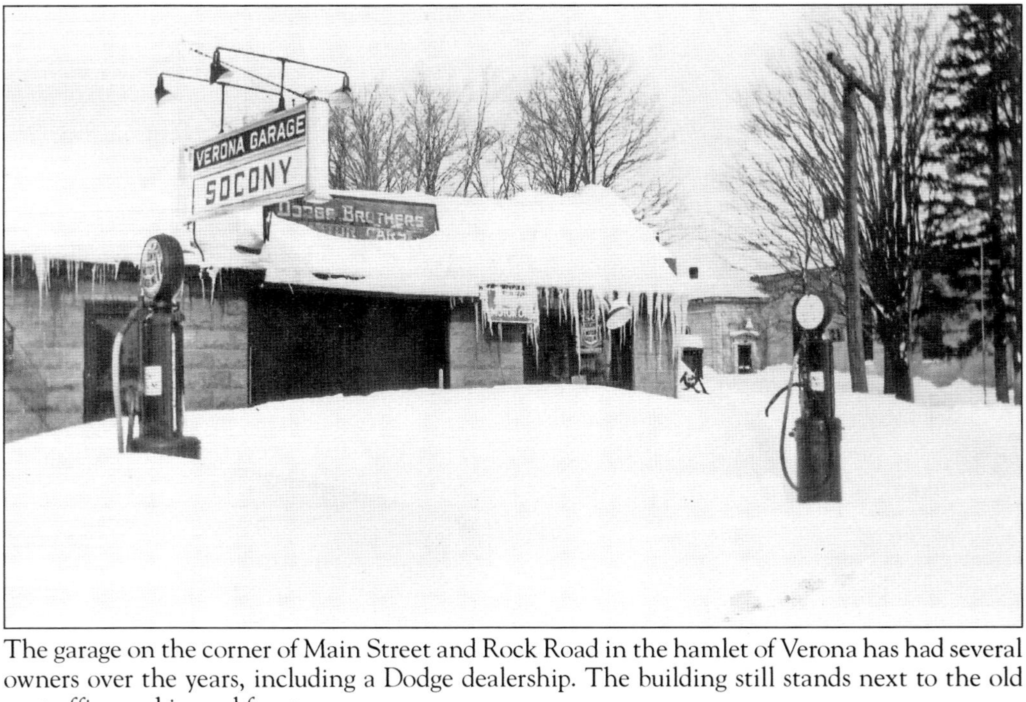

The garage on the corner of Main Street and Rock Road in the hamlet of Verona has had several owners over the years, including a Dodge dealership. The building still stands next to the old post office and is used for storage.

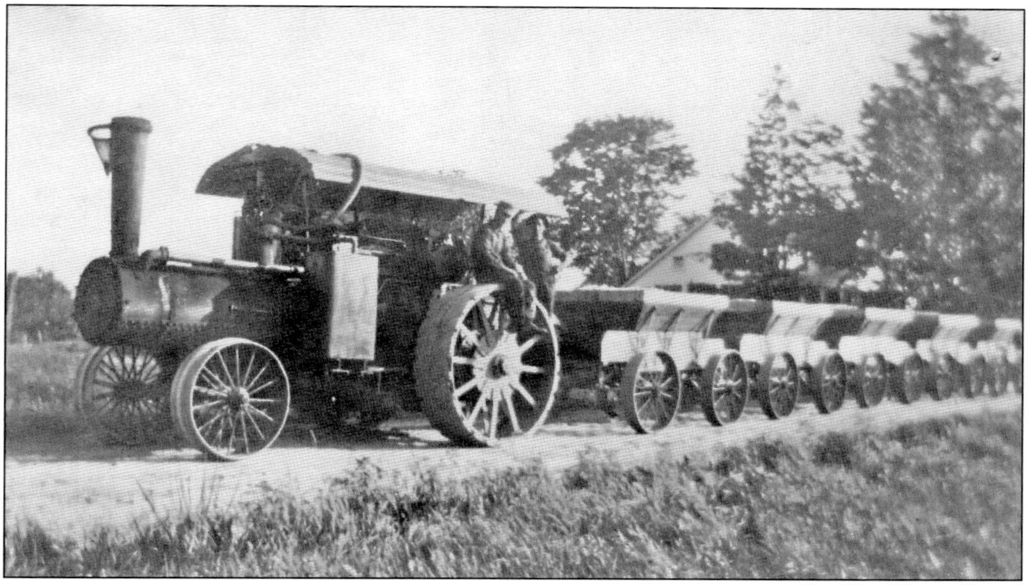

This was the last run of the steam tractor being driven down Main Street in Verona. This tractor transported materials from origin to the train depot for destination.

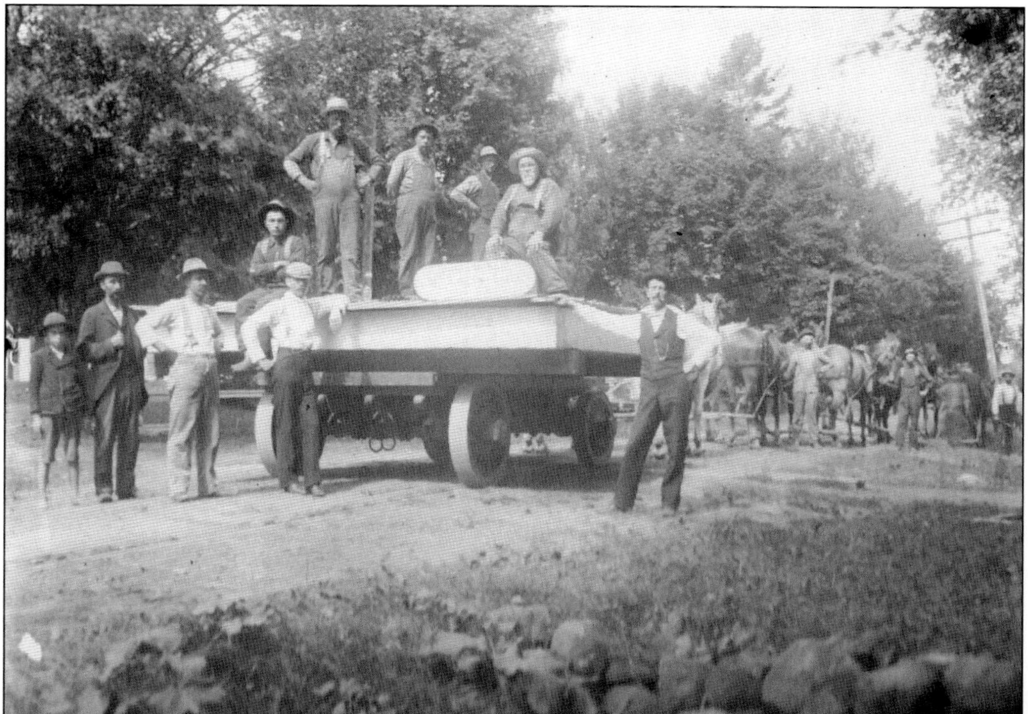

The Horace W. Soper Monument is the largest monument in the Verona Cemetery. It stands at a height of 30 feet on a base of 12 feet. The 50-ton structure constructed of grey Barre granite from Vermont was transported to Verona on four train cars. This photograph shows the base being transported to the cemetery in 1899 by a wagon pulled by a team of eight horses. The size of the monument's base takes up the space of 48 burial plots.

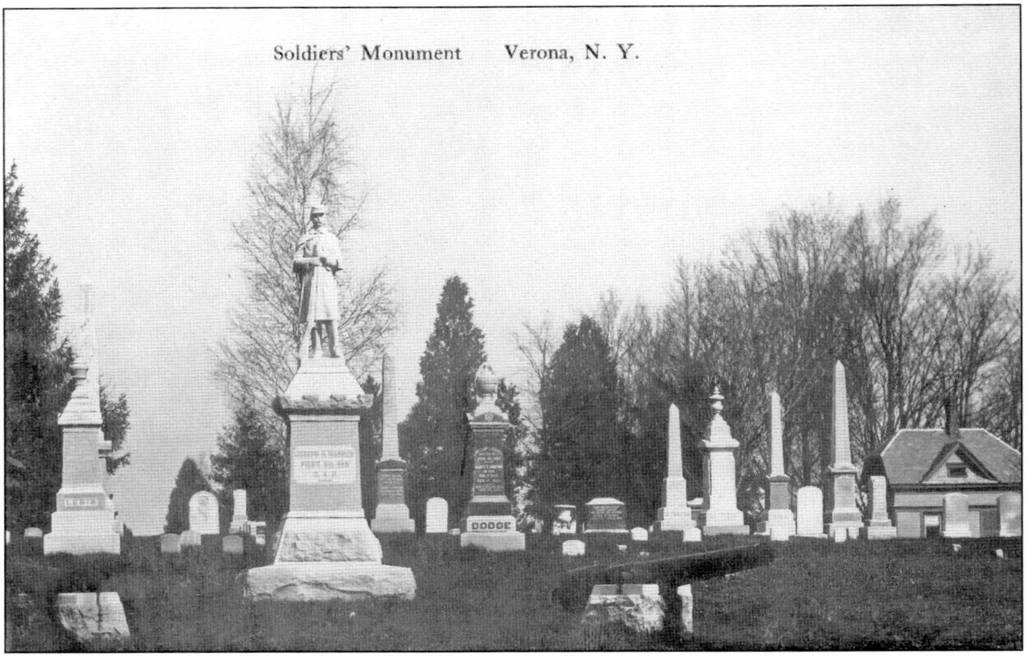

The Soldier's Monument in the Verona Cemetery was erected in 1902 by Joseph Warren Post No. 615 Grand Army of the Republic in honor of the men who fought for and maintained the union of the states, not for themselves but for their country, between 1861 and 1865. Flanked by two cannons presented by Horace Case, the monument was produced of Barre granite from Vermont and stood 17 feet high. The cannons were later removed and melted down to help the war effort at the beginning of World War II.

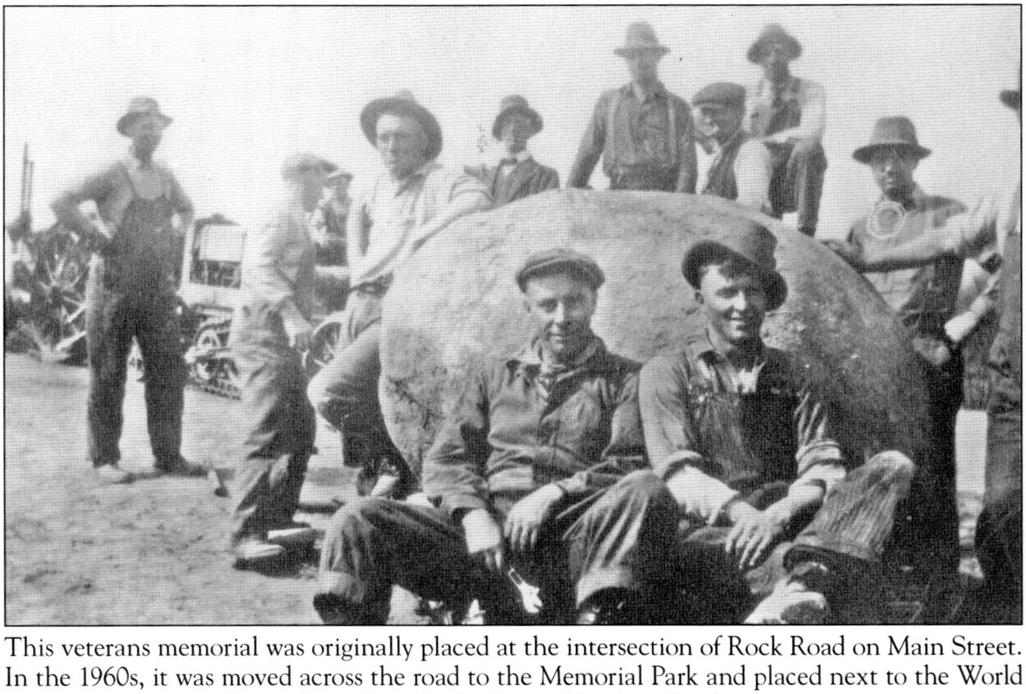

This veterans memorial was originally placed at the intersection of Rock Road on Main Street. In the 1960s, it was moved across the road to the Memorial Park and placed next to the World War II monument. This park is where the Lafayette Hotel used to be.

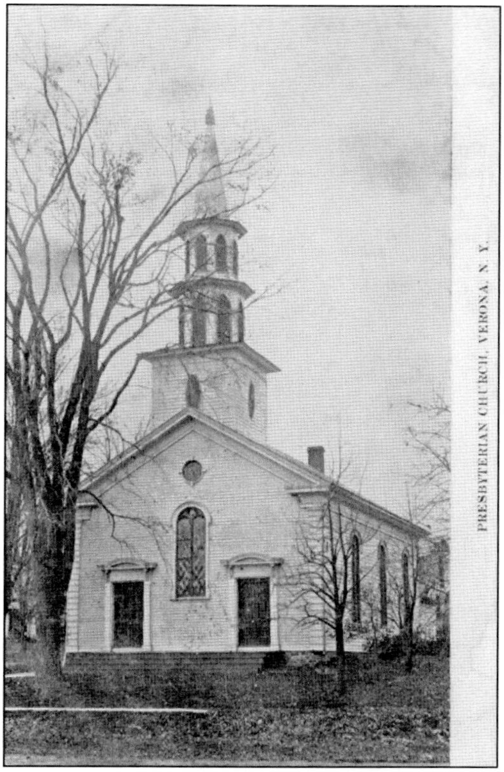

This picture shows what was once the Congregational church, formed in 1803 at Blackman's Corners. In 1829, the membership joined the Presbyterian church in the hamlet of Verona. The old Congregational church was moved on logs and pulled by horses in the winter across the road in Churchville from St. Peter's Lutheran Church to become the German Lutheran Church, then later moved to New London to become the Methodist church. It was later abandoned and converted into a barn that is still standing today.

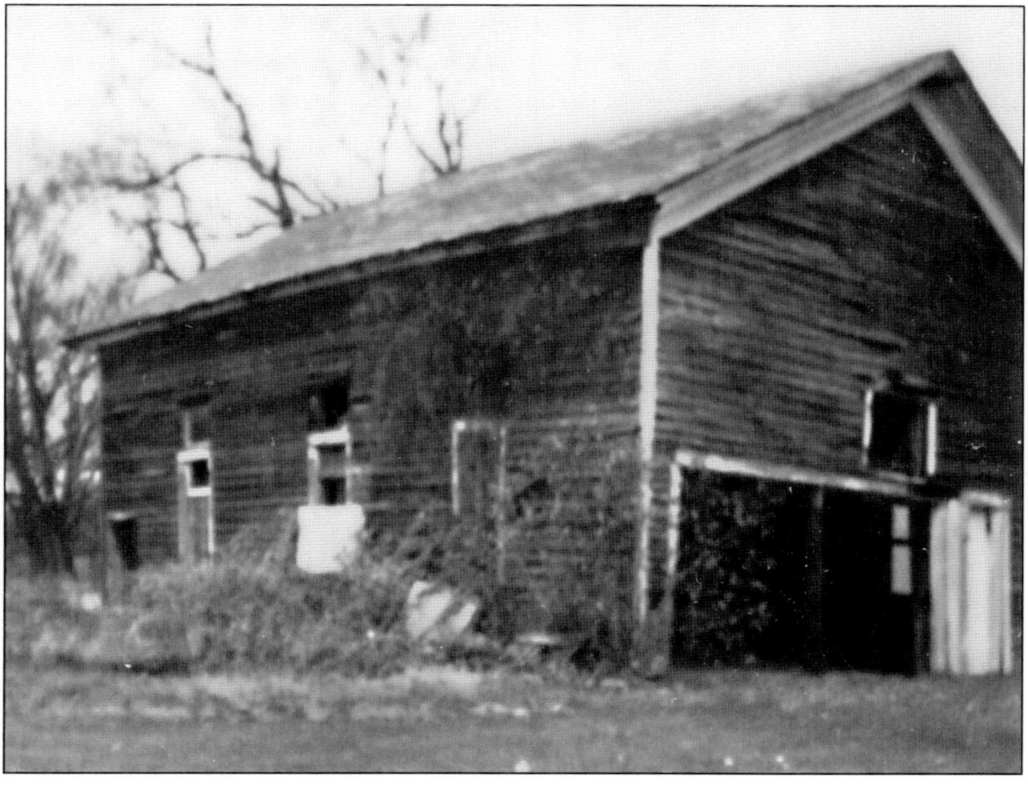

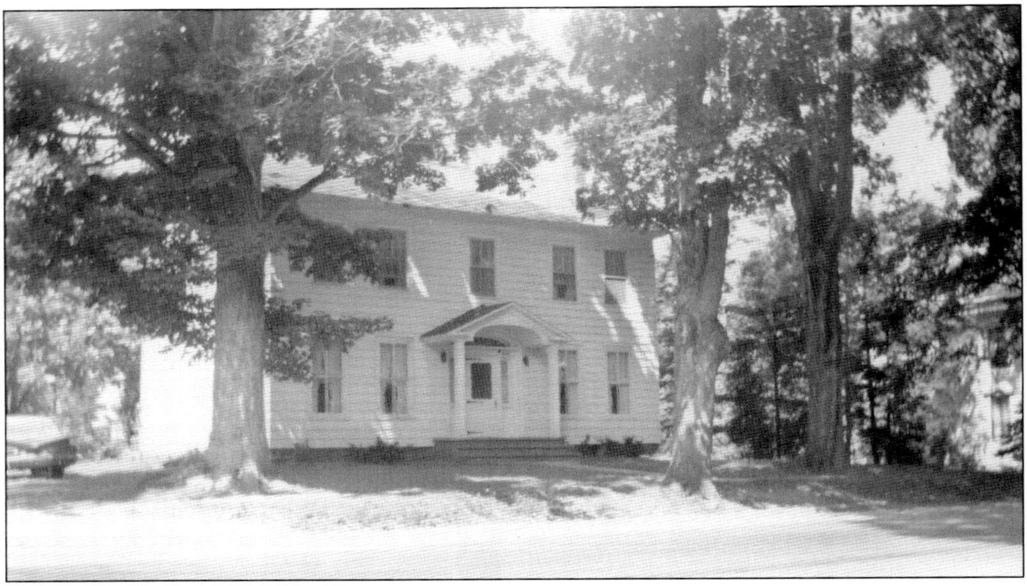

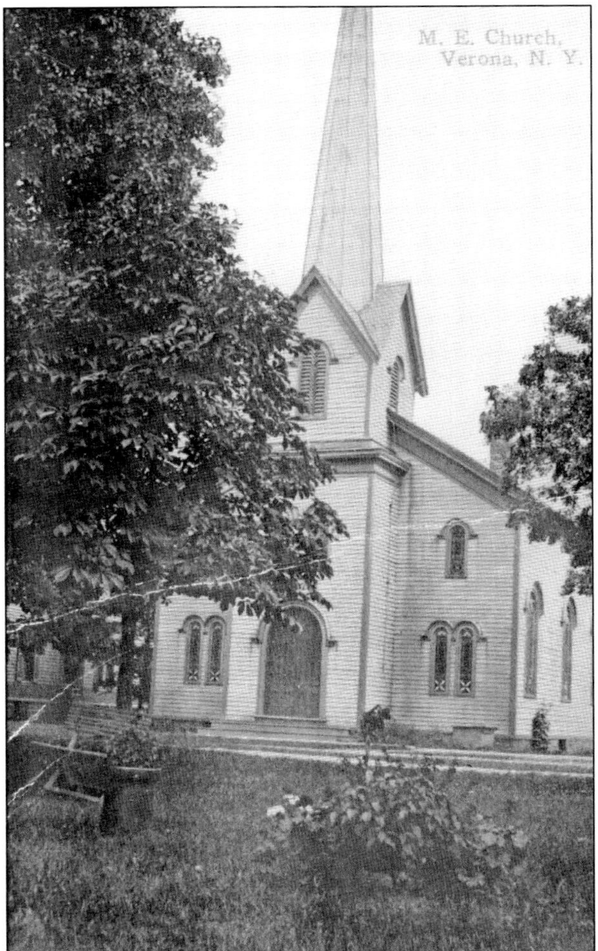

This photograph shows the old Presbyterian manse, the pastor's home, located about a quarter mile from the church. It was sold in the mid-20th century and is now a private home owned by Joseph and Margaret Cmaylo.

In 1818, Baruch Cooley preached the first sermon in the Methodist church in town. The church first met in the Langdon schoolhouse, later purchasing land at Hand's Village on July 1, 1831. In 1832, the church edifice was built and the Methodist Episcopal Church of Verona was formed in 1833. The church is still active today.

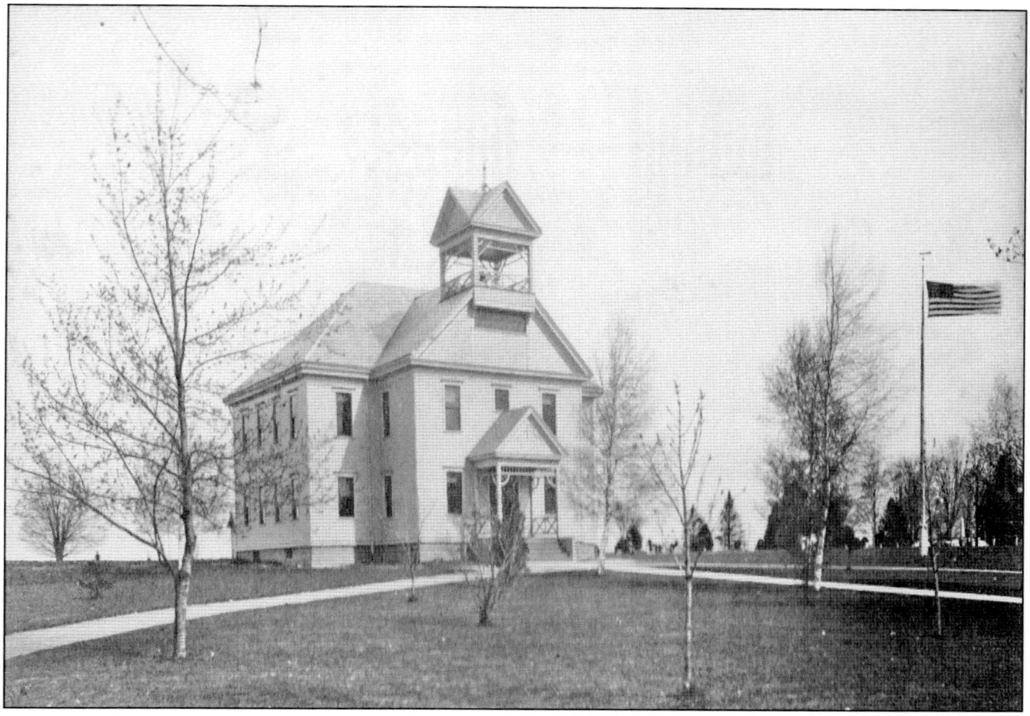

Upon graduation from the more than 20 one-room schoolhouses throughout the town, students attended Verona High School, pictured here in 1915.

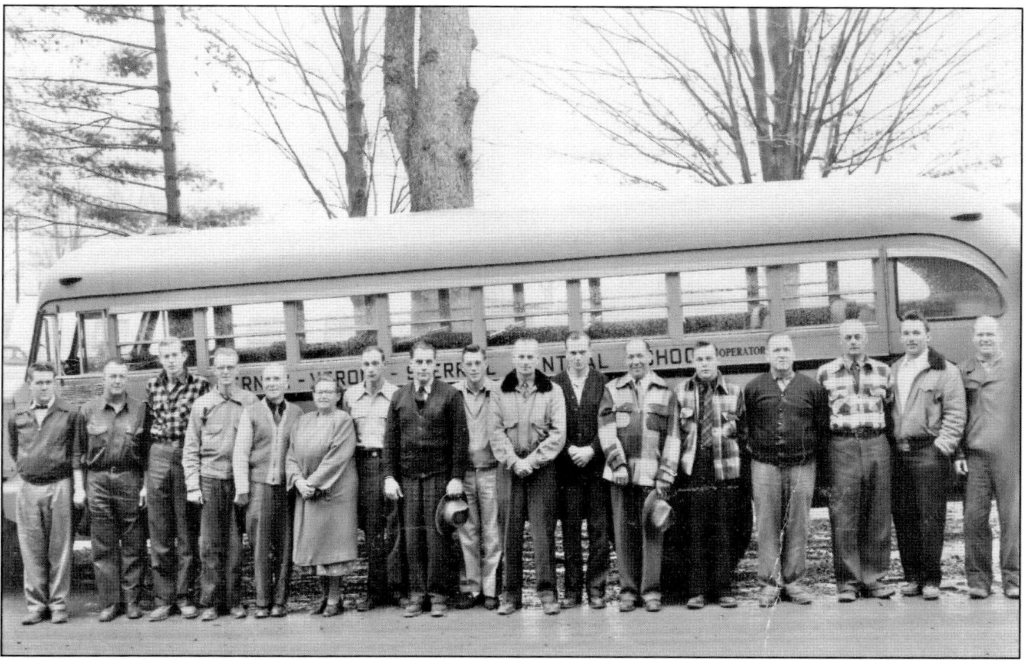

Pictured are the bus drivers for the Verona High School during the 1952–1953 school year. From left to right are R. Brown, C. Lampman, Al Smith, R Grant, Mr. and Mrs. Chamberlain, W. DeBlois, J. Avery, R. Mantor, Seward Cole, G. Schneible, Art Sable, D. Lane, Jacob Stook, Albert Dam, G. Seifert, and Ed Dailey. (Photograph courtesy of Chuck and Marion Tallman.)

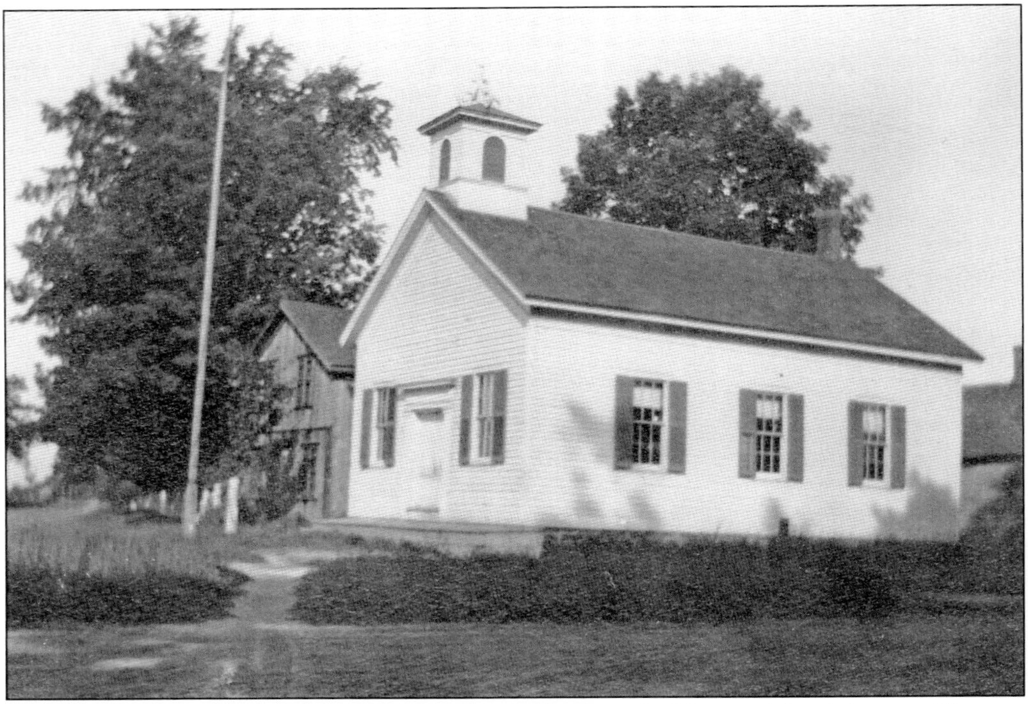

Greenway Rural School is one of the one-room schools in the Verona School district. This was on Greenway Corners and is now a home.

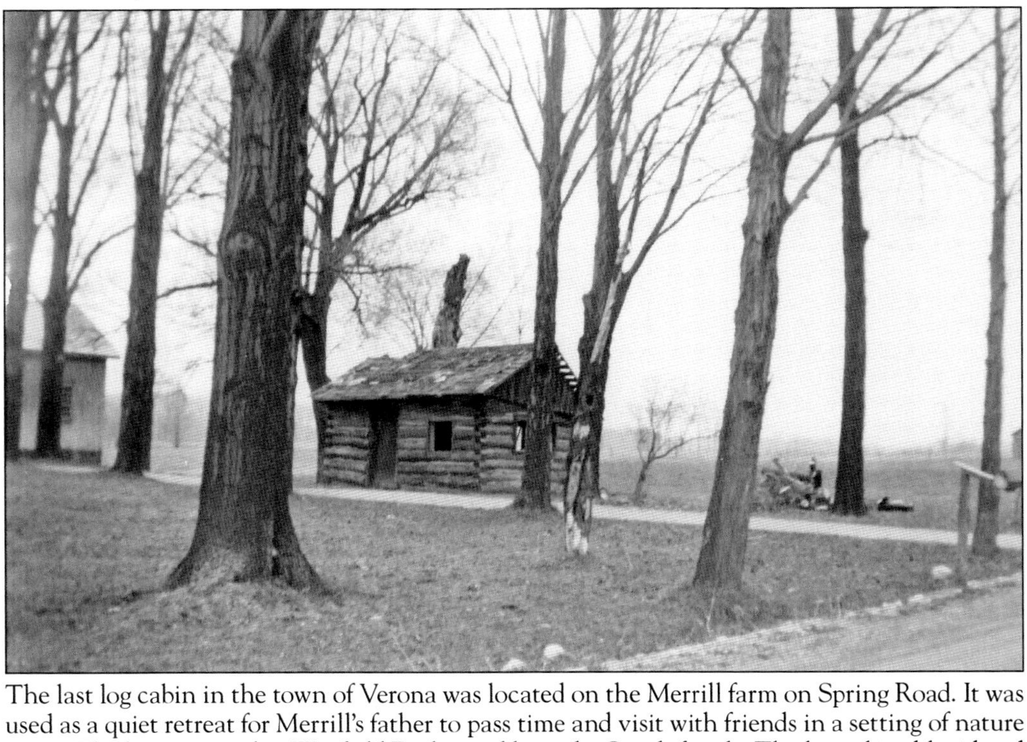

The last log cabin in the town of Verona was located on the Merrill farm on Spring Road. It was used as a quiet retreat for Merrill's father to pass time and visit with friends in a setting of nature items. The home passed to Winfield Dodge and later the Smith family. The log cabin dilapidated and was demolished several years ago.

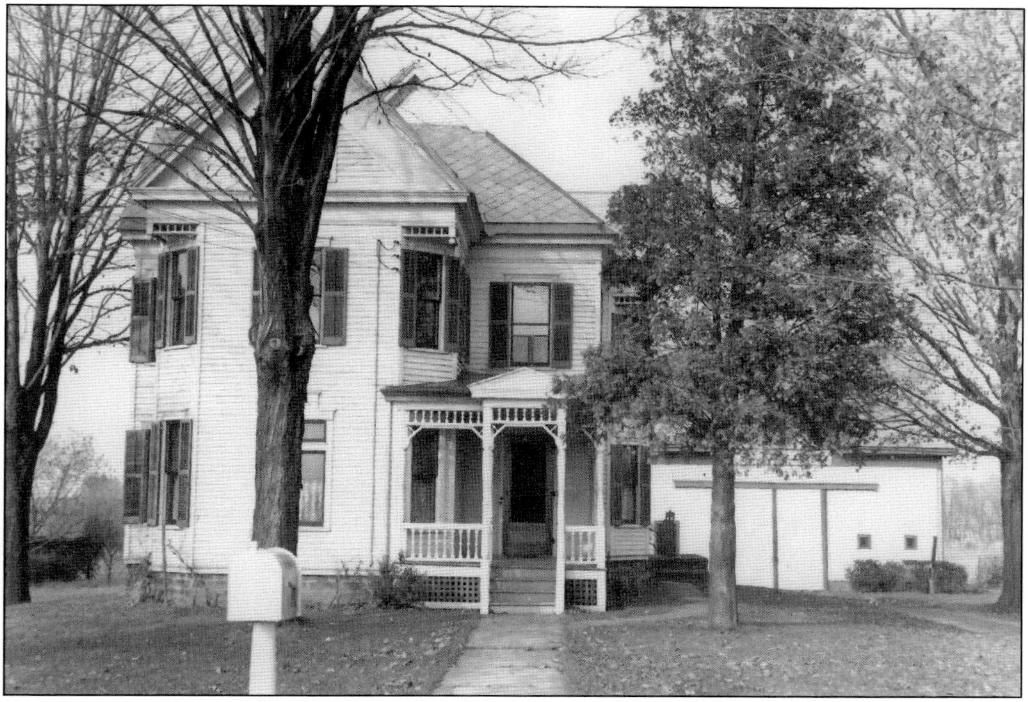

This home was originally built for Reuben West and later owned by Grace Cagwin until 1950, when it was purchased by Albert and Elizabeth Anderegg. In 1968, the property passed to their daughter, Katherine E. Anderegg, who was at one time the town historian of Verona. It has recently been restored.

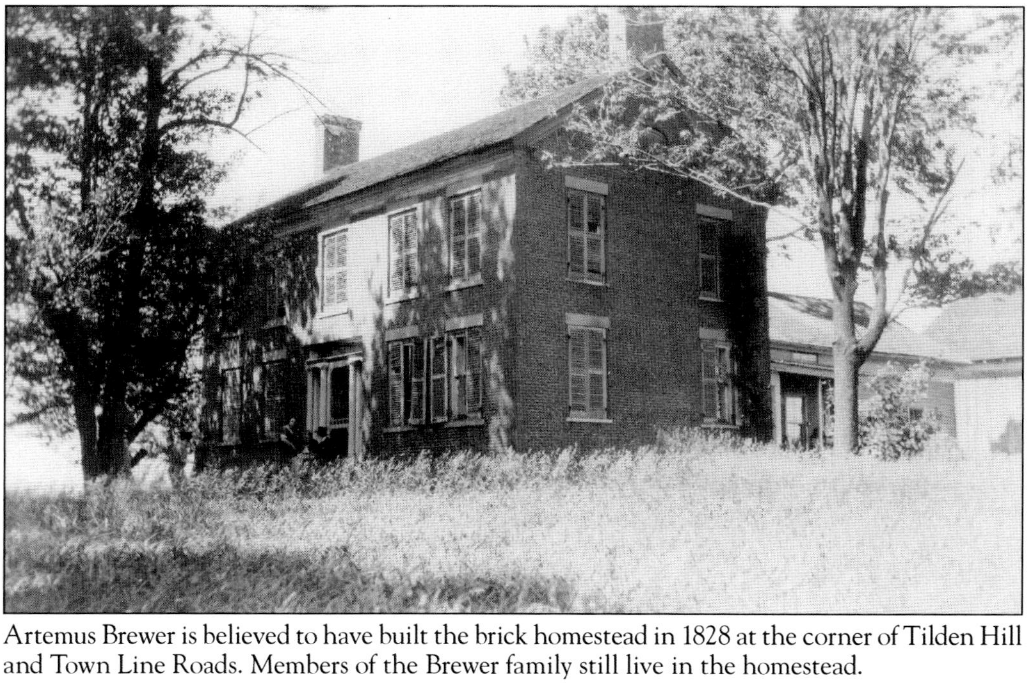

Artemus Brewer is believed to have built the brick homestead in 1828 at the corner of Tilden Hill and Town Line Roads. Members of the Brewer family still live in the homestead.

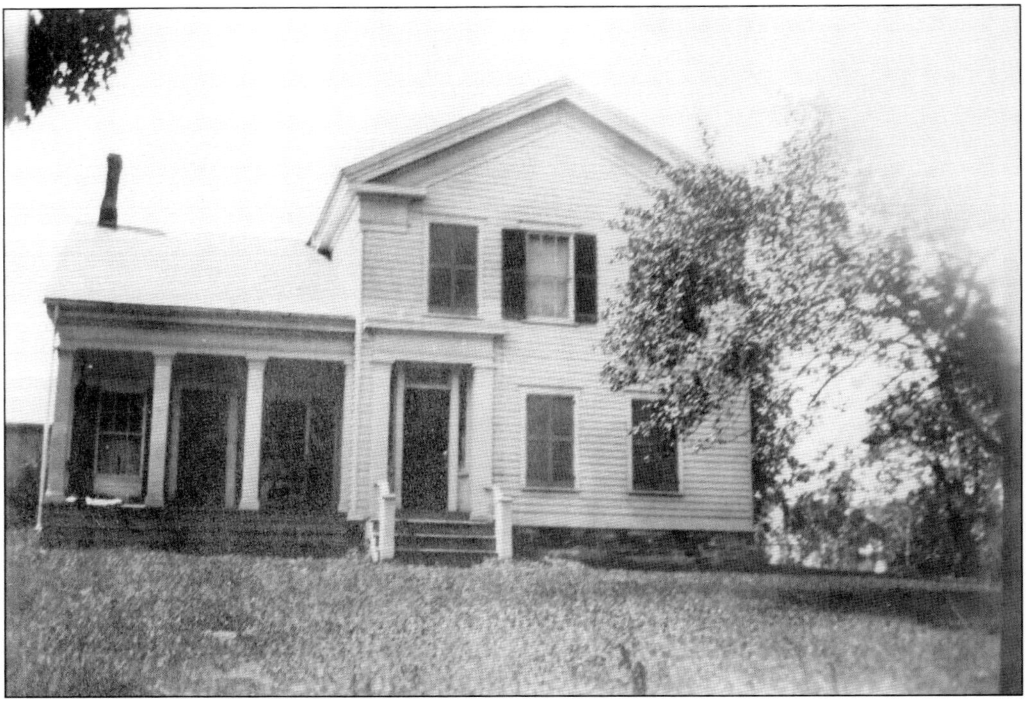

These are known as the Whaley-Beaver homes. The home above was built by Dr. Alex Whaley in the late 1700s. The land on which this home was built was given to Whaley by the Oneida Indians in return for his medical services. Originally a two-room log home, in 1899 the house was sold and enlarged and became the family home of H. D. Beaver and his bride, Sarah Whaley. The picture below shows a house built in 1802 by Alex Whaley and now lived in by his great-great grandson, Thom Beaver.

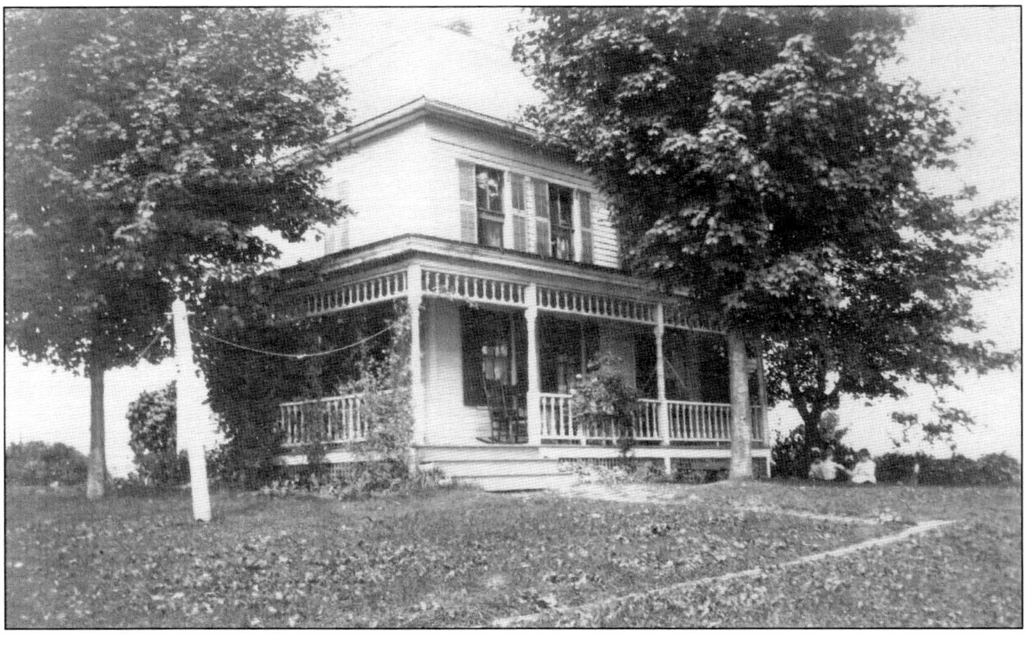

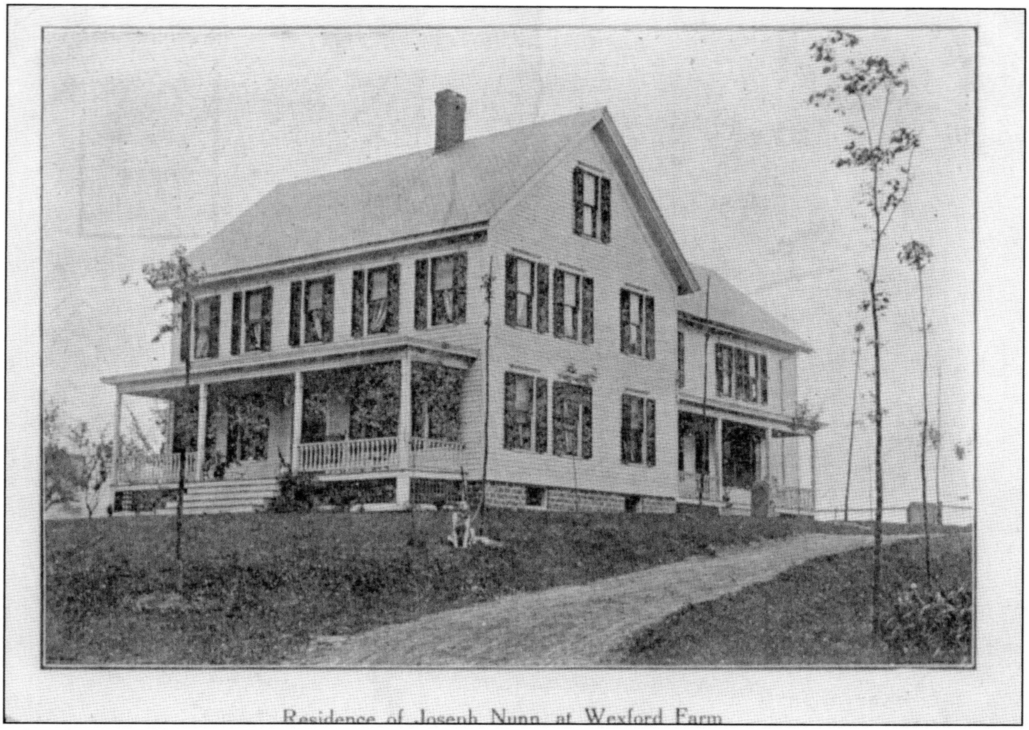

This farm and barn were originally owned by the Wexford family. Later owned by Joseph Nunn, this farm is where Martin J. Nunn, a funeral director from Rome, was brought up. This is also where the Nunn pumps were made. The Nunns began the Catholic Church of Verona in their living room; it was later named Our Lady of Good Counsel. This home at one time was a State Farm colony where the mentally handicapped were provided with work and living quarters. Both the house and barn are now apartments owned by the Oneida Indian Nation.

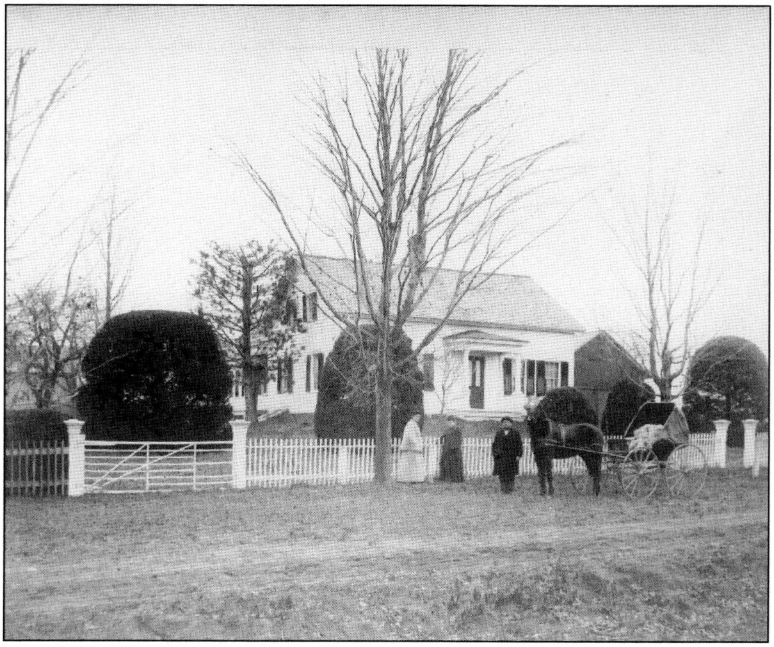

This is known as the Sleight home. It is on the corner of old Route 365 and new Route 365. Franklin and Helen M. Sleight are getting ready to enter the carriage for a drive. Sleight was a Civil War veteran. This home has been owned by several people and is still standing.

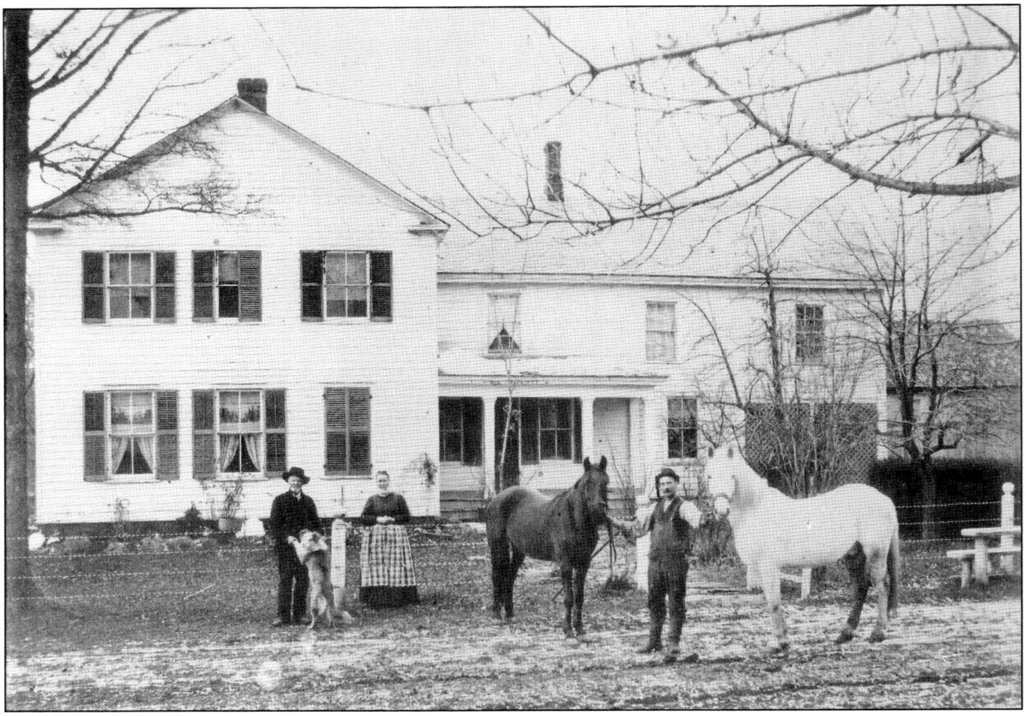

Called "Flower of the Woods," because the wood came from the surrounding forest, this was the home of the Joslyn family, built in 1816 on Rock Road. The house burned down many years later.

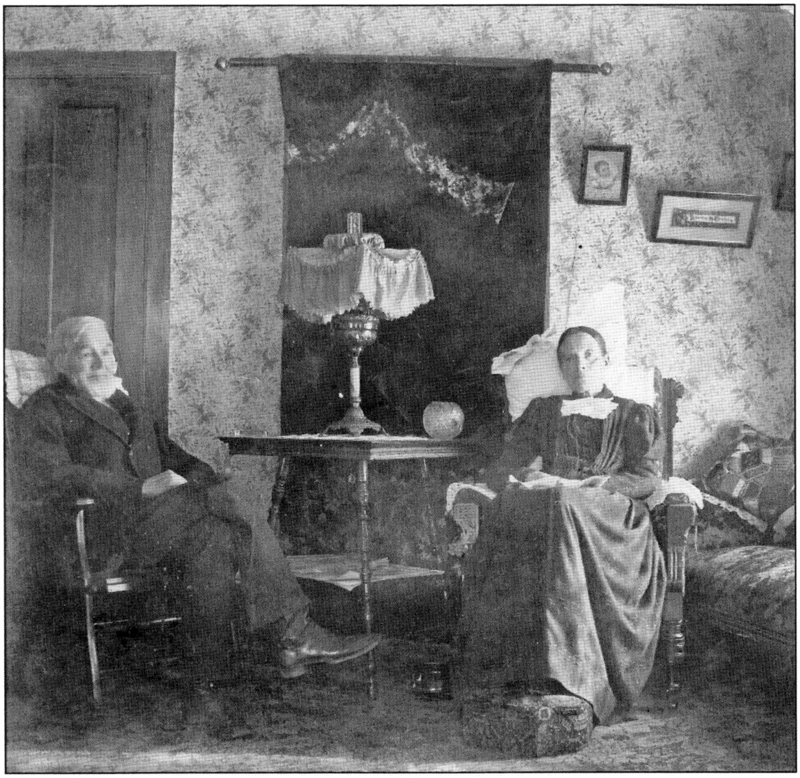

This photograph shows the interior of the home of William and Betsey Wyman on Spring Road around 1900. Wyman, born in England, was a dairy farmer who lived in Verona for 50 years. The decor was typical of Victorian farmhouses. Note the oil lamp with the cloth shade, the heavy drapes, and the flowered wallpaper.

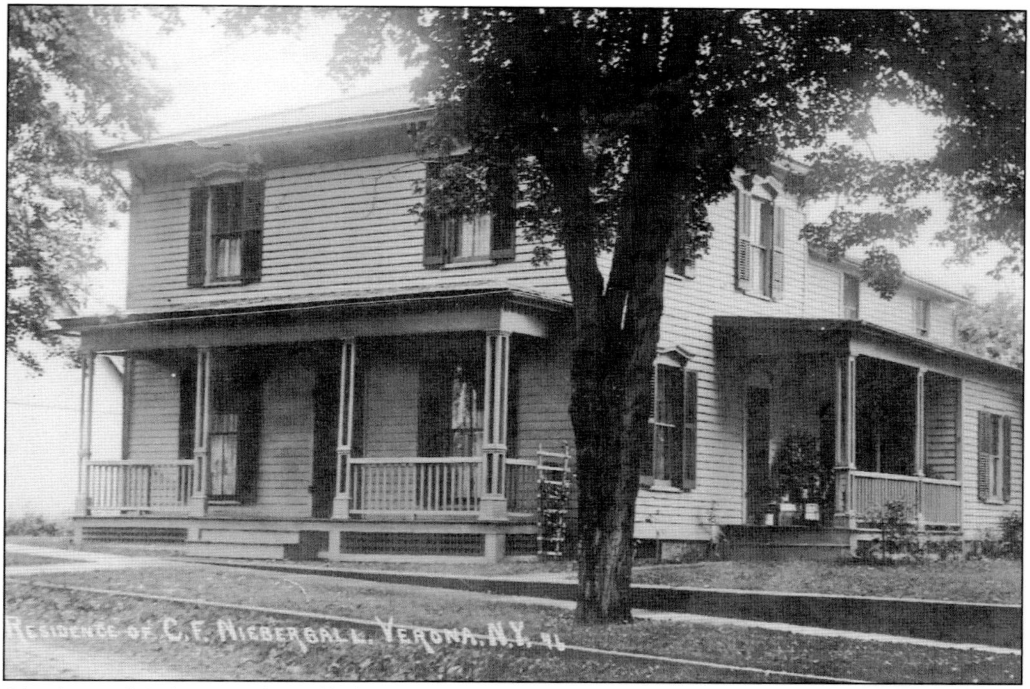

Charles and Celeste Neibergall's home on Rock Road was in back of the Presbyterian church. It was originally a schoolhouse, which they built up and out to convert into a house. It was later acquired by the church for the purpose of Sunday school rooms and minister's office and later torn down.

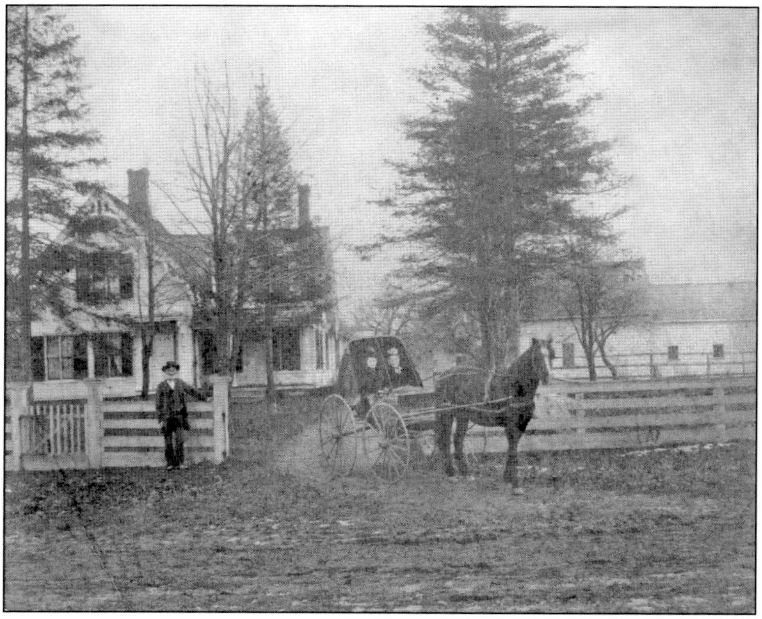

The John Hull Brewster home and farm was located on Rock Road. The distinctive gingerbread-style architecture is still visible on the roofline.

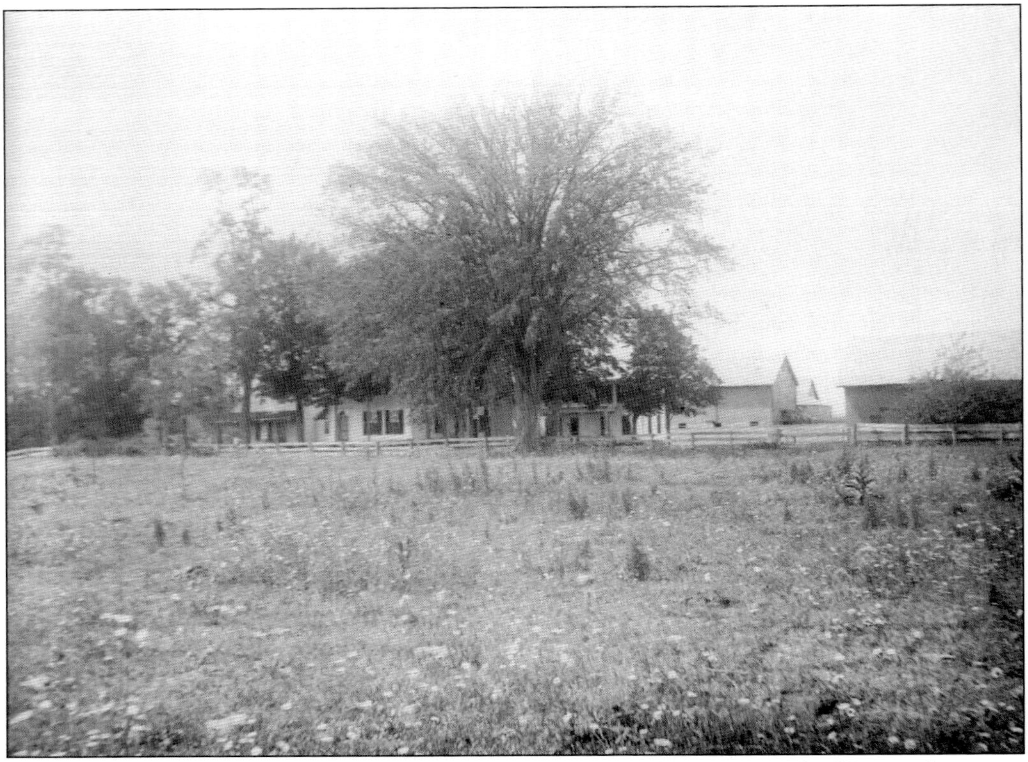

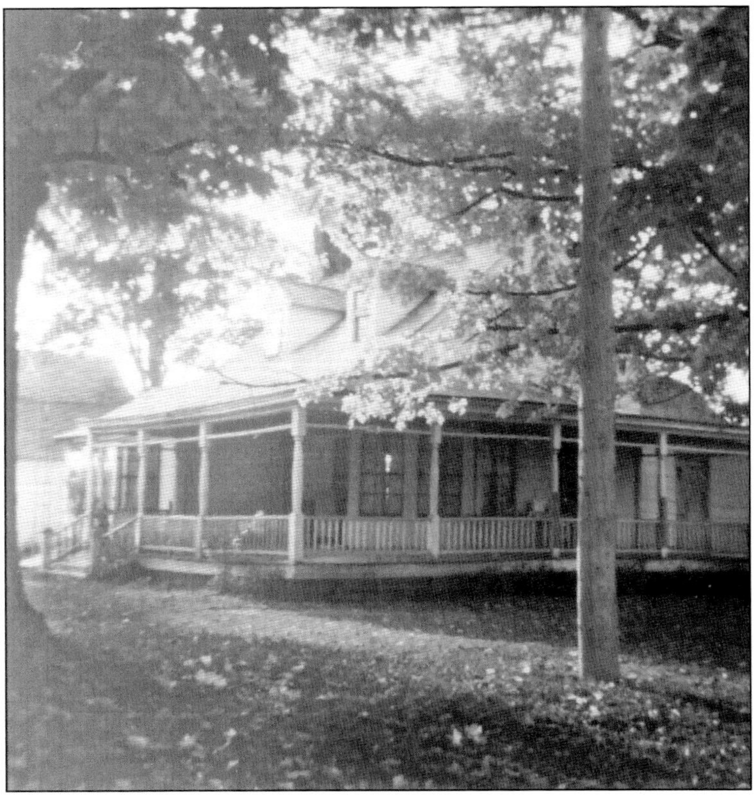

The Warren farm was built in 1888 on Tilden Hill Road by Charles and Leila Whaley Warren. Their main industry was dairy farming. It was a palatial home and farm. The Warrens traveled extensively to foreign countries and spent their winters at a large apartment in Utica. The house and barn were torn down to make way for the New York State Thruway in 1947. Mrs. Barbour, a sister to Charles, lived in the cottage near the farm during the summers. Her husband was a Barbour of the Irish Linen Thread Company.

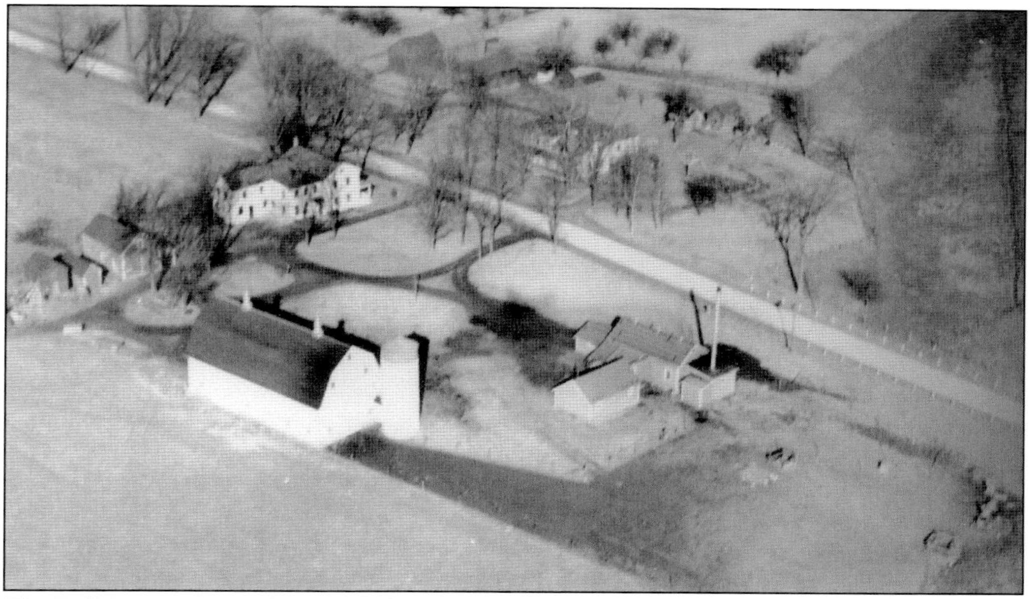

The Toll farm was once known as the Home School for Girls. Originally opened in Verona in 1874, it was moved to New Hartford in 1876, returning to Verona in 1883, and closing its doors in 1895. It stood on Beacon Light Road and Route 31 where Vernon-Verona-Sherrill High School now stands.

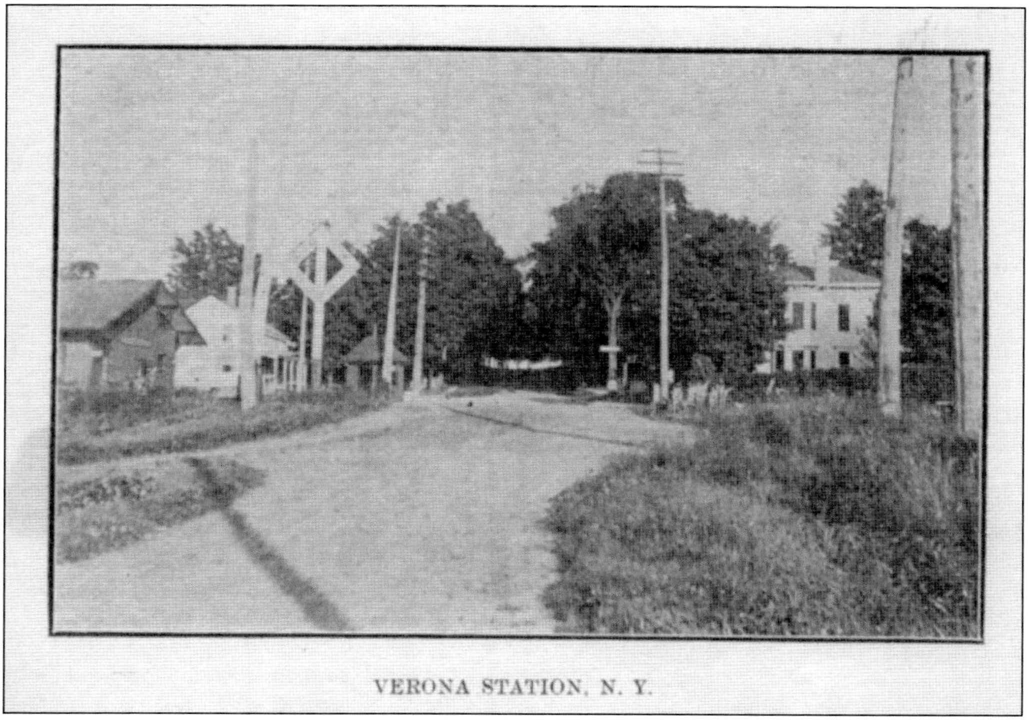

This photograph shows the area of Verona Station where traffic crossed the New York Central Railroad tracks. Due to the high number of deaths at the crossing, a bridge was built to cross above the tracks and many homes and businesses were moved to other locations in the hamlet of Verona.

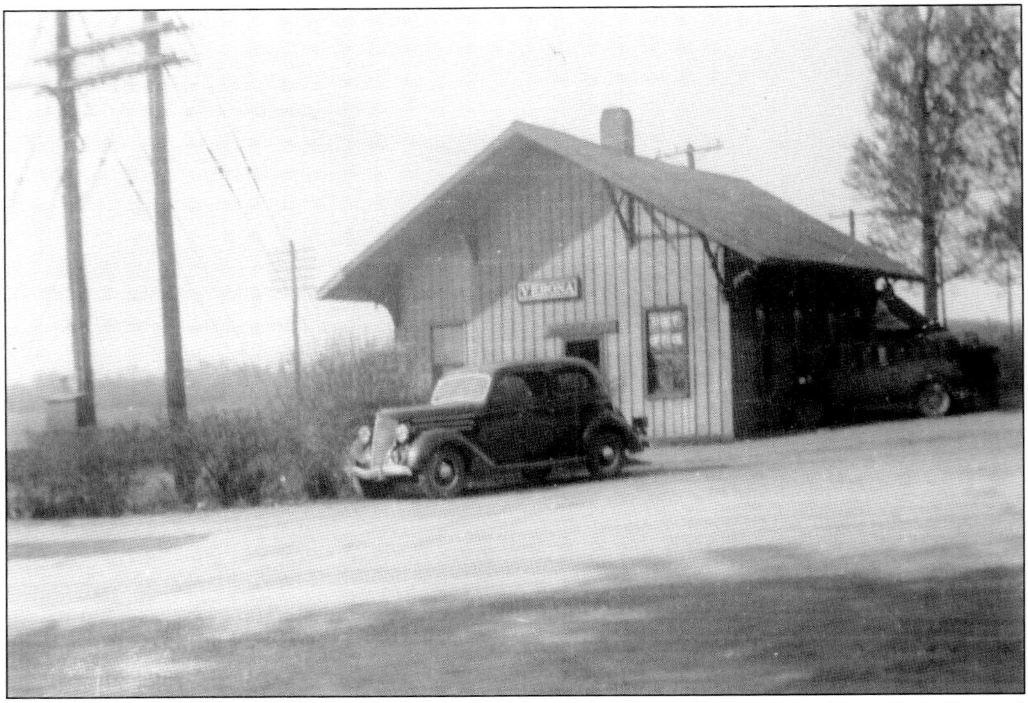

The Verona Station train depot was located on Station Street. Trains of the New York Central Railway traveled through from Rome in the east and continued on to Oneida in the west. This station was replaced by a bridge on Route 31, which crossed over the railroad tracks.

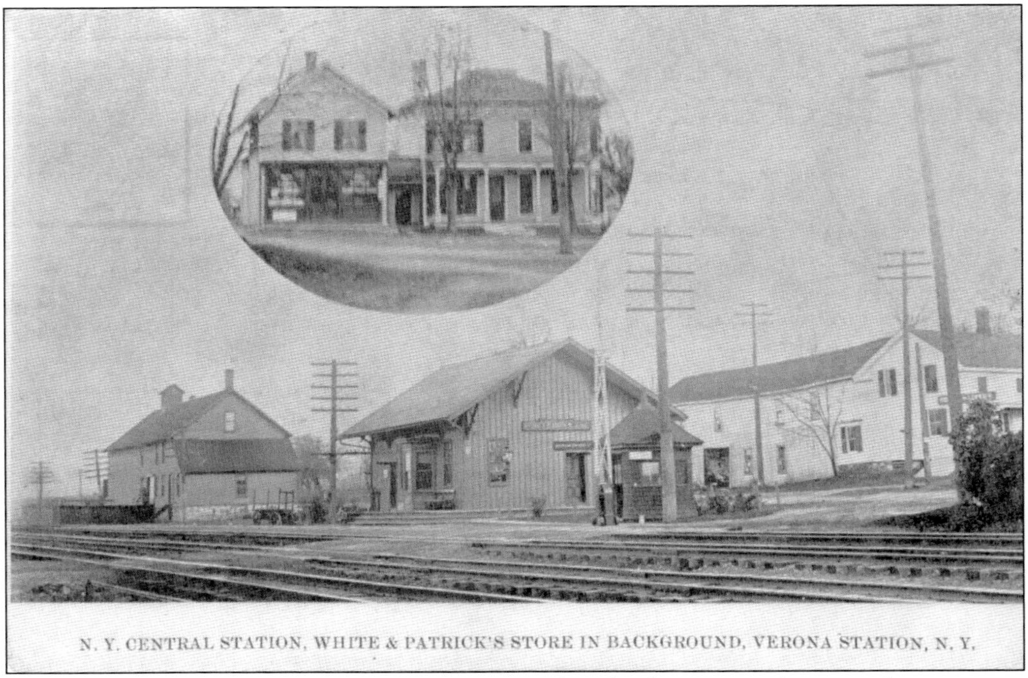

White and Patrick's Store, later Tom Ray's first Red and White Store, shown in the inset, was located in Verona Station. The photograph shows the milk plant to the left, the train depot with multiple rail tracks in the center, and the Berical-Williams Hotel at the right.

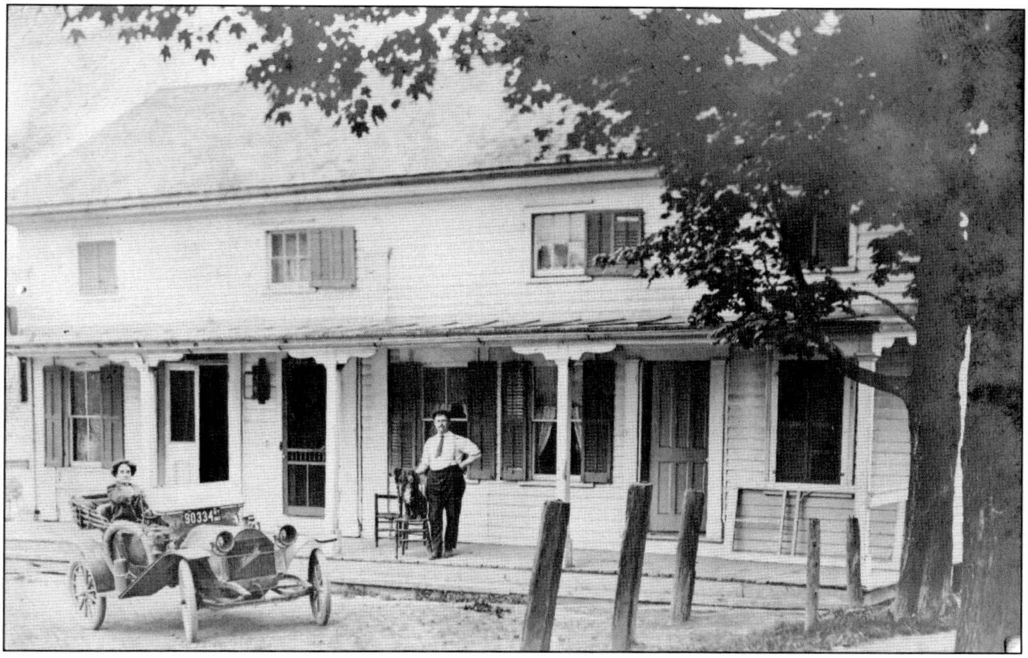

William Berical purchased the Shearwood Hotel in Verona Station in 1900. In 1937, New York decided to build a bridge over the railroad, which required extensive fill to reach the same level as the hill on the Verona side. The hotel was partially torn down and the main portion was moved to Route 31 where it later became the Williams's home.

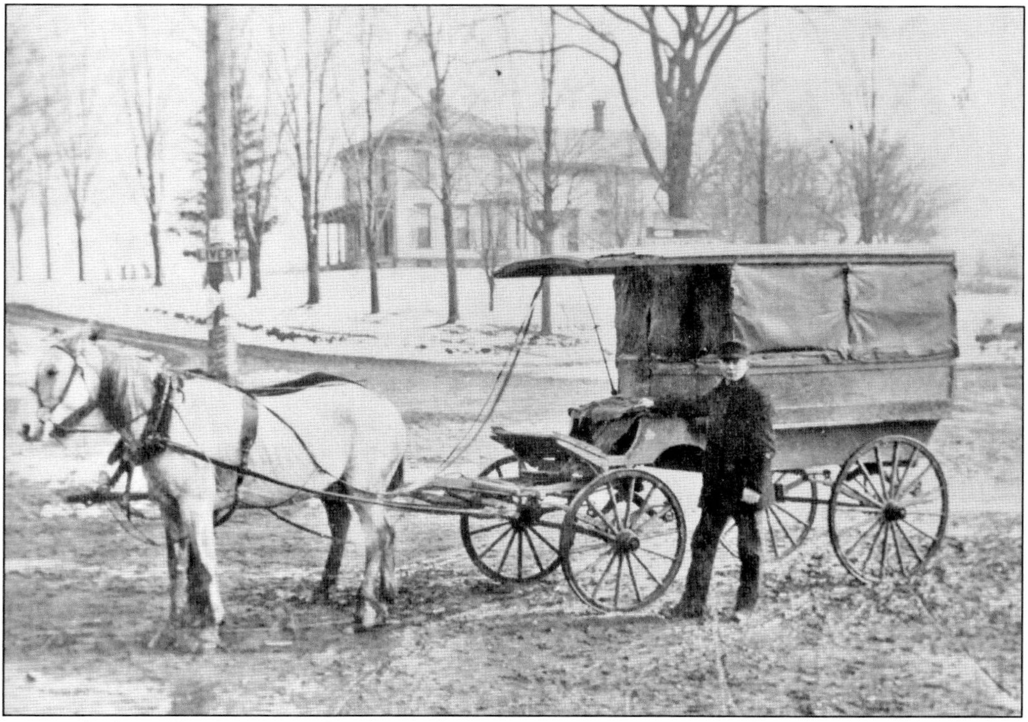

Jon Link drove his taxi as early as 1901, escorting passengers from the train station at Verona Station to their destinations.

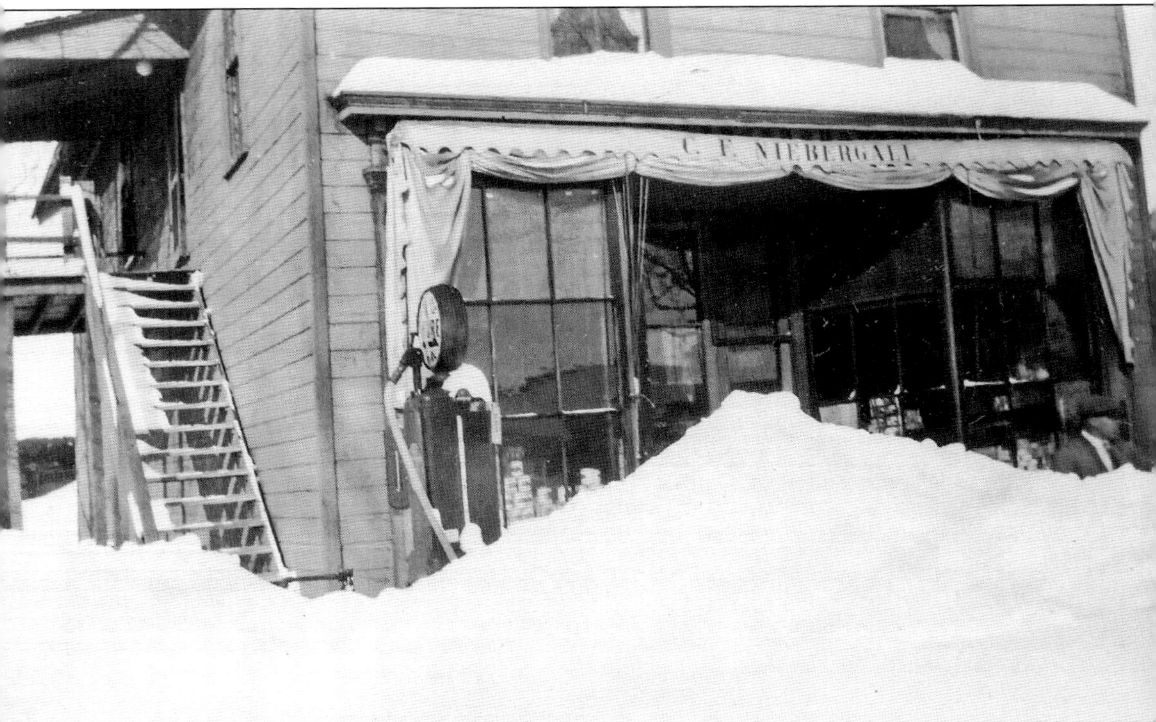

Charles and Neibergall's store was located on Main Street in Verona, next to the Verona Hotel with the Grange hall upstairs. The store flourished in the late 1800s but later burned.

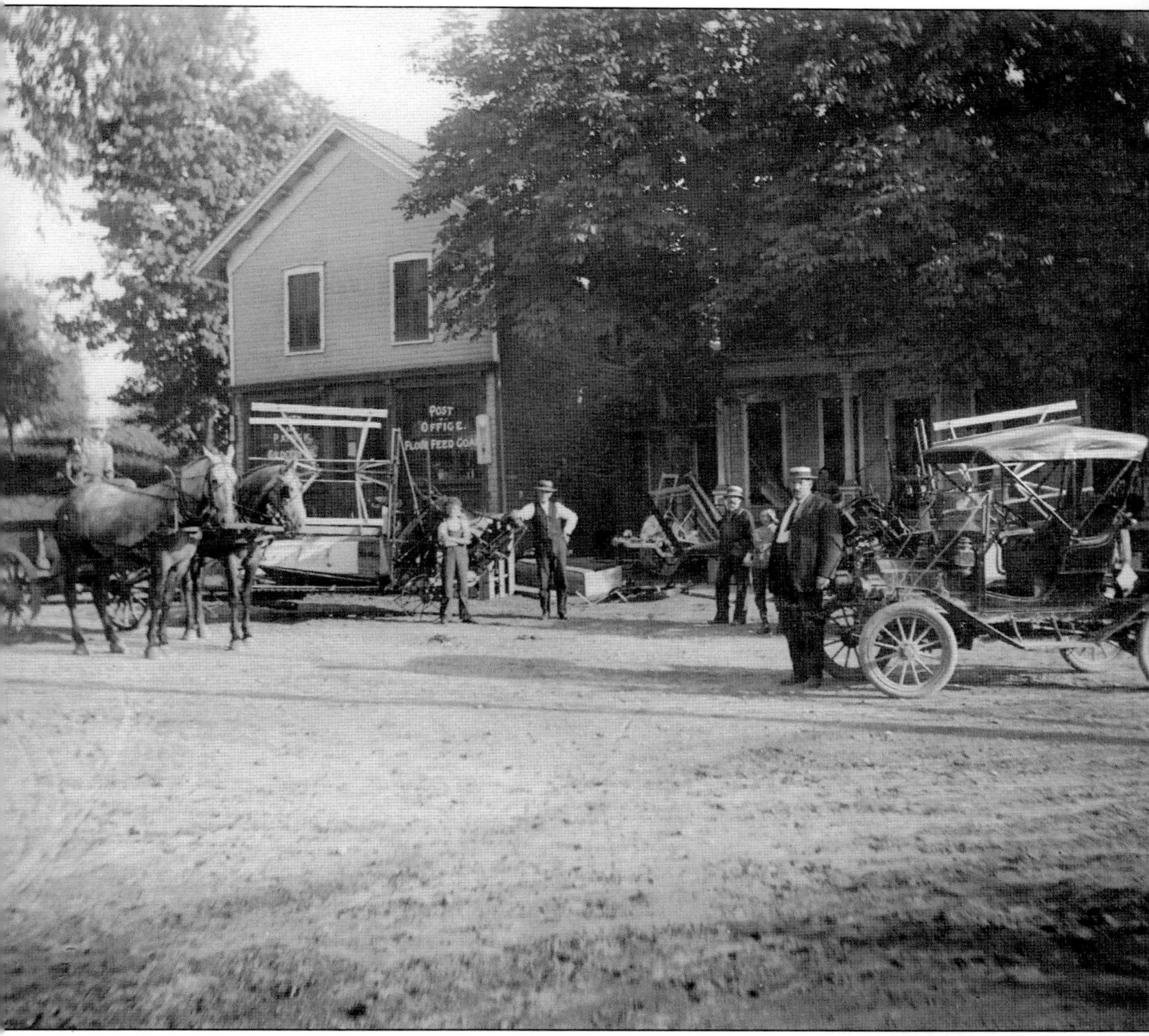

White and Patrick's was a mainstay of Verona Station, providing services and goods to people of the area. This photograph shows a variety of village transportation and activity. Once the bridge over the railroad tracks on Route 31 was erected, Verona Station dwindled.

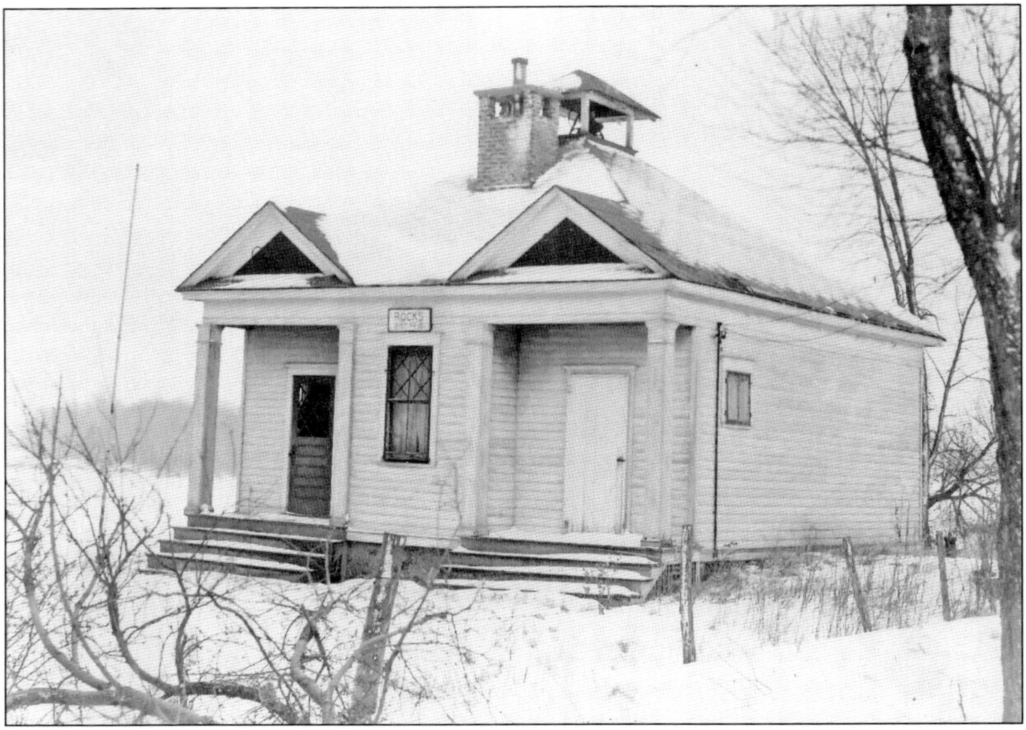

The Rock Road School commonly known as "The Rocks" was District No. 16, located on the corner of Stook and Rock Roads. The original school burned and the new schoolhouse, pictured above, was built. The Rocks was closed before 1945.

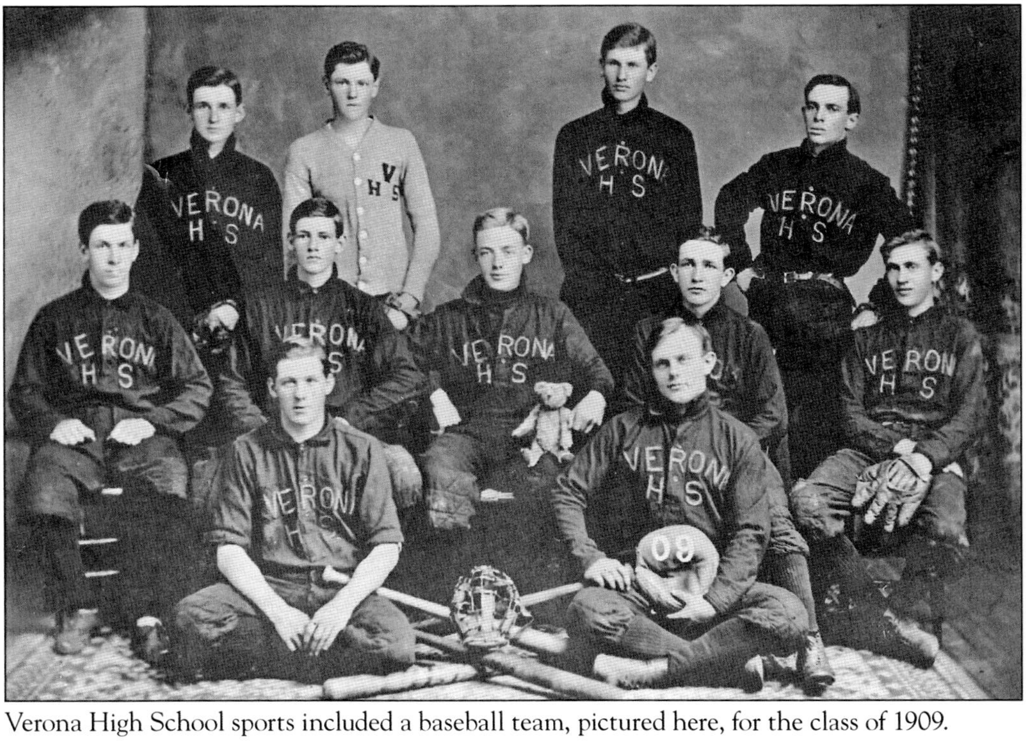

Verona High School sports included a baseball team, pictured here, for the class of 1909.

Six

Verona Beach

Pine-covered woods in the northwest corner of the township on the shore of Oneida Lake made this area an attractive spot for its first settlers.

George A. Smith was the town of Verona's first inhabitant, who settled his family inland from the lake near the Royal Blockhouse, the fortification built along Wood Creek that the English had since abandoned. However Verona Beach was not settled as quickly as some of the other areas of the township.

In the 1840s, the Roberts brothers, William, Harmon, Seth, and George, settled on the south side of Wood Creek, first known as Wood River, where it intersects with Fish Creek. Other families began to settle further to the south near what is now the intersection of Jug Point Road and Oneida Street.

About this time, James D. Spencer began acquiring land along Oneida Street and towards the lake. Ownership of the nearby sand beds and the ample forests for lumber were prosperous enterprises. By the early 1900s, improvements, including a new road near the shore of the lake, Cove Road, two railroads, and widening of the canal to accommodate larger barges, brought more people to the area, including summer residents who had built cottages here.

After World War II, Verona Beach became a destination for vacationers and summer residents, with the construction of the Verona Beach State Park, New York State Route 13, and a new bridge crossing the canal. Small shops, restaurants, and marinas were established to support the tourism industry and people who used the canal and lake for recreation.

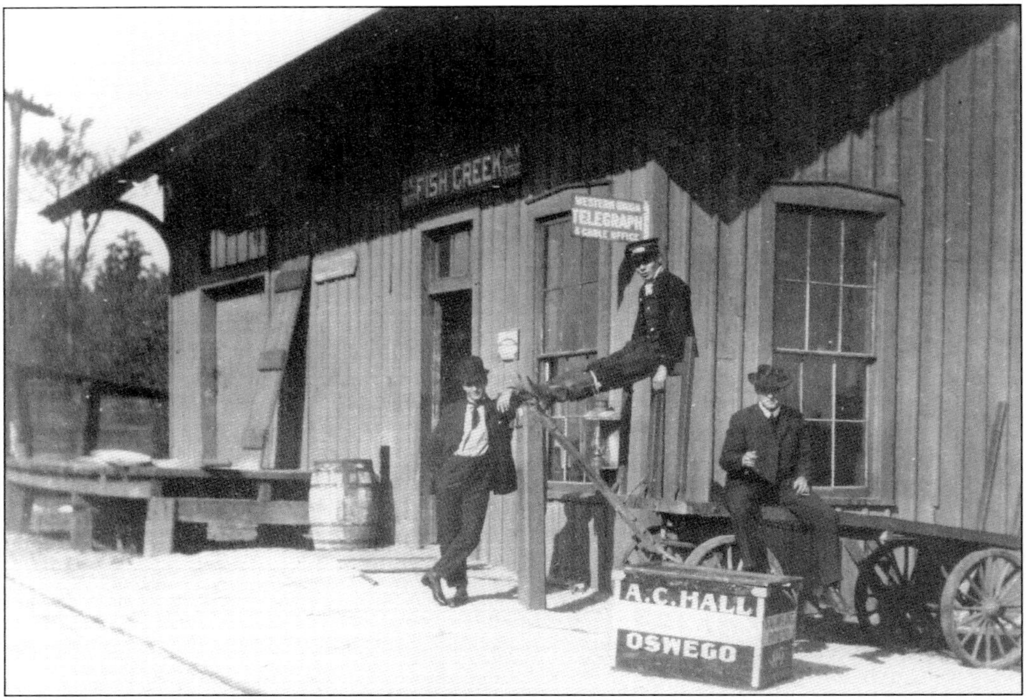

Pictured here is the Fish Creek Rail Station of the New York Ontario and Western Railroad. William Erwin Bentley is the boy pictured on the truck along with a railway employee.

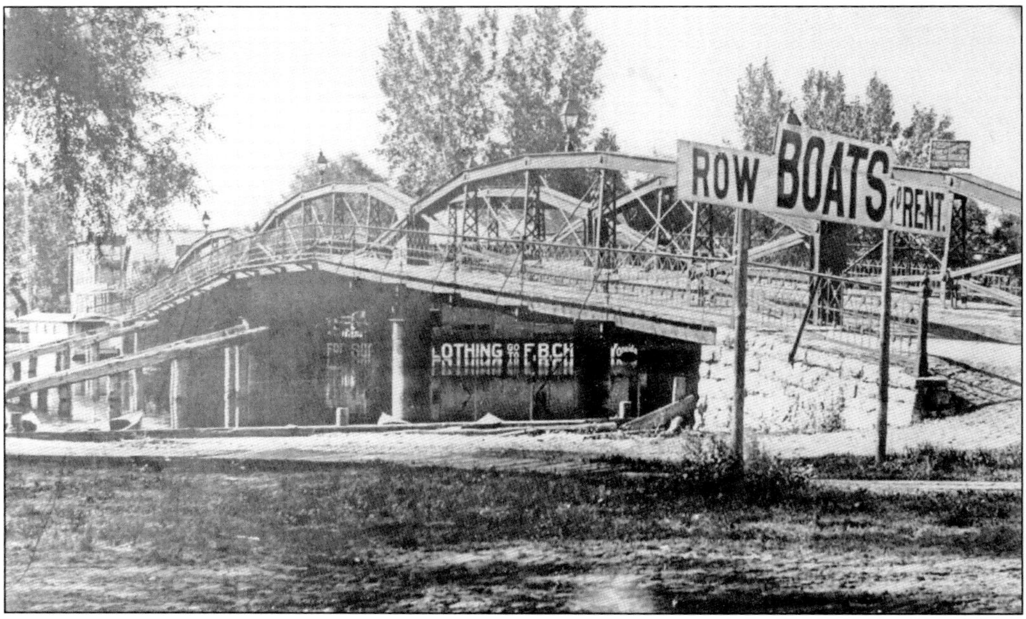

This photograph is of the first bridge built over Wood Creek between Verona and Sylvan Beach. Construction took place in the late 19th century.

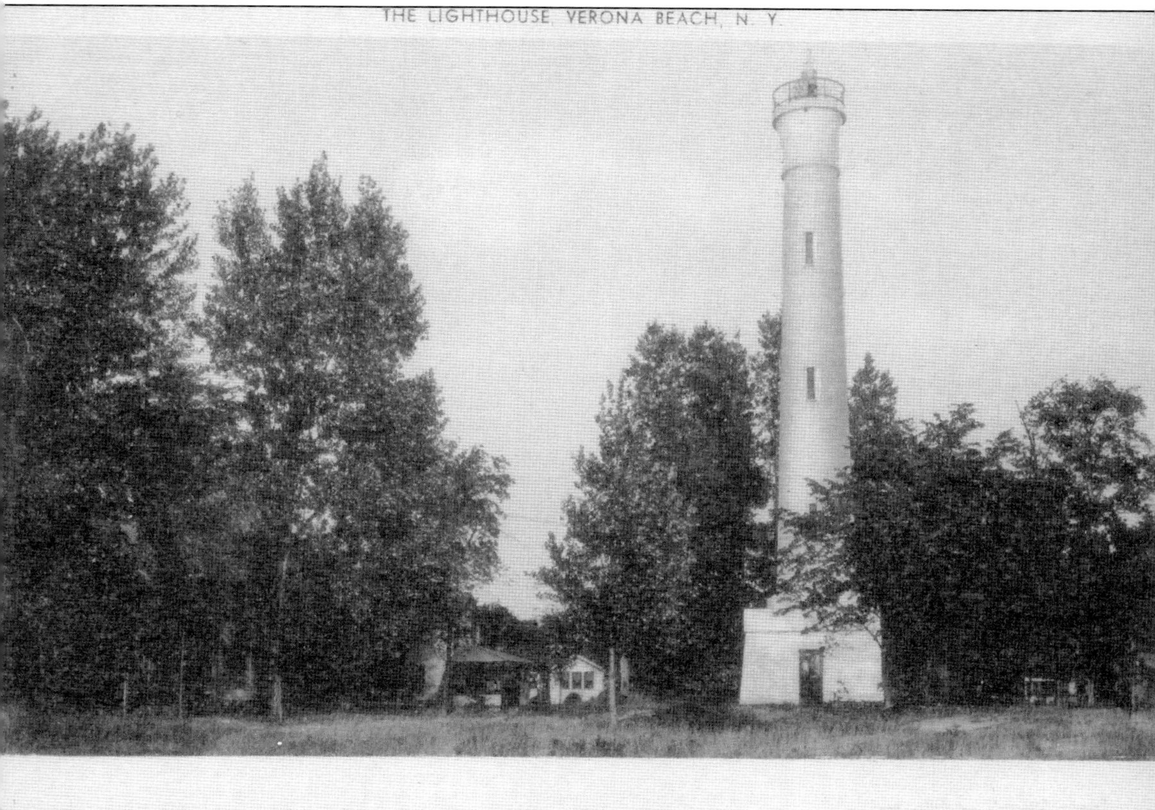

The lighthouse of Oneida Lake was located at Verona Beach. Built in 1915 during the construction of the Barge Canal and powered by gas, it was modified in 1927 to run electric gas and more recently restored. It stands today across the beach from the popular amusement park at Sylvan Beach.

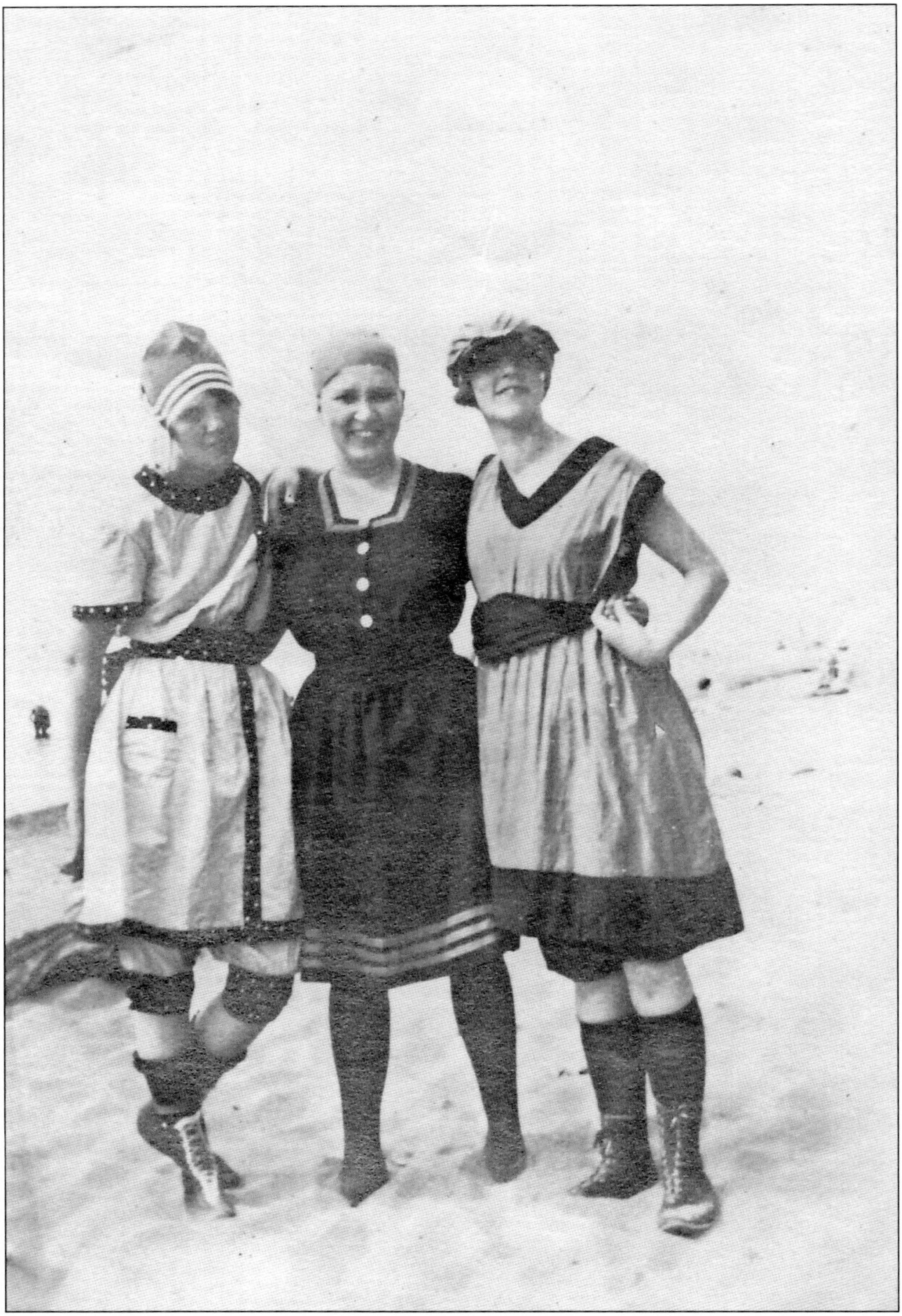

What a lovely day to spend at the lake. Pictured here are young ladies enjoying the sun, sand, and water at Verona Beach. Their bathing suits reflected the latest styles of the day.

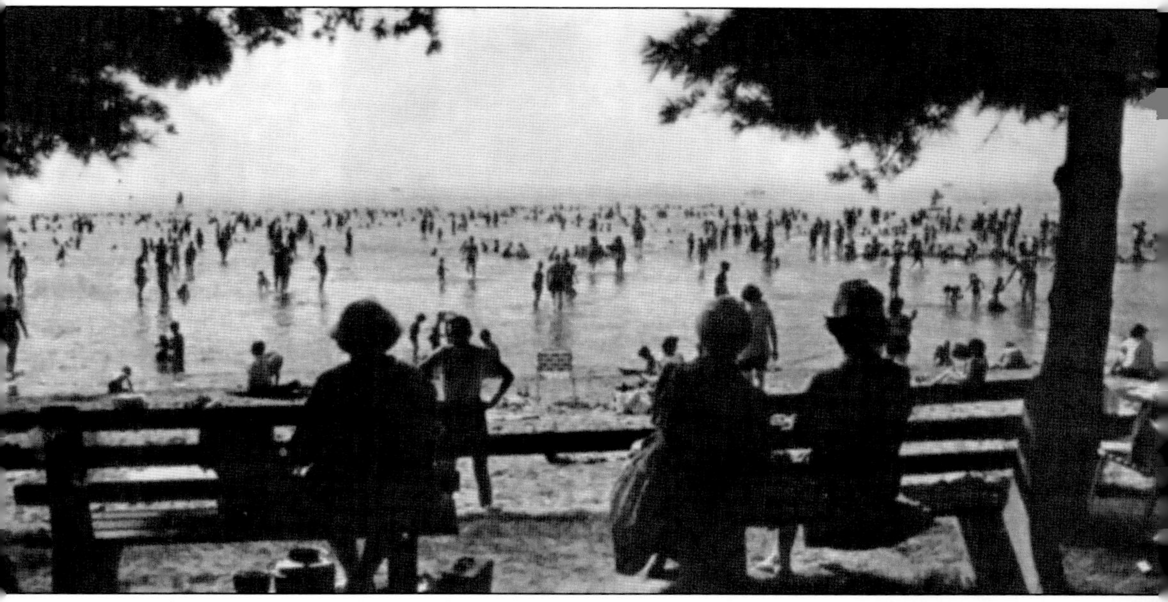

Verona Beach was a very popular spot for sunbathing and swimming, attracting large numbers of people as seen in the photograph from the early 20th century. (Photograph courtesy of Oneida County Historical Society.)

BIBLIOGRAPHY

Beer's Atlas of Oneida County, 1874.

Cookinham, Henry J. *History of Oneida County, New York: From 1700 to the present time*. Chicago, IL: S. J. Clarke, 1912.

Durant, Samuel W. *History of Oneida County, New York: with illustration and biographical sketches of some of its prominent men and pioneers*. Philadelphia, PA: Everts and Fariss, 1878.

Ernenwein, Raymond P. *Verona Town History*. Sherburne, NY: Heritage Press, 1970.

Jones, Pomroy. *Annals and Recollections of Oneida County*. Rome, NY: Self-published, 1851.

New Century Atlas of Oneida County, 1907.